FAMILY VIOLENCE FROM A COMMUNICATION PERSPECTIVE

FAMILY VIOLENCE FROM A COMMUNICATION PERSPECTIVE

Edited by

Dudley D. Cahn & Sally A. Lloyd

SAGE Publications
International Educational and Professional Publisher
Thousand Oaks   London   New Delhi

For information address:

SAGE Publications, Inc.
2455 Teller Road
Thousand Oaks, California 91320
E-mail: order@sagepub.com

SAGE Publications Ltd.
6 Bonhill Street
London EC2A 4PU
United Kingdom

SAGE Publications India Pvt. Ltd.
M-32 Market
Greater Kailash I
New Delhi 110 048 India

Printed in the United States of America

Library of Congress Cataloging-in-Publication Data

Family violence from a communication perspective / editors, Dudley D. Cahn,
    Sally A. Lloyd.
        p.   cm.
    Includes bibliographical references (p.) and index.
    ISBN 0-8039-5982-6 (cloth: acid-free paper).—ISBN 0-8039-5983-4
(pbk.: acid-free paper)
        1. Family violence—United States.   2. Communication in the family—
United States.   3. Wife abuse—United States.   4. Child abuse—United
States.   5. Dating violence—United States.   I. Cahn, Dudley D.
II. Lloyd, Sally A.
HQ809.3.U5F343   1996
362.82'92—dc20   95-50233

This book is printed on acid-free paper.
96 97 98 99   10 9 8 7 6 5 4 3 2 1

Sage Production Editor: Tricia K. Bennett   Sage Typesetter: Marion Warren

Contents

Preface

Violence is alarmingly prevalent in today's American family. If one focuses on physical violence, a number of studies report startling findings. Sugarman and Hotaling (1989a) averaged the results of studies on premarital violence, revealing a prevalence rate of 30%. Straus and Gelles (1990) reported that physical violence occurred in one of every six marriages. Estimates of physical violence by a parent against his or her children range from 3.5 to 24 cases per 1,000 children (Lloyd & Emery, 1993). Perhaps one should not overlook the fact that 6% of all police officers who died in the line of duty between 1972 and 1984 were killed while dealing with domestic violence cases.

Another form of violence—sexual abuse—exists in the family and premarital relationships as well. Fifty to 75% of women report some type of sexual aggression in their dating relationships (Lloyd & Emery, 1993). Finkelhor and Yllö (1985) reported marital rape of 10% of women in intact couples and 25% of women in divorced couples. Using a random national sample, Finkelhor, Hotaling, Lewis, and Smith (1990) observed that over 6% of women and nearly 2% of men had experienced childhood sexual abuse.

Other forms of violence—verbal, emotional, and psychological abuse—likely occur more often than physical violence (Marshall, 1994). Sugarman and Hotaling (1989a) reported that over 75% of the people in their study had expressed threats of violence to their partners. In a recent study of students, 77% of males and 76% of females had expressed threats of violence to their partners, and 72% of males and 79% of females had received threats from their partners (Marshall, 1994).

Because of the extent of family and premarital violence in the United States, the subject is increasingly receiving the interest of family theorists and researchers. Much of the research in the past has concentrated on the personality factors and characteristics of aggressors and their victims. Lloyd and Emery (1994) have noted that recent work indicates that communication factors are better at differentiating relationships that are abusive from nonabusive relationships. Today, more researchers are attempting to investigate the communicative factors associated with family violence, to clarify some of the interrelationships among the different types of communication and different types of family violence, and to discuss the implications of current communication research on family violence for theorists and practitioners. In this vein, *Family Violence From a Communication Perspective* is designed to make several contributions to the domestic violence and family abuse literature.

First, this book presents a communication perspective on family violence. Other perspectives of violence and abuse appear to focus on behaviors that inflict physical or psychological pain, injury, or suffering or both on another person. From a communication perspective, these behaviors are redefined as acts or actions with intention (from a message sender's point of view) or with perceived intention (from a message receiver's point of view). In addition, these acts or actions may be verbal (words) or nonverbal (symbolic actions besides words) or both. A communication perspective is useful for examining abusive family relationships because verbal and nonverbal communication is the essence of an interpersonal relationship. Communication is the tool partners use to create, perpetuate, and redefine their relationship.

Second, this book is multidisciplinary in that it includes contributions from the disciplines of communication studies, family studies, sociology, and psychology. The contributors include teachers of family communication and related college courses, interpersonal conflict and violence researchers, and family therapists. They represent the north, south, east, west, and middle of the United States. Some chapters present more traditional or quantitative views of the subject whereas others take a qualitative approach. The strength of this book lies in its diversity. Taken together, these chapters present an emerging communication perspective on family and premarital physical violence, sexual abuse, and verbal aggression.

Third, this book takes a developmental view of violence in the family—beginning with courtship violence, proceeding through marital violence, and ending in parent-child violence. Some of the chapters interrelate these subjects in interesting ways to show how violence at one stage leads to violence at other stages of family development. Although more communication-oriented research has been done on marital violence, in this book an attempt has been made to take a more balanced approach by including courtship and parent-child physical, sexual, and verbal abuse.

Fourth, although *Family Violence From a Communication Perspective* reports numerous research findings, discusses some methodological issues, and relates empirical findings to theory, it also attempts to offer practical applications of research, especially in family therapy. Practitioners will find a number of useful insights that should be valuable in their daily work with perpetrators and victims as well as with parents and children in abusive families. Although therapists may find this book to be useful, researchers and theorists will benefit from a fruitful and comprehensive treatment of the subject.

Finally, this book consists of some chapters that summarize existing studies to emphasize principles that underlie family violence and other chapters that report the results and analyze data to break new ground. Reviews of family violence in general as well as specialized topics like coercion, power, and control in abusive families and marital and parent-child verbal aggression create a foundation for generating future hypotheses. Meanwhile, specific research reports on dating violence, processes of seduction and entrapment in violent dating relationships, negative and positive interaction in abusive marriages, parents' relationship to adolescent sex offenders, patterns of relational control in violent marriages, and the link between parental interaction and parent-child interaction in abusive families extend existing research into new territory.

Acknowledgments

We thank our contributing authors without whom this book would not exist. They devoted a great deal of time from their busy schedules to meet deadlines, revise, and meet new deadlines as they tried to apply their knowledge and expertise to the study of violent families. We also express our appreciation to the loved ones of the contributing authors and the editors for their patience, understanding, help, and emotional support as we worked together to bring our efforts to a close.

1

Family Violence From a
Communication Perspective

DUDLEY D. CAHN

This chapter reviews recent studies on courtship, marital, and parent-child violence that illustrate a communication approach. Family violence refers to physical violence, sexual abuse, and verbal aggression by a family member (or prospective family member—e.g., a date) who does physical or psychological, emotional, or mental harm or both to another. In this chapter, family violence is related to the three primary dimensions of communication: instrumental, relational, and identify.

Although violent behavior is probably as old as civilization, most recently family violence took center stage in the media with the much televised trial of O. J. Simpson, once a professional football star, famous Hertz rental car promoter, and handsome TV sports announcer. He stood accused of knifing to death his attractive ex-wife, Nicole, and a man outside her residence, following her decision to move from the West coast to the East. Although O. J. Simpson was later declared not guilty by the jury, bits and pieces of information publicized during the trial painted a picture of an abusive husband. Tape recordings allegedly showed a hysterical Nicole Simpson screaming for help as O. J. Simpson beat down the door to get at her. Records showed her attempts to get police protection, and neighbors reported prior incidents of wife beating. A woman who was allegedly a member of Nicole's therapeutic support group described on television how Nicole was beaten, blamed herself, tried to hold the marriage together, and continued to love O. J.

Infante, Chandler, and Rudd (1989) claim that "when violence occurs it is not an isolated event in [spouses'] lives, but is embedded firmly in the process of interpersonal communication which people use to regulate their daily lives" (p. 174). However, much of the research on family abuse in the past has treated violence as an isolated form of behavior by concentrating on describing the personality factors and social characteristics of both the abusers and their victims (Lloyd & Emery, 1994). This past research fails to place violent behavior within broader and more extended sequences of human interaction. Lloyd and Emery point out that such noncommunication-oriented research is a relatively poor predictor of domestic violence compared to communication research.

In addition to setting the scene for the chapters that follow, the purpose of this chapter is to describe a communication perspective on domestic violence research, to suggest a direction for future research, and to frame the literature in a way that is useful for family therapists who must create ways to help abusers and victims. Before describing a communication perspective, a few points must be made about family violence.

For the purposes of this chapter, family violence includes physical violence, sexual abuse, and verbal aggression. As a first step to combating family violence, it is important to have definitions of these terms to clarify the difference between normal or acceptable types of behavior and violations. Physical violence is defined by Straus and Gelles (1990) as "an act carried out with the intention, or the perceived intention of causing physical pain or injury to another person" (p. 467). Gelles and Conte (1990) define child sexual abuse as "forced, tricked, or coerced sexual behavior between a young person and an older person" (p. 1050). When applied to courtship, Sugarman and Hotaling (1989a) define abuse as "the penetration or threat of an act of violence by at least one member of an unmarried dyad on the other within the context of the dating process" (p. 5). Verbal aggression is defined by Infante et al. (1989) as a verbal attack that "attempts to inflict psychological pain, thereby resulting in the (other's) feeling less favorable about self, i.e., suffering self-concept damage" (p. 164). Verbal aggression often plays a role in conflict that gets out of hand. In actuality, physical, sexual, and verbal abuse often occur together, sequentially, or simultaneously.

It is also important to better understand who are the abusers and the victims of abuse. Research shows that men are more likely to be the perpetrators of violence toward their female partners who are more likely to be the victims. Bograd (1990) reports that "wives suffer significantly more physical injuries than do husbands" (p. 133). According to Marshall (1994), males are more likely to hit or kick a wall, door, or furniture; drive dangerously; act like a bully; hold and pin; shake or roughly handle; grab; and twist an arm, whereas more females sustain these acts. As Dobash and Dobash state (1988), "certainly, there is a vast body of evidence confirming the existence of persistent, systematic, severe, and intimidating force men use against their wives . . . [that] does warrant the use of terms such as *wife beating* or *battered woman*" (p. 60). More than half of all women homicide victims are killed by former or current boyfriends or husbands, usually after they are separated (Walker, 1989). Research shows that women and children are more likely than male partners and fathers to be harmed by physical force in the family (Marshall, 1994).

Using a social exchange model, Margolin (1992) frames abuse into a phenomenon of gender. Noting that abusers are more likely to use violence in the home, where they expect the costs of abuse to be less than the rewards, Margolin argues that women suffer greater penalties than do men for domestic violence. If abusive behavior is more "costly" to women, men are more likely than women to beat or abuse their partners and children who love them. Furthermore, if violence committed by men is more likely to avoid sanctions, such as police intervention, loss of status, and public humiliation, men's violence toward family members is less subject to social control. Finally, due to their greater size and economic-social status, men may abuse family members "with less fear of reprisal." When one combines the privacy of the home with the lack of stigma, lack of social sanctions, and lack of social control, the costs of a man's being violent are less than the rewards.

Also, for the purposes of this chapter, family violence includes courtship, marriage, and child abuse. At first glance, it would seem that these topics are quite different subjects and are in fact often treated in separate articles and books. The different types of family violence, however, may be more interrelated than their definitions imply. For example, courtship violence is important because the origin of spouse abuse in many cases may be traced to courtship patterns that are also abusive. When physical abuse between husband and wife is present, the risk of physical abuse of the child is increased by as much as 150% (Straus & Smith, 1990). Moreover, sons who observe their father's violence are 10 times more likely to engage in wife abuse in later marriage than are boys from nonabusive parents (Straus, Gelles, & Steinmetz, 1980). According to Williams and Finkelhor (1990), approximately one in five parents abused as children are sexually abusive to their own children. The relationship between courtship, spouse, and child abuse may be due to the fact that they share common features unique to the family in which members experience high levels of emotional involvement and spend a lot of time in face-to-face contact (Burgess, Anderson, Schellenbach, & Conger, 1981). As early as the 1970s, some researchers emphasized the similarities in patterns, causes, and remedies between child abuse and other forms of family violence (Breines & Gordon, 1983).

Having made a few introductory comments about family violence, I will describe what I mean by a communication perspective. I will also explain what it means to take a communication perspective on domestic violence research.

A Communication Perspective on Domestic Violence

A common way to view communication is as a process of sending and receiving messages. Some communication studies focus primarily on the sending or encoding of messages and how people in certain situations tend to engage in certain kinds of message behaviors. These studies raise questions related to goals, purposes, and intentions of message senders. Other studies examine the decoding of messages and how people are likely to respond to messages. These studies raise questions related to the effects of messages in receivers.

Some communication scholars (e.g., Clark & Delia, 1979) argue that communicators produce messages to attain one or more of the following three goals: (a) instrumental goals that concern solving problems or accomplishing tasks, (b) relationship goals that concern creating and preserving a particular relationship between interactants, and (c) identity goals that concern establishing or maintaining a desired image of the communicator with others. Concomitantly, Benoit and Cahn

(1994) point out that a message has potential effects on receivers in these three same areas whether intended or not by message senders. The instrumental, relationship, and identity goals or effects may be considered as dimensions of communication, each varying from more to less.

By focusing on these dimensions of communication rather than simply the goals (sender's orientation) or the effects (receiver's orientation), researchers view the interaction between communicators as joint ventures (i.e., human actions) and meaning as jointly created. Presumably, humans construct their reality and coordinate their actions by intentionally (or perceived as intentionally) using verbal and nonverbal symbols whose meanings are shared by others. Symbols arouse meanings according to commonly shared conventions (e.g., rules, norms, and customs). Verbal and nonverbal communication is regulated by these social conventions that vary from one culture to another and that govern what is appropriate, expected, permissible, or prohibited in specific social contexts. *Communication competence* refers to the ability to appropriately and effectively use verbal and nonverbal symbols within a given speech community (e.g., culture). Appropriate communication avoids the violation of valued social conventions, whereas effective communication obtains valued goals or effects (Spitzberg, Canary, & Cupach, 1994). A communication approach views abusive and violent acts as the dark side of communication and the abusers and violators as communicatively incompetent (Lloyd, 1991).

A communication perspective is useful for examining family relationships because "interaction is the sine qua non of relationships; it is through communicative action that persons initiate, define, maintain, and terminate their social bonds" (Baxter, 1985, p. 245). Given a communication perspective, what are the interpersonal dynamics—the patterns of interaction—that typify abusive family relationships? In the remainder of this chapter, I will define violence from a communication perspective, review recent studies on family violence that take a communication perspective, and relate them to the three primary dimensions of communication.

Defining Violence and Abuse From a Communication Perspective

Many definitions of violence and abuse appear to focus on behaviors that inflict physical or psychological pain, injury, or suffering or both on another person. From a communication perspective, these behaviors are redefined as acts or actions with intention (from a message sender's point of view) or with perceived intention (from a message receiver's point of view). In addition, these acts or actions may be verbal (words) or nonverbal (symbolic actions besides words) or both. Moreover, because violence appears to involve elements or power and control, a definition of violence should include the ability to impose one's will (i.e., wants, needs, or desires) on another person.

Finally, in most definitions of violence, the question of degree, type, and appropriateness arises. For example, when are parental discipline and punishment abusive? Some argue that physical violence is never justified even if it is effective (gets intended results); there are always better ways to solve problems if one takes the time to consider options and makes the effort to use nonviolent alternatives. At the other extreme, others respond automatically to violent behavior with no thought to alternatives simply because it gets results. Finally, somewhere in the middle are those who believe that one might resort to violence in situations of self-defense and the prevention of abuse. At least some effort should be made to determine which behaviors are appropriate and which ones violate socially acceptable standards.

In summary, violence or abuse may be defined as the ability to impose one's will (i.e., wants, needs, or desires) on another person through the use of verbal or nonverbal acts, or both, done in a way that violates socially acceptable standards and carried out with the intention or the perceived intention of inflicting physical or psychological pain, injury, or suffering, or both. The range of abusive behaviors includes mild forms of verbal intimidation, severe beatings, and extremely violent rapes and homicides. Violence ranges from carefully planned attacks to sudden emotional outbursts inflicting injury on other persons.

The description of a communication perspective on domestic violence includes the goals and effects of message behaviors that are intended or perceived as intended. These goals or effects represent the dimensions of communication. The next section considers how these dimensions may be applied to the study of domestic violence.

Violence and the Dimensions of Communication

When applied to the subject of family violence, the three dimensions of communication—instrumental, relational, and identity—provide an alternative view from the traditional study of the subject. Typically, research on family violence distinguishes between instrumental and expressive behaviors (Breines & Gordon, 1983; Finkelhor, 1983). Although the instrumental dimension clearly appears to be purposive and functional, the expressive category becomes a catchall for more than one type of noninstrumental behavior. In addition to the instrumental dimension, communication researchers are finding it useful to distinguish two additional categories of abusive behaviors—relationship and identity—depending on the abuser's goals or effects of the behaviors or both. Such a view reveals how communication functions differently in abusive and nonabusive families.

Family Violence as the Instrumental Dimension of Communication

The instrumental dimension of family violence is task accomplishing, goal attaining, or issue resolving. Among the types of behavior (on the part of victims) that supposedly precipitate violence, the only discernible pattern is that the behavior represents the victim's failure or refusal to comply with an abuser's wishes. Of course, there are many ways to get others to cooperate, so why do abusers resort to physical and sexual aggression?

Violence may occur in the family because one cannot easily walk away from disagreeable others. In contemporary American society, attempts to leave one's spouse or young children may be met with harsh social sanctions. Even breaking off living together arrangements may be complicated for some romantically involved but unmarried couples. Unable to break off easily from companionate, marital, and familial obligations, individuals may become frustrated, angry, and resentful. According to the frustration-aggression hypothesis, when goal attainment is blocked frustration increases and, as a result, persons become more aggressive, increasingly more threatening, and eventually violent (DeTurck, 1987).

According to Lloyd and Emery (1994), physical and sexual aggression is self-reinforcing due to the fact that it often is an effective way to get what one wants:

> If the aim of engaging in conflict is achieving one's desires or meeting one's needs, and if aggression helps ensure that one "wins," then aggression will be reinforced to the extent that winning is more important than the emotional and physical well-being of the partner. (p. 30)

When these feelings and abusive behaviors occur in the privacy of the household, the immediate rewards of using violence to work off anger or frustration may appear preferable to reasoned and rational conversation with one's children or partner that would take longer and offer less predictable results (Gelles & Straus, 1988). Thus, abusive men who see their wives or children as blocking their goals experience mounting frustration and turn violent to coerce them into compliance.

Another reason for the use of aggression is due to a temporary loss of control. Theories of impulsive aggression focus on three factors: (a) high levels of emotional arousal or sympathetic excitation, (b) loss of cognitive control, and (c) heavy reliance on learned (and hence automatic) behaviors (Zillmann, 1990). Loss of cognitive control may result from emotional overload (Zillmann, 1990), but researchers have documented the link between alcohol and family violence (Leonard & Senchak, 1993; Straus & Kantor, 1991).

Finally, heavy reliance on learned behaviors in the family of origin also appears to help explain family violence. Suh and Abel (1990) report that the abuser's childhood history of violence is a significant predictor of later child abuse. Children witnessing family violence are likely to be abusive toward siblings but are not more likely to hit their parents or those outside the family. Also, child witnesses of spousal abuse are potential targets of physical and emotional abuse later in their own marriages. Moreover, Straus and Kantor (1991) report that the use of severe physical punishment by parents in the family of origin is associated with subsequent physical abuse of children and physical assaults on wives. It should be noted, however, that verbal abuse and other destructive communication behaviors are probably passed on to children along with physical abuse.

Understanding how frustration leads to aggressive behavior that is often effective at goal attainment does not mean that one must accept violent behavior from another. Efforts need to be aimed at educating violent partners on alternative ways that are just as effective but more beneficial to the relationship and the well-being of their partners and children.

Family Violence as the Relationship Dimension of Communication

The relationship dimension of communication focuses on degree of commitment to a premarital or marital relationship, love and emotional involvement, jealousy, conflict, influence of friends and relatives, interpersonal trust, separation-breakup-divorce, compatibility, frequency of sex in marriage, satisfaction with sexual relations, and balance of power. Regarding this dimension of communication, there are two ways in which it emerges in an abusive family. First, relationship issues may be the focus of abuse. For example, violence may result from a jealous outrage in which a couple suffers serious conflict over one partner's lack of commitment to their relationship. Second, and possibly more commonly, abuse over nonrelationship concerns may have effects on the relationship that were not intended by the abuser. For example, a conflict over instrumental concerns, such as sex, money, or relatives, that ends up in violence may also result in separation and eventually divorce. Although it may be thought that violence harms relationships, this is not always the case. As will be shown below, violence is sometimes seen by some romantic partners as a sign of love and commitment. Moreover, some abusive relationships are described by the spouses as satisfying.

Relationship Problems. Violence due to relationship problems often occurs before a couple marries. Lloyd, Koval, and Cate (1989) described abusive dating relationships as characterized by repeated attempts to persuade the partner that one's own way is right and a belief that it is possible to change the partner. Riggs (1993) found that partners in abusive dating relationships reported more relationship problems (e.g., jealousy, conflict, breakdown of the relationship, and the interference of friends) than did those who were nonabusive.

At other times, violence due to relationship problems occurs after marriage. Duhon-Haynes and Duhon-Sells (1991) report that in these cases violence usually enters a marriage early, in a relatively innocuous form, but over time it changes as does the marital relationship.

Is abuse or violence bad for a relationship? Cate, Henton, Koval, Christopher, and Lloyd (1982) report that one third of those who had experienced courtship violence interpreted violence as "a sign of love," and only 8% said it meant "hate." Some dating partners attribute the occurrence of violence to situational factors that produce undue stress, such as pressures from school, family, or wedding plans (Lloyd, 1991). Similarly, Billingham (1987) reported that violence in courtship occurs much earlier in the development of emotional commitment than previously thought. His results suggest that for some couples violence serves as a catalyst for moving the relationship to more committed levels of involvement. In addition, Billingham and Sack (1987) claim that some men use violent behavior as a test of their partner to determine whether or not she is "safe" before they take the "ego risk" to move the relationship to greater levels of emotional involvement. They conclude that when violence is observed in committed romantic relationships, it may be due to the fact that the partners have accepted violence as a legitimate form of conflict management since the beginning of their relationship.

Although some dating partners may see value in partner abuse, many married partners report disastrous consequences. Eventually, spouses report a high level of conflict and a low level of marital satisfaction (Edleson, Eisikovits, Guttmann, & Sela-Amit, 1991). According to Apt and Hurlbert (1993), victimized wives report significantly lower levels of intimacy and compatibility in their marriages. In addition, victimized wives evince a more traditional sex role ideology, greater erotophobia, and a stronger desire to avoid sex than do nonvictimized wives. Also, compared with nonvictimized wives in distressed marriages, the victimized wives rate themselves as having a lower degree of sexual assertiveness, arousability, and satisfaction. Despite these findings, the victimized wives report a significantly greater frequency of sexual intercourse in their marriages than do nonvictimized wives.

Relationships With an Imbalance of Power. As Bograd (1984) reports, "male-female relationships are structured by the unequal distribution of power based on gender" (pp. 558-559). This is not to say that all powerful men abuse their female partners. Some evidence, however, supports the view that violence tends to gravitate toward the partner with the greatest power and toward relationships with the greatest power differential (Finkelhor, 1983). Lloyd and Emery (1993) view physical and sexual aggression in dating as a result of the power imbalance between men and women. Coleman and Straus (1986) claim that equalitarian couples had the lowest rates of conflict and violence, and male-dominant and female-dominant couples had the highest rates.

Power is also manifest in parenting styles. The authoritarian type of parent maintains traditional relations, teaches values of order, conformity, and obedience, and discourages expressions of autonomy, whereas the authoritative style attempts to raise children in a rational, issue-oriented manner with relatively few restrictions on their behavior (Osborne & Fincham, 1994). Bayer and Cegala (1992) examined the constructs of trait verbal aggressiveness and verbal argumentativeness in relationships to patterns of self-reported parental behavior. Those parents who scored negatively on argumentativeness and positive on verbal aggressiveness displayed parenting behaviors that are associated with the authoritarian prototype. Those parents (of children in kindergarten to sixth grade) who scored positively on argumentativeness and negatively on verbal aggressiveness reported behaviors consistent with an authoritative parenting style.

To the extent that a power differential is translated into dependency, violence is likely to occur. Once violence occurs, the threat of further violence is always present, which may be viewed as a powerful form of psychological abuse. Because of a man's use of threats after first relying on physical violence, some women find themselves trapped in their abusive relationships. As Hilberman and Munson (1977-1978) found, women's physical and psychological symptoms result from the constant threat of violence. Moreover, as an example of "learned helplessness," some women have learned through experience that they cannot stop the beatings and hence cannot control their own fate (Breines & Gordon, 1983). Where greater power has fallen to males rather than to females, statistics show that the greatest volume of violence is directed toward dependent girlfriends or wives. Thus, the different types of couple violence are cases in which the strong victimize the weak, especially those who perceive that they are trapped.

Several studies paint a bleak picture of entrapment in which the woman is the one most likely made to suffer. In a review of the literature on black and white women who endured marital violence, Coley and Beckett (1988) discovered that domestic violence crosses racial and socioeconomic boundaries, and regardless of race, battered women share the psychological pain of guilt, emotional and economic insecurities, and fear of reprisals from their men if they seek help. Lloyd et al. (1989) described abusive dating relationships as characterized by a feeling of being "trapped." Duhon-Haynes and Duhon-Sells (1991) report that there are often numerous personal, social, and material reasons why women feel they cannot make a permanent break from an abusive relationship.

Spouse Interaction Patterns. The nature of a relationship is characterized by its communication pattern. Interaction between spouses with a history of violence has distinguishing characteristics:

> The observed problem-solving discussions by couples with a history of marital violence appear more negative and emotional than those of nonabusive couples (Burman, John, & Margolin, 1992; Burman, Margolin, & John, 1993; Davidovich, 1990; Margolin, Burman, & John, 1989; Margolin, John, & Gleberman, 1988).
>
> The observed interaction between abusive spouses reveals that male abusers manifest a more depressing, gloomy atmosphere and engage in more antisocial behavior than their nonabusive counterparts (Davidovich, 1990; Margolin, Burman, et al., 1989).
>
> Observed interaction shows that abusive couples behave in a more rigid, predictable, and escalating fashion (Cordova, Jacobson, Gottman, Rushe, & Cox, 1993; Margolin, John, & O'Brien, 1989; Stets, 1990; Zillmann, 1990).
>
> The interaction patterns reveal that abusers (and often the victims) manifest few constructive communication, social, negotiation, problem-solving, and argumentation skills (Else, Wonderlich, Beatty, & Christie, 1993; Holtzworth-Munroe, 1992; Holtzworth-Munroe & Anglin, 1991; Infante et al., 1989; Infante, Sabourin, Rudd, & Shannon, 1990; Launius & Jensen, 1987; Margolin, Burman, et al., 1989).

Parent-Child Interaction Patterns. According to Lloyd and Emery (1993), "one of the most consistent interaction patterns found in abusing families is a greater proportion of parental negative and aversive behavior . . . [and] very low levels of positive interaction" (pp. 131-132). Abusive parents are often intrusive, insensitive, and controlling. Abused children may display insecure attachment to their parents, aversive behavior, or compliance just to avoid the parental abuse.

Parental skill deficits occur in child management and parent-child interaction, anger and stress control, and problem solving (Burgess et al., 1981; Hansen & MacMillan, 1990). For example, abusive and neglectful mothers show poorer problem-solving skills for child-rearing problems than do comparison mothers. Meanwhile, fathers who are often sources of stress and maltreatment are rarely the focus of research.

Parental Violence and Subsequent Child Behavioral Patterns. Abused children often have problems relating to other children. Vissing, Straus, Gelles, and Harrop (1991) reported that children (of both sexes and all ages) who frequently experienced verbal aggression exhibited high rates of physical aggression, delinquency, and interpersonal problems. Salzinger, Feldman, Hammer, and Rosario (1993) found that victimized children had lower peer status and less positive reciprocity with peers chosen as friends, were rated by peers as more aggressive and less cooperative, were rated by parents and teachers as more disturbed, and exhibited more insular social networks than nonmaltreated children.

Moreover, abused children may as adults become abusers. About 20% of those abused as children become sexually abusive of their children (Williams & Finkelhor, 1990). Regarding physical violence, Kaufman and Zigler (1987) estimate that the likelihood of abused children becoming abusive adults is 30%. Even some children who witness their parents abusing one another are more likely to engage in spouse abuse in their own marriages.

Unfortunately for some, the end justifies the means even at the cost of an enduring, supportive, and loving relationship. Greater efforts are needed to help partners and parents understand the importance of mutual respect, interpersonal trust, responsibility for one's actions, positive self-esteem, and self-control.

Family Violence as the Identity Dimension of Communication

The identity dimension of communication includes self-esteem, sexual esteem, a male's manhood or masculinity, a female's womanhood or femininity, impression formation and management, egocentrism, appearing to be in control of others, perceptions of oneself, and traditional stereotypes regarding sex roles. As with the relationship dimension, the identity dimension emerges in an abusive families in two ways. First, identity issues may be the focus of a serious conflict. For example, calling into question a male's manhood may result in his becoming overly aggressive just to "prove himself." Second, and possibly more commonly, arguments over instrumental or relationship concerns may have unintended effects on the identities of the combatants (e.g., violence resulting from a conflict over a task or relationship issue may make one appear immature or selfish).

Abusers may use their aggression for ego satisfaction. Hurlbert and Apt (1991) compare abusive with nonabusive husbands to show that abusers evidence greater sexual preoccupation and greater sexual esteem than do the nonabusers. They conclude that an egocentric pattern of sexual behavior appears in the marital relationships of abusers.

Similarly, violence allows the abuser to have an identity as "the one who wears the pants in the family"—as one who is in control of others. This identity includes one's attempts to appear dominant. According to Bograd (1990), "men use extreme violence to control and dominate while women use lethal violence in order to escape" (p. 133). As Frieze and McHugh (1992) observed, women with abusive husbands have less overall influence in terms of decision making than do those with nonabusive husbands. Abusive husbands have been found to hold more traditional stereotypes regarding sex roles, are more possessive, and are more controlling than nonabusive husbands. For example, Smith (1990) showed that husbands who adhere to an ideology of familial patriarchy are more likely to beat their wives than husbands who do not adhere to such an ideology. Moreover, Babcock, Waltz, Jacobson, and Gottman (1993) report that, of the abusive husbands, those who have less power are more physically abusive toward their wives. The authors suggest that violence may be compensatory behavior to make up for husbands' lack of power in the marriage. I would add that their compensatory behavior may have been motivated by identity concerns (appearing dominant) to make up for their lack of power, which is a relationship concern.

Finally, the abuser may encourage submissive behavior by manipulating a victim's identity, namely, one's perceptions of himself or herself. According to Finkelhor (1983), victimized children are often told that they are bad, uncontrollable, and unlovable, and in cases of sexual abuse they may be told that their father's sexual attentions are normal and testimony of his affection for them. Victimized wives are often told that they are incompetent, hysterical, and frigid. A common end result for these different victims is a similar long-term pattern: "depression, suicidal feelings, self-contempt, and an inability to trust and to develop intimate relationships in later life" (Finkelhor, 1983, p. 21).

As for men who may be victims of verbal abuse, Harris (1993) examined the differences in anger-provoking behaviors and in verbal insults as a function of the gender of the aggressor and the target of the provocation. Responses of female and male undergraduates revealed that it was considered worse for men than for women to be called sexually inadequate, worthless, cowardly, or to be called an obscene name. This would indicate that for some men, identity concerns may outweigh instrumental and relationship concerns.

Following a violent act, abusers may engage in communication to rectify their partner's impression of them. Along with blaming others for one's behavior or denying that an event occurred at all, abusers may offer accounts for their transgressions (Cahn, 1987). Accounts are explanations offered for actions called into question because they are unexpected or untoward. They are linguistic devices that function to change the potential pejorative meanings of one's actions and to repair one's identity (Buttny, 1990). According to Cahn (1987), excuses are accounts in which one denies responsibility for an action but admits that the act is reprehensible (e.g., "the alcohol made me do it"), whereas justifications are accounts in which one admits responsibility but interprets the act in a "socially acceptable" manner (e.g., "I didn't hit her. I just shook my fist at her.") In many cases, neither an excuse nor a justification actually solves a problem but may be used to explain one's actions. Thus, accounts often function to transform what might initially be seen as reproachable behavior to an action seen as justifiable or understandable. Wolf-Smith and LaRossa (1992) claim that abusers generally are not likely to stop accounting for abusive behavior, but battered women who seek shelter are progressively less likely to honor their men's accounts.

In summary, violence may alter identity directly when identity issues are the subject of discussion and may produce unintended effects when nonidentity goals (instrumental or relationship) are being pursued.

Specifically, the research shows that the abuser's ego is often a key factor in domestic violence and that abusers may attempt to offer accounts in an attempt to justify their actions and repair their identities. Again, the end does not justify the means when ego satisfaction occurs at the expense of significant interpersonal relationships. Greater efforts are needed to get partners and parents to understand the importance of caring about both self and other, empathic understanding, and sensitivity to the needs and feelings of other family members.

Violence and the Interrelationship of the Three Dimensions of Communication

Previous research suggests that (a) one or more of the dimensions (goals or effects) apply to male abusers who want to attain their goals, want to control their partners, or want to prove themselves by asserting their "manhood," and (b) although victimized females might suffer all three as effects, many score high on the relationship dimension as a common reason for tolerating violence. Future research, however, might relate different levels of abusive behavior to different dimensions of communication.

Some research that has revealed different degrees, levels, or intensities of abuse may be useful here. In their research using the Conflict Tactics Scale (CTS; Straus, 1974), Margolin and colleagues (see Margolin, Burman, et al., 1989; Margolin, John, et al., 1989) differentiated between low and high levels of physical aggression. Caulfield and Riggs (1992) subjected data obtained by Straus's CTS to factor analysis techniques and observed that a fourth factor could be identified—that is, severe aggression. Using a national sample, Gelles (1989) reported that single fathers' levels of severe violence—kicking, biting, or hitting with a fist or objects, beating up the child, and so on—were notably higher than those for single mothers, especially for low-income single fathers.

If future research relates degree or different levels of abuse to the three dimensions of communication, investigators might find that low levels of abusive behavior (including verbal aggression) may be associated more with the instrumental dimension, whereas high levels of abuse (such as severe physical or sexual aggression or both) tend to be associated more with the relationship and identity dimensions. Perhaps in date rape, men who use comparatively low levels of abusive behavior (such as holding the woman down) do so for instrumental purposes (getting sex), whereas men who use more extreme abusive behaviors (beating, threatening with a knife, or choking) may do so for relationship (to have power over women) or identity purposes (to convince their buddies of their manhood in their presence or to later confirm their manhood by bragging to them about their physical exploits). Similarly, partners married or living together may use comparatively low levels of abusive behavior (hitting, slapping, grabbing, and verbal abuse) to get their way or win an argument (i.e., to attain some instrumental goal) but resort to more extreme forms of violence for relational or identity purposes. In child physical and sexual abuse, parents may punish their children for instrumental purposes but sexually or physically abuse their children for relationship and identity purposes. Along these lines, Finkelhor (1983) claims that parents often resort to physical violence or start to sexually abuse their children when they are unemployed or are failing financially or sense that they have lost control of their children and of their own lives. Attempts to satisfy relational and identity goals may be behind the phrase, "kicking them when they are down."

This is not to say that people never take extreme measures for instrumental purposes (e.g., one spouse could murder the other for a financial gain) or that they never use low-level abusive behaviors for relationship or identity purposes (such as a husband's slapping his wife to prove his manhood), but that research might show that there may be a tendency for partners to use lower levels of force when their goals are instrumental and higher levels of force to attain relationship or identity goals or both.

Conclusion

This review of recent studies on family violence that take a communication perspective reveals that a great deal of communication often takes place in abusive relationships. First, sometimes abusive behavior consists of verbal and nonverbal messages. Such behavior takes the form of verbal and symbolic aggression as when one insults, threatens, or swears, engages in putdowns or name calling, and ignores or neglects one's partner or child. Second, an abusive relationship often includes verbal and nonverbal messages that (a) trigger a particular abusive situation, (b) occur with abusive behaviors, and (c) are produced to repair damage done to the relationship or reinforce abuse.

The aim of this chapter has been to examine the contribution of the communication approach to domestic violence by first describing the communication perspective and then by applying it to the study of domestic violence. In so doing, domestic violence was defined as the ability to impose one's will (i.e., wants, needs, or desires) on another person through the use of verbal or nonverbal acts, or both, done in a way that violates socially acceptable standards and carried out with the intention or the perceived intention of inflicting physical or psychological pain, injury, or suffering or both.

This chapter related empirical findings on physical violence, sexual abuse, and verbal aggression to the dimensions of communication. The instrumental dimension reflects the degree to which physical and sexual aggression is self-reinforcing because it is often an effective way for abusers to get what they want. The relationship dimension indicates the degree to which abusers are willing to sacrifice enduring, supportive, and loving relationships to get what they want. The identity dimension involves the abusers' egos and their attempts to offer accounts to justify their actions and repair their identities. Future research might show that there may be a tendency for partners to use lower levels of force when their goals are instrumental and higher levels of force to attain relationship or identity goals or both.

The focus on the key elements of abusive relationships that are communicative in nature should be of interest to family violence researchers regardless of their academic discipline. First, when studying abusive family relationships, it is important to examine the meanings members attribute to one another's messages. Second, when studying abusive family relationships, it is important to include the major communication variables that play a role in the process of exchanging messages between partners; the verbal and nonverbal codes, the channels of communication, and the social contexts may have important effects on the development, maintenance, and deterioration of relationships. Third, it is important to identify the instrumental, relationship, and identity dimensions of communication.

It was also the purpose of this chapter to contribute to the development of domestic violence prevention and intervention. In their work, therapists can help victims and abusers (a) become aware of the interactional context characterized by patterns of abusive and communication behavior; (b) realize that violence occurs in families characterized by certain relationship structures; and (c) appreciate the fact that due to circular causality or reciprocal interactions, violence may serve a functional (instrumental, relationship, and identity goal or effect) but harmful role in the maintenance of some relationships.

Today, more published studies are taking a communication perspective on physical, verbal, and sexual abuse in the family. Many of these studies focus on interaction behavior involving dating partners, married couples, parent-child relationships, and other social systems that lend themselves to a communication approach to the conduct of research and inquiry. Many of these studies are part of an explanation that falls on the "dark side" of interpersonal communication.

I view these studies as a first step that I hope will lead to a better understanding of domestic violence by emphasizing the dynamics, the broader and more extended sequences of human interaction, and the interpersonal factors that are communicative and relational in nature. Moreover, I hope that such efforts will lead to improved prevention programs that "include a variety of efforts such as conflict management and interpersonal skills training, elimination of adversarial attitudes between the sexes, efforts to increase equality between the sexes, and work to reduce the romantic [and sometimes blinding] veneer of intimate relationships" (Lloyd & Emery, 1994, p. 43).

2

The Catalyst Hypothesis
Conditions Under Which Coercive Communication Leads to Physical Aggression

MICHAEL E. ROLOFF

This chapter examines the degree to which coercive communication (e.g., threats and insults) is a catalyst for physical aggression. Rather than assuming that verbal assaults always lead to physical violence, four factors are identified that cause such escalation: face loss, desire for control, coercive potential, and anger. Research associated with each of the factors is reviewed and future research directions are suggested.

Tedeschi and Felson (1994) define coercive behavior as "an action taken with the intention of imposing harm on another or forcing compliance" (p. 168). In effect, coercion involves the threatened or real use of negative sanctions to control another's behavior. Given that real or threatened aversive stimulation is a defining characteristic of physical aggression, it can be appropriately viewed as a form of coercive power. As such, actions typically labeled as physically aggressive can be grouped with other actions into larger categories of threats and punishments (Tedeschi & Felson, 1994).

Coercive forms of communication are evident within each of these larger categories. Threats are expressions of an intent to do harm to another (Tedeschi & Felson, 1994). Contingent threats forecast that the target will be punished unless he or she complies and noncontingency threats communicate impending, unavoidable punishment. Threats appear frequently as a basic strategy used to influence others (e.g., Wiseman & Schenck-Hamlin, 1981) and are a common way in which parents attempt to control their children (Trickett & Kuczynski, 1986).

Punishments are acts intended to do harm to another. Tedeschi and Felson (1994) distinguish between three types of harm. First, an individual may exert control over another by inflicting physical or emotional pain. Typically, such harm is achieved through direct bodily contact or by the use of weapons or objects. In some cases, communication is used to induce negative emotional states. For example, individuals who want to control, punish, or get even with their romantic partners often induce jealousy by exaggerating their attraction to rivals, flirting, or actually going out with others (White, 1980). Although not resulting in tissue damage, such emotional states may be accompanied by physiological reactions symptomatic of anger or depression (Shettel-Neuber, Bryson, & Young, 1978).

Second, punishment may be aimed at depriving another of needed resources. Although infrequently studied, strategic need depravation does occur. For example, relational influence is sometimes exerted by giving a partner the "silent treatment" during which individuals are unresponsive to their partner, ignore the partner, quit talking to the partner, and refuse to do favors until the partner complies (Buss, Gomes, Higgins, & Lauterbach, 1987).

Third, individuals may try to do social harm by attacking their partner's self-concepts. Communication is a fundamental process by which a person's identity is formed and maintained and, typically, communicators support each other's image or face (McCall & Simmons, 1978). Interactants, however, sometimes engage in insults and criticism that can aversively impact self-image and psychological well-being (e.g., Baron, 1988).

Thus, communication can be a coercive means of achieving relational control. It can forecast impending aversive stimulation or may itself serve as a punishment. Because of its punitive nature, coercive communication may prompt physical retaliation and could play a role in physically violent episodes. Therefore, in this paper I will (a) examine the conditions under which coercive communication might lead to interpersonal violence, and (b) articulate research directions arising from my analysis.

Coercive Communication and Interpersonal Violence

Researchers interested in interpersonal violence have often employed measures of coercive communication. Although frequently containing similar items, such measures have been variously labeled aggression (Scanzoni, 1978), emotional abuse (Dutton & Starzomski, 1993), negative affect (Bird, Stith, & Schladale, 1991), psychological abuse (Mason & Blankenship, 1987), psychological aggression (Stets, 1991), symbolic aggression (Cloven & Roloff, 1993), verbal aggression (Straus, 1974), verbal aggressiveness (Infante, Chandler, & Rudd, 1989; Infante, Sabourin, Rudd, & Shannon, 1990), and verbal coercion (Frieze & McHugh, 1992).

Generally, a positive correlation exists between the frequency of coercive communication and the use of physical aggression (Stets, 1990; Straus, 1974). This statistical association might be taken as evidence that verbal aggression serves as a catalyst for physical aggression. In effect, verbal aggression prompts or, perhaps, provokes physically aggressive responses. Although there is evidence to support this analysis, a close examination of research suggests that the "catalyst effect" is not a universal phenomena. The results of two studies illustrate the point.

Stets (1990) investigated the relationship between the frequency of verbal and physical aggression in marriage. A significant positive correlation emerged between the two forms of aggression that held across biological sex and race (correlations ranged from .15 to .27). A somewhat different picture emerges, however, when one examines the percentage of individuals who engaged in the tactics. Roughly 64% of the sample indicated that they had experienced or used verbal aggression within the past year without a single occurrence of physical aggression. Thus, for the majority of the sample, verbal aggression was not a prelude to physical aggression.

A similar conclusion can be reached from an analysis performed by Stets and Henderson (1991). They asked individuals to describe in detail the most coercive episode in which they had participated during the previous year. Consistent with the "catalyst hypothesis," 53% of the victims of physical aggression reported that it resulted from verbal aggression (e.g., an insult). Forty-seven percent, however, cited other causal factors, such as miscommunication, physical aggression, and alcohol-drug use. Among those who admitted using physical aggression against their relational partner, only 33% cited verbal aggression as a causal factor, whereas 67% attributed their violent behavior to other causes.

Although each of the aforementioned studies has methodological limitations, they suggest that coercive communication has the potential to lead to violence but does not always do so. Indeed, several scholars have noted that verbal aggression is a necessary but not sufficient condition for producing physical aggression (Infante et al., 1990; Stets & Henderson, 1991). Given that substantial numbers of individuals report being involved in verbally aggressive episodes, it is essential that researchers identify the conditions under which the catalyst hypothesis might be true. At least four factors might cause verbal aggression to lead to physical aggression: face loss, desire to control, violence potential, and anger.

Face Loss

Felson (1978) created a theory that highlights the causal role of impression management in aggressive episodes. Essentially, he argues that attacking another person's identity results in aggressive retaliation aimed at restoring face. Successful physical retaliation against a verbally aggressive person might (a) clearly establish one's physical dominance over the attacker, (b) humiliate the attacker, (c) prevent future face attacks, and (d) force the aggressor to make amends. The tendency to retaliate, however, is not unqualified. Although every insult and threat may inherently constitute an attack on another's identity, aggressive retaliation occurs only when the loss of face exceeds some threshold. A face attack is most likely to prompt retaliation when it is viewed as illegitimate, unmitigated, central to the victims' self-concept, public, and when the target lacks self-control.

Illegitimate Attacks. A face attack may be viewed as illegitimate if it is an inaccurate characterization of the target. As a result, the target is likely to disagree with the assessment and feel greater need to retaliate. Conversely, if the face attack is accepted by the target as being at least somewhat accurate or truthful, the pressure to retaliate may be lessened. It is possible that insults have a "grain of truth" to them. If face attacks result from a real grievance, they may be exaggerations rather than complete fabrications. Indeed, three quarters of a sample of college students indicated that they better understood their own deficiencies after a confrontation with a person who was angry with them (Averill, 1983). In such cases, the pressure to retaliate through physical aggression is attenuated.

Unmitigated Attacks. Although all forms of coercive communication constitute an attack on the hearer's face, the degree to which they do so may be affected by the linguistic elements of conflict messages. For example, not all phrasings of a given insult are equally insulting. Benoit and Benoit (1990) found that phrasings such as "You're a jerk for spending so much time with that friend" are perceived to be less appropriate and less effective than alternative phrasings such as "You've never given me reason to be jealous before but you're acting like a jerk now." Although both phrasings characterize the target in a negative way, the latter qualifies the characterization. Furthermore, they found that linguistic forms such as commands, unjustified requests, or refusals aggravate the attack on a target's face, whereas others, such as indirect requests or positive regard, mitigate the degree of face loss.

Such mitigation devices can be observed within conflict interactions. Power, McGrath, Hughes, and Manire (1994) found that mothers and fathers did not differ in the degree to which they used threats to control their children, but that mothers were significantly more likely to soften their control attempts by minimizing the size of their requests, justifying the request, expressing affection for the child, and expressing commonality with the child. Furthermore, Trickett and Kuczynski (1986) discovered that in disciplinary encounters, abusive and non-abusive parents did not significantly differ in their use of verbal punishments (threats or reprimands), but nonabusive parents were more likely to supplement coercive communication with requests and reasons for compliance.

Although never directly tested, it is possible that such mitigation may lessen the likelihood that coercive communication will lead to aggressive retaliation. For instance, Burman, Margolin, and John (1993) found that during an argument nonaggressive married couples were just as likely as physically aggressive ones to reciprocate each other's negative attacks (e.g., scorn or sarcasm), but that nonaggressive couples interspersed their negative behaviors with positive, supportive communication (e.g., affection, humor, and caring). It is possible that such "mixed" behavior mitigates the degree of face loss and prevents violent retaliation.

Centrality. Just as different phrases of the same insult may impact the degree to which it is insulting, not all types of insults are equally insulting. The most aversive insults are those that call into question critical features of a person's self-concept and they may be most likely to provoke aggressive retaliation. For example, based on interviews with the victims of physical aggression, Gelles (1972) hypothesized that certain verbally aggressive acts are more likely to prompt physical retaliation than are others. Nagging elicits violent reactions only occasionally, but the probability of physical aggression increases when a person engages in name-calling (profanity or ethnic slurs), verbal attacks (insults aimed at specific, personal traits), and all-out verbal attacks (assault on everything about a person). Consistent with this reasoning, Infante et al. (1990) found that violent episodes contain greater amounts of coercive communication (attacks on competency, background, physical appearance, and threats) than do nonviolent conflicts, but the most distinctive feature of violent episodes is the greater number of attacks on a person's character.

Although character attacks appear to be aversive, not all aspects of the self-concept may be so central that an alleged deficiency would be seen as terribly insulting. For example, Harris (1993) asked undergraduates the "worst thing" that individuals of the same or opposite sex could call one another. Regardless of the sex of the speaker, being called cowardly was perceived to be worse for males than for females and being referred to as promiscuous was thought to be worse for females than for males. For males, being called sexually inadequate or worthless and being characterized in an obscene way (e.g., bastard) was perceived to be worse when the communicator was female rather than male.

To the extent that these expectations are grounded in reality, males and females may be more reactive to some insults than others and their sensitivity might also vary with the sex of the speaker. For example, Briere (1987) asked undergraduate males how likely they would be to hit their wife under a variety of conditions. Roughly 15% indicated that they would consider hitting her if she refused to cook and keep the house clean, but 65% indicated that they might hit her if she told friends that they were "sexually pathetic." Thus, verbal aggression is most likely to serve as a catalyst for physical aggression when it attacks areas in which the parties are especially vulnerable.

Public Attacks. When others observe a verbal attack on one's face, humiliation may be greater than when the assault occurs in private, especially so for males. Self-reports reveal that males are more likely than females to become aggressive if challenged or argued with in public (Campbell, Muncer, & Coyle, 1992). Moreover, Briere (1987) discovered that 48% of a sample of male undergraduates indicated that they were at least somewhat likely to hit their wife if she "made fun" of them at a party.

The characteristics of onlookers, however, also affect the likelihood of male aggression. Shope, Hedrick, and Geen (1977) found that males were more physically aggressive toward females who aggressed against them in front of a male rather than in front of a female. The researchers interpreted this pattern as suggesting that males were more sensitive to a female's attack when in the presence of another male. Moreover, males were more physically aggressive toward another male who attacked them in the presence of a female rather than in the presence of a male. This might indicate that males are motivated to reassert their strength relative to another male so as to impress a female observer.

Although many abusive episodes occur in private (e.g., Gelles, 1972), some take place in public settings (e.g., Stets & Henderson, 1991) and it is possible that physical aggression can be precipitated by face attacks made earlier in the presence of others (cf. Briere, 1987). Thus, public insults may stimulate either an immediate or a delayed physical attack.

Self-Control. Given their face-threatening nature, it is not surprising that insults are capable of inducing feelings of anger that may become expressed and eventually escalate into physical aggression (Felson, 1982). Retaliation, however, might not occur if insulted individuals can exert emotional self-control. For example, Sadler and Tesser (1973) found that insulted individuals who were immediately distracted from thinking about the verbal attack became less hostile than individuals who dwelled on the negative event. This implies that people might be able to control their emotional reactions to coercive communications. Although individuals find it hard to ignore negative information and to remain physiologically unaroused, some are able to focus their attention away from their emotional reactions (Bonanno, Davis, Singer, & Schwartz, 1991; Weinberger & Davidson, 1994) and repress their expression of them. If so, these individuals may be less easily provoked by coercive communication.

This analysis suggests that coercive communication can serve as a catalyst for physical aggression but only when conditions increase sensitivity to identity attacks. If most people avoid these conditions, then the catalyst effect is a rare phenomenon.

Desire to Control

Stets (1993) argues that individuals have a fundamental need to control their environment. By doing so, they gain needed resources. Given the fact that interpersonal relationships are important sources of social need satisfaction, control may be a recurrent goal of intimate interactions (Stets, 1995). Indeed, as relational intimacy increases, there is increased desire to control a partner's behavior (Stets, 1993, 1995).

Although generally higher than in nonintimate relationships, the degree to which individuals wish to control their intimate partners varies. Stets (1993) likens interpersonal control to a cybernetic process in which control attempts are relatively infrequent until a person's level of control falls below some minimum threshold. Thus, when a person feels that he or she cannot master the environment, he or she will try to control it. One such challenge to a person's mastery is relational conflict, and conflict increases a person's desire to exert control (Stets, 1993, 1995).

A person who is trying to control his or her partner may engage in a variety of strategies. In initial attempts, noncoercive strategies may be the strategy of choice. White and Roufail (1989) asked undergraduates to rank order 43 influence strategies in terms of how likely they would use them in an initial influence attempt. Those most likely to be used were reason, stating desires, and offer to compromise. Individuals indicated that they would initially avoid verbally aggressive techniques, such as stating negative consequences for not complying, forcefully asserting one's way, getting angry, and arguing and yelling. The least likely strategies were physical force and threats of physical force. Although self-reports are sometimes suspect, there is evidence garnered from actual aggressive encounters that initial control attempts rarely entail insults and threats (Felson, 1984).

If initial, noncoercive influence attempts are met with resistance, however, individuals are willing to switch to more coercive tactics. For example, people are more willing to use high-pressure tactics (e.g., arguing and yelling, threatening to use force, and using force) and to express negative emotions (e.g., getting angry and demanding compliance) as measures of last resort than as initial influence attempts (White & Roufail, 1989).

If so, then the catalyst effect may result from a process by which individuals increase their level of force to overcome the level of experienced resistance. This principle is different from that suggested by reciprocal behavior. Instead of matching the degree of force associated with resistance, individuals apply greater pressure as a means of extinguishing further defiance. In the process, the conflict escalates to verbal and eventually physical coercion.

This analysis has several implications for conflict escalation. First, during the initial stages of a conflict, aggressive and nonaggressive episodes are indistinguishable. A person engages in an action that appears to another to be unacceptable and a noncoercive confrontation takes place (Felson, 1984).

Second, resistance plays a critical role in the likelihood that aggression will be used. Aggression emerges in later stages of a conflict as individuals attempt to overcome continued resistance. Indeed, Felson (1984) found that noncompliance to initial influence attempts was a critical feature of aggressive episodes. Although it is unclear as to whether noncompliance causes physical aggression or vice versa, studies of family interactions indicate that abused children are less likely than their nonabused counterparts to comply with their parents' control attempts (Oldershaw, Walters, & Hall, 1986; Trickett & Kuczynski, 1986).

Simple noncompliance, however, may be insufficient to trigger violent responses; resistance must be expressed in a manner that challenges another's sense of control. Indeed, abused children are not only less likely to comply with their parents' influence attempts but do so in an openly defiant manner (Trickett & Kuczynski, 1986). Kuczynski, Kochanska, Radke-Yarrow, and Girnius-Brown (1987) have speculated that children who have negotiation skills might successfully resist their parent's control attempts without the negative consequences associated with direct defiance. Conversely, an attack on another's right to control one's behavior may not prompt aggression if it is accompanied by compliance. Thus, a person might say, "I am going to do what you want but I think you are a jerk" and receive a less aggressive response than if the insult accompanied a refusal.

Third, an individual's inability to competently perform noncoercive techniques may promote a faster escalation sequence. Individuals who have limited persuasive skills are less likely to achieve compliance through noncoercive means and may switch to verbal and physical aggression much earlier in a dispute. Conversely, individuals who are persuasive may be better able to gain compliance and the control attempt stops. Although there are no direct tests of this notion, Infante et al. (1989) found that violent spouses relative to their nonviolent counterparts are less able to logically advance to attack positions during an argument but are more likely to be verbally aggressive. Furthermore, Follingstad, Wright, Lloyd, and Sebastian (1991) discovered that the inability to express oneself verbally was cited as a cause of a violent dating episode by about a third of a sample of victims and one quarter of the perpetrators.

Perhaps the most suggestive evidence comes from a study of the interaction patterns observed between abusive and nonabusive mothers and their children (Oldershaw et al., 1986). Abusive relative to non-abusive mothers were more likely to initially respond to their child's misbehavior with a command that contained no reason for compliance or with a command that also contained a power assertive tactic such as a threat, condemnation, or insult. Moreover, when encountering non-compliance, nonabusive mothers switched their strategies to other noncoercive ones, whereas abusive mothers continued with their coercive attempts. Finally, when children did comply, nonabusive mothers were more likely to respond with positive reinforcement rather than with power assertion; abusive mothers were equally likely to respond with positive reinforcement or continued verbal coercion. Although this study contained no direct measure of verbal skill, it is possible that abusive mothers are less able to employ arguments and other noncoercive techniques to gain compliance and switch much earlier to coercion. Alternatively, they may know how to do so but are unwilling to for some reason.

Regardless, the catalyst effect may result from a "battle for control" during which relational partners try to dominate each other while resisting being dominated (Babcock, Waltz, Jacobson, & Gottman, 1993). Indeed, such power struggles have been observed in studies of marital abuse (e.g., Anson & Sagy, 1995). If individuals are unable to secure compliance, they may shift to more forceful coercive strategies to overcome resistance. If the target is openly defiant or the communicator is unskillful, then the conflict may escalate to aggression much faster.

Violence Potential

A person's potential for violence constitutes the perceived amount of bodily harm that might be inflicted on another. As defined, violence potential is an attributed phenomena and, accordingly, the judgments of others may be at variance with a person's conception of his or her own potential. In some cases, an individual may appear to be more powerful to others than he or she thinks and in other instances a person may underestimate his or her violence potential.

Every person has a degree of potential for violence that can be brought to bear against another. A person who is ambulatory is capable of striking another. Some individuals, however, have greater coercive potential than others (i.e., they are bigger, more skilled at physical aggression, or have a weapon) and a person's potential for violence may vary with the situation. Because of their greater size, involvement with physical activity, and exposure to aggression, many males typically possess greater potential than some females. Some adult females, however, have many of the same advantages over children of both sexes and will have greater violence potential in dealing with them.

The possession of violence potential may predispose an individual to use it. Hence, when trying to control another, they are prone to turn to physical aggression to overcome resistance. Indeed, individuals who have access to coercive resources tend to use them (Lawler, Ford, & Blegen, 1988). Moreover, if their aggression results in compliance, then that response is reinforced and may be repeated in future conflicts (cf. Stets & Pirog-Good, 1987).

This trend, however, is not universal. In at least three cases, violence potential may not be acted on. First, the mere perception of the potential for violence may be sufficient to force compliance; hence, it is unnecessary to activate it. For example, individuals who think that their dominating partner might physically aggress against them if confronted tend to withhold their relational complaints (Cloven & Roloff, 1993). In effect, they are "chilled" from expressing grievances (Roloff & Cloven, 1990) and thereby allow their partners to control them (cf. Follingstad, Rutledge, Polek, & McNeill-Hawkins, 1988). Thus, violence potential may be sufficiently intimidating such that arguments rarely arise.

Second, a person's willingness to act on his or her potential for violence may be restrained by the partner's coercive potential. In some cases, the likelihood of acting aggressively is attenuated by the possibility that the partner might hit back. In other cases, the likelihood that the partner might leave the relationship, call the police, or that the aggressor might be stigmatized by families and friends is sufficient to reduce the likelihood that a person with violence potential might use it (Lackey & Williams, 1995).

Third, even if a person has greater violence potential than his or her partner, he or she may be constrained by societal norms about the use of aggression. For example, given that many males tend to have greater potential for physical aggression than do some females, one would expect that many males should show a greater willingness to enact it than will many females. Indeed, many males are more willing to be aggressive in the initial stages of a dispute than are many females (White & Roufail, 1989) and males often become increasingly aggressive against a resisting target who has insulted them (White, 1988).

Male aggression, however, is also limited by societal norms. Campbell and Muncer (1987) found that males are aware of prohibitions against physically aggressing against weaker individuals. To do so is to lose face. To aggress against an equal, however, is a "fair fight" and to "take on" a stronger individual is heroic. If so, then the willingness of males to act on their coercive potential against females should vary with the situation. Strangely, males who view females as equals may be more willing to aggress against them than those who view females as weaker. For example, Young, Beier, Beier, and Barton (1975) investigated how males with traditional sex role orientations (e.g., believed in male dominance) differed from those with more egalitarian ones when playing a game in which they and a female confederate were to try to hit one another with padded clubs. When the female was instructed to play the game defensively (i.e., do not attack him, only ward off his blows), males with egalitarian attitudes were far more aggressive (i.e., hit her with more intense blows) than were males with traditional attitudes. Those with traditional attitudes openly said that they could not hit a female. Only when the female shifted her strategy to play the game more offensively did the traditional males become more aggressive and then their attacks approached the intensity level of those of the egalitarian males. The egalitarian males were equally aggressive when the female played the game defensively or offensively.

Although the context is considerably different from that of an interpersonal conflict (i.e., it was a game in which aggression was appropriate), the results suggest that a fair fight rule may restrain some instances of male aggression. When a male regards females as equals, there is no societal stigma attached to being aggressive and there is evidence that egalitarian males can act aggressively toward their female partners (DeMaris, 1987). When the male views a female as weaker, however, the fair fight norm may inhibit violence unless he perceives that he is being challenged.

Just as having greater potential for violence does not always result in its use, having relatively little violence potential does not always preclude the use of aggression. Individuals in relatively powerless roles may use their limited potential for aggression as self-defense. Gelles (1972) observed what he described as "protective-reaction violence" during which abused wives (a) engage in a preemptive attack after seeing signs that their husband might attack them; (b) retaliate for his attack at a later time when the husband is vulnerable (e.g., he is drunk or sleeping); or (c) delay retaliation until she can acquire a weapon. Under these conditions, she is employing her limited violence potential in a manner to maximize its impact or, in the last case, is trying to increase her potential for violence.

Thus, a person may retaliate against verbal aggression by using his or her aggressive potential. Although there are societal norms that restrain individuals with coercive power from using it against weaker parties, the possession of violence potential may tempt an individual to employ it. Moreover, individuals whose potential for physical aggression is limited may use it selectively or seek to increase it when dealing with those with greater potential.

Anger

The mere expression of disagreement is physiologically arousing and this arousal can significantly reduce attraction even toward someone who is initially liked (Gormly, 1974). If so, then a verbally aggressive argument is especially likely to generate anger that may increase the likelihood of aggression. For example, both the accounts of victims and perpetrators of dating violence implicate anger as a cause (Follingstad et al., 1991).

Notwithstanding the aforementioned research, anger itself is not necessarily bad for conflict. It is possible that without anger, a person is insufficiently motivated to confront ongoing problems. Moreover, a person's muted emotional response to a complaint could be interpreted as indifference to the partner's concerns or as "stonewalling," which may result in resentment and further attacks (Scanzoni, 1978).

Prolonged and uncontrollable anger, however, is dysfunctional. When a person is unable to control his or her anger, it may be difficult to resolve a dispute. For example, Burman et al. (1993) examined the interaction behaviors of married couples whose typical conflict style could be characterized as primarily physically aggressive, verbally aggressive, withdrawing, or nonaggressively confrontational. When comparing the groups, they found that, to some degree, all spouses respond in kind to the angry or contemptuous attacks made on them by their partner. Physically aggressive couples, however, respond with greater anger that persists longer into the argument. Furthermore, the anger expressed by physically aggressive couples reduces the likelihood that they will engage in positive, neutral, or nonhostile negative interaction behaviors. From these data, the researchers speculate that although anger and contempt are reciprocated in all couples, those who have no history of physical aggression are able to break out of the cycle. Although verbally aggressive couples attack each other through the content of their communication (e.g., insults or criticisms), they control and reduce their affective displays of anger as the argument progresses (e.g., yelling, disdain, and sarcasm) and apparently avoid escalation. This may be a sign that verbally aggressive couples are able to attack one another but still stay in control of their anger.

Given these data, it is possible that the ability to control one's anger or at least the display of one's anger may be central to reducing the likelihood of physical aggression. Indeed, individuals who are adept at emotional control are also less aggressive and less likely to have engaged in criminal behavior (Weinberger & Schwartz, 1990). As a result, one might speculate that the lack of emotional control might play a role in the catalyst effect.

Although there is no research focused directly on this link, there are suggestive findings. Mason and Blankenship (1987) found that highly stressed females who had a high need for affiliation but were low in impulse control were most likely to inflict physical and psychological abuse on their romantic partners. These findings suggest that when stressed individuals are unable to control their impulses, they may act out their negative emotions against their relational partners. Interestingly, this pattern is also evident in how females describe their use of physical aggression. In general, females are more likely than males to characterize their physical aggression as a failure to control their anger (Campbell & Muncer, 1987; Campbell et al., 1992). This may result from the greater tendency of many males to internalize or repress their emotions rather than to externalize them (Weinberger & Davidson, 1994).

Research, however, has also uncovered a lack of emotional control in violent males. Several studies find a positive relationship between the propensity to become angry and inflicting both psychological and physical aggression (Dutton, Saunders, Starzomski, & Bartholomew, 1994; Dutton & Starzomski, 1993). Furthermore, Margolin, John, and Gleberman (1988) found that, during a conflict interaction with their spouse, physically aggressive husbands exhibited greater degrees of nonverbal anger and contempt than did nonviolent husbands. Thus, uncontrolled anger appears to be related to interpersonal violence among males and females.

Although the presence of an anger-prone person increases the probability that verbal aggression results in physical aggression, it may not assure it. It is possible that a nonaggressive partner may move to close off the argument before it escalates to violence. When seeing insults and threats, they act to "cool off" the dispute and prevent further escalation. For example, Vuchinich (1987) discovered that mothers and daughters play a critical role in bringing family quarrels to a close. They typically initiate compromises and, when a conflict results in a standoff, they are more likely to focus family attention on nonconflict activities than are male family members.

This implies that the likelihood of conflict escalation is greater when both relational partners lack impulse control than when only one does. In such cases, there is no one to close off the dispute before it erupts into violence. Moreover, the mutual absence of impulse control implies that violence may be initiated by either partner. As a result, there are a greater number of potentially violent interchanges.

Research Directions

Although the catalyst hypothesis is both intuitive and empirically supported, my analysis suggested that it might not be a universal phenomena. I articulated four perspectives that might provide insight into the conditions when the catalyst hypothesis holds. Although I was able to find research that seemed to support all four perspectives, much more work is necessary to establish their veracity. By and large, my review constituted a post hoc attempt to piece together research into coherent frameworks. In most cases, the cited research was not conducted with my perspectives in mind. Although my inductive approach to formulating the perspectives yielded some plausible insights, research needs to be executed that directly tests the various paths.

When conducting this research, scholars should be mindful of the relationship among the four perspectives. It is possible that there are multiple determinants of the catalyst effect; hence, each perspective constitutes a viable and distinct path from coercive communication to physical aggression. Consequently, no single path can account for all instances of the catalyst effect.

Furthermore, when studying the catalyst effect, researchers need to employ diverse methodologies. Assessing the frequency of aggressive acts can be useful for categorizing relationships in terms of their primary conflict management styles, but it does not provide the kind of information needed to analyze the causal factors involved in the catalyst effect. Researchers must employ methods that richly test the communication variables that occur during conflict episodes. Reenactments of conflict interactions (Burman et al., 1993), written accounts of prior conflict episodes (Stets & Henderson, 1991), diaries (Trickett &

Kuczynski, 1986), and taped observations of naturally occurring conflicts (Power et al., 1994) yield the kind of detailed data necessary to study escalation processes. Although none of the aforementioned are error free, each can provide useful information about the communication patterns that distinguish aggressive from nonaggressive episodes.

Finally, I end on a cautionary note. Although coercive communication does not always lead to physical aggression, one should not view it as an appropriate way to manage disputes. It can lead to physical violence. Furthermore, coercive forms of communication, such as verbal aggression, typically lead to more psychologically and emotionally destructive outcomes than do noncoercive conflict management techniques (Infante, Myers, & Buerkel, 1994). Hence, it is not surprising that criticism and verbal assaults appear prominently among "things people wish they hadn't said" (Knapp, Stafford, & Daly, 1986).

3

Family Interaction Process

An Essential Tool for
Exploring Abusive Relations

GAYLA MARGOLIN
RICHARD S. JOHN
CHANDRA M. GHOSH
ELANA B. GORDIS

This chapter examines whether aggression in the marital relationship is associated with family processes observed during a dyadic play task and a triadic family discussion. Fathers' physical and emotional marital aggression was linked to fathers' authoritarian and controlling behaviors with sons. Marital aggression also was linked with boys' participation and emotional reactions during the tasks, with fewer findings for girls. These data suggest that understanding the effects of interparental aggression requires examination of parent-child relationships.

A story titled "The Forgotten Victims" (Baum, 1994) appearing in the *Los Angeles Times* recounts the following episode, which had occurred in Tampa, Florida, as two sheriff's deputies responded to a complaint of wife beating:

> The deputies, who had been to this home several times, said they didn't know if the couple had children. This time, while one deputy was

AUTHORS' NOTE: Preparation of the manuscript was supported by the National Institute of Mental Health Grants 1RO1 36595 and 1F31 10947. Correspondence regarding this chapter should be addressed to Gayla Margolin, Department of Psychology, SGM 930, University of Southern California, Los Angeles, CA 90089-1061.

subduing the fuming man, the other noticed a spelling book on a coffee
table and began to search. Finally, in the master bedroom, she heard a
noise coming from the closet. Inside, three small children were huddled
together. The older brother had a gun. Whenever a fight broke out, he
would grab the gun and hide the other children. (pp. E1, E6)

As this incident suggests, children who observe physical aggression
between their parents often are the forgotten or unidentified victims of
chaotic and violent family systems. In this case, deputies had been in
this family's home on several previous occasions without noticing
whether or not children were present.

Over the past 20 years there has been increasing attention to
identifying appropriate legal and mental health responses for male
perpetrators of violence and for female victims of assault, yet relatively
little attention has been paid to the children who are exposed to such
violence between their parents. Watching one parent physically lash out
against another parent can have significant cognitive and emotional
impact on a child even if the child suffers no direct physical harm.

Extrapolating from prevalency data on marital violence, it is estimated that 3.3 million children in the United States are at risk each year
for exposure to interparental violence (Carlson, 1984). The situation of
most children who witness marital violence may not be as poignant as
the one described above. There is variability in the chronicity and
severity of violence observed by children. Some children may see an
occasional slap or shove, whereas others may witness frequent beatings.
Likewise, there is variability in the resources and coping mechanisms
available to children who are exposed to interparental violence. Some
child witnesses may enjoy a supportive relationship with an adult,
whereas others may be more isolated and lonely. Overall, the literature
indicates that children exposed to marital violence are at risk for a
variety of emotional, social, and behavioral problems (e.g., Fantuzzo &
Lindquist, 1989; Holden & Ritchie, 1991; Hughes, Vargo, Ito, & Skinner,
1991; Jaffe, Wolfe, & Wilson, 1990; Margolin, in press; McDonald &
Jouriles, 1991; Sternberg et al., 1993). There is considerable range in
the outcomes for children, however, with some child witnesses showing
severe disturbance and others surviving relatively unscathed.

One of the key questions surrounding the impact of marital violence
on children is whether families that engage in violence exhibit other
types of coercive and destructive interaction patterns that also have a

negative impact on children. Not surprisingly, there is evidence that physical aggression often is accompanied by high levels of verbal aggression in the marriage (Murphy & O'Leary, 1989). Exposure to marital conflict even if it does not include physical aggression has also been linked with negative child outcomes (Cummings & Davies, 1994; Emery, 1982; Fincham & Osborne, 1993). Less is known about the linkages between physical aggression in the marriage and hostile, punitive parent-child relationships. To make sense of the variability in children's outcomes, it is important to examine how marital violence is related to other risk factors in the family context. In this chapter, we explore whether interparental violence is associated with other types of disruption in family interaction. In particular, we examine the relationship between interparental aggression and parents' abilities to engage in typical, everyday types of parent-child interactions, such as discussing problem issues and playing a game with their children.

The focus on the relationship between marital abuse and typical parenting activities has both theoretical and clinical implications and should interest anyone studying family violence or working with violent families. As noted some time ago by Patterson (1982), the study of day-to-day interactions is the key to understanding long-term changes in the family process. Although often thought to be innocuous, these day-to-day interactions set into motion short-term changes in mood and set the stage for significant developmental outcomes. Because of the frequent, repetitive nature of these interactions, they also can be a good choice as a target of intervention.

This chapter presents an overview of what is known about the relationship between exposure to marital violence and family process. This literature is, in some regards, an outgrowth of a more general literature on marital conflict (rather than violence) and its effects on children. We will then present data from our own laboratory examining the association between marital abuse and parent-child relations. We are interested in distinguishing the effects of physical abuse from emotional abuse and thus explore how both types of abuse relate to family process.

Generalizing from the marital conflict literature (Emery, Fincham, & Cummings, 1992; Fauber & Long, 1991) on marital violence, it can be suggested that exposure to marital conflict takes its toll on children through direct and indirect risk factors (Margolin, in press). Direct risks refer to those reactions reflecting the psychic trauma or posttraumatic stress that develop when faced with an overwhelming and generally dangerous situation. In addition to the potential risk for injury to the child, there is also the fear, helplessness, and horror of witnessing an attack on a loved one (Peled, Jaffe, & Edleson, 1995). The reactions shown are similar to responses to other traumatic experiences or to witnessing other types of violence (Bell & Jenkins, 1993; Garbarino, Dubrow, Kostelny, & Pardo, 1992). Witnessing interparental violence may be even more confusing and frightening because the child is witnessing the injury of one parent at the hands of another.

Indirect risks refer to those reactions that are due to the parents being compromised in their caretaking functions. Interparental abuse is likely to take its toll on children by making each parent less emotionally and physically available to the child and less effective as a caretaker. There is a growing literature lending support to the idea that parents embroiled in their own conflicts may be compromised in their parenting roles. The majority of this literature is based on the reactions of parents who experience marital discord not even as extreme as marital violence, although a handful of studies also have examined parenting by perpetrators and victims of abuse. Recent reviews have summarized the link between disturbance in the marriage and disrupted parenting (Easterbrooks & Emde, 1988; Engfer, 1988; Erel & Burman, 1995) due to disagreement specifically over the child (e.g., Block, Block, & Morrison, 1981), overly punitive discipline (Fauber, Forehand, Thomas, & Wierson, 1990; Jouriles, Pfiffner, & O'Leary, 1988), or triangulation whereby the child is drawn into the marital conflict through pressure by one parent to side against the other parent (Maccoby & Mnookin, 1992; Minuchin, Rosman, & Baker, 1978; Westerman, 1987).

With regard to marital violence per se and not just conflict, there is evidence that husbands who abuse their wives are more likely to abuse their children. Early reports suggested that both perpetrators and victims of spouse abuse are more abusive to their children (Straus, Gelles, & Steinmetz, 1980). Recent data, however, suggest that it is abusive men in particular who tend to be physically aggressive with their children (O'Keefe, 1994) and mostly toward their sons (Jouriles & LeCompte, 1991). Holden and Ritchie (1991) provide the most comprehensive evaluation of parenting in abusive couples—using maternal reports and mother-child observations to compare abusive and nonabusive couples. Batterers, compared to nonbatterers, were portrayed by their wives as more irritable, less involved in child rearing, less physically affectionate, less likely to use reasoning in response to misbehavior, and more likely to use physical punishment and power-assertive responses. Although abused wives reported high levels of parenting stress, these wives did not differ from control wives in their discipline approaches. Thirty-four percent of the battered women, however, compared to 5% of the control sample, reported frequently changing their child-rearing behavior in the husbands' presence, presumably to avoid inciting the fathers' anger.

The primary question to be examined here is whether abuse in the marital arena is associated with particular styles of family processes that involve the child. Is marital abuse associated with negativistic, controlling styles of parenting? Is marital abuse associated with a greater likelihood of particular responses by the child? Direct observations of family interaction have been obtained rather than relying on family members' recollections and interpretations of family process. The present study is similar to previous studies in its treatment of marital aggression as a global and historical variable. It is set apart from previous studies, however, in its focus on actual interactional processes and children's immediate reactions during those interactions.

A "common-factor" hypothesis (Engfer, 1988) suggests that the interpersonal style of a parent may be a common determinant of both the marital and the parent-child relationship. That is, an individual may exhibit a harsh, authoritarian interpersonal style that generalizes across relationships and creates tensions with both the spouse and the child. Hostile, coercive interpersonal styles, for example, have been found to characterize spouse-abusing males (Margolin, John, & Gleberman, 1988) and have also been associated with childhood problems (Patterson, 1982). Although the marital interaction literature and parenting literature point to similar features that are destructive to the communication process, these literatures have remained relatively distinct.

A major contribution of the study presented here is the ability to examine the link between marital abuse, interparental communication style, and parenting style within the same individuals. The data to be presented are based on two types of interpersonal tasks. One task, surrounding a play activity, examines the separate relationships of each parent with the child. From these data, we can examine the differential relationship between abuse and the mother-child and father-child relationships. The second task, a three-person problem-solving discussion, simultaneously involves both parents and the child. This task allows us to examine the child's reaction to possible interparental and parent-child conflict that may occur in the presence of both parents. Data from each of these tasks will be used to examine whether the amount of physical and emotional aggression exhibited in the marital relationship is related to (a) the parents' behavior as they interact with the child, (b) the child's behavior when interacting with the parents, or (c) associations between specific parent and child behaviors.

Overall Design

Participants

Ninety-one families participated in this study, which was the second phase of a two-part study on marital conflict and family interactions. The original sample of 180 families was recruited through various public announcements and direct mailings in the Los Angeles area. At the time of the first stage, all families had two parents living in the home and had a child age 8 to 11 years inclusive (89 male and 91 female). The eligibility criteria for the study were (a) both parents were required to read and speak English fluently; (b) at least one adult was required to be the biological parent of the child, and any nonbiological parents were required to have lived with the child since the child's second birthday; and (c) the parents were required to have a telephone in the home. Of the original sample, 123 families were invited back, and 103 (84%) indicated that they were interested in participating. The goal of the second stage of the study was to see half of the families, so once this target was reached the remaining families were not scheduled.

Due to video equipment problems, 3 families were not videotaped during the parent-child interaction task, and 1 of the 3 also was not videotaped during the triadic interaction task; therefore, the sample size for this study is 88 for the dyadic interaction and 90 for the triadic interaction. Demographic data for the 90 families reveal the ethnic composition of the couples in the sample to be primarily Caucasian (70%) and African American (21%). Of the 90 children, 15.5% were only children, 36.7% had one sibling, 25.5% had two siblings, and 22.2% had three or more siblings. The mean age of the children was

11.4 for boys (standard deviation [*SD*] = 1.09, range = 9.4-13.1) and 11.2 for girls (*SD* = 1.1, range = 9.4-13.4). *T*-tests and chi-square analyses revealed no significant differences for boys and girls on any of these demographic variables. For further details about the sample, see Gordis, Margolin, and John (in press).

General Procedures

Families that participated in the second stage of the study returned to the laboratory for a 3-hour session that included a number of videotaped interaction tasks and several questionnaires. For our purposes here, we focus on the Domestic Conflict Inventory (DCI), a self-report questionnaire used to assess emotional and physical aggression in the marriage, and two interaction tasks.

Domestic Conflict Inventory

Scores on physical and emotional marital aggression derived from the DCI (Margolin, Burman, John, & O'Brien, 1990) serve as our measure of children's exposure to marital abuse. The DCI is a 51-item inventory of marital conflict behaviors containing a 14-item index of physical abuse and an 11-item index of emotional abuse (see Margolin, John, & Foo, 1995). Participants were presented with a list of 51 behaviors and asked to indicate (a) whether the behavior has ever happened in the relationship with the spouse, (b) whether it has happened in front of the child, and (c) the number of times the behavior has occurred in the previous 12 months using a six-category response system (0, once, 2-5 times per year, 6-12 times per year, 2-4 times per month, and more than once per week). Each spouse is presented with the list of behaviors twice. First they are asked whether they have exhibited the behaviors toward the spouse, and then they are presented with the list and asked to consider if their spouse has exhibited the behaviors toward them. To examine emotional and physical aggression within the past year, we used the frequency data, corresponding to the six categories of responses (0-5). When there were discrepancies between a husband's and wife's report about a specific behavior, the maximum report between the two was used based on the assumption that underreporting is more likely than overreporting (Margolin, 1987).

The 14-item physical aggression summary score was composed of the following behaviors: (1) physically twisted your spouse's arm; (2) pushed, grabbed, or shoved your spouse; (3) slapped your spouse; (4) physically forced sex on your spouse; (5) burned your spouse; (6) shaken your spouse; (7) thrown or tried to throw your spouse bodily; (8) thrown an object at your spouse; (9) choked or strangled your spouse; (10) kicked, bit, or hit your spouse with a fist; (11) hit your spouse or tried to hit your spouse with something; (12) beat your spouse up (multiple blows); (13) threatened your spouse with a knife or gun; and (14) used a knife or gun on your spouse. The 11-item emotional aggression summary included (1) damaged a household item or some part of your home out of anger toward your spouse; (2) deliberately disposed of or hid an important item of your spouse's; (3) purposely hurt your spouse's pet; (4) purposely damaged or destroyed your spouse's clothes, car, or other personal possessions or all three; (5) locked your spouse out of the house; (6) told your spouse that he or she could not work or go to school or to other self-improvement activities; (7) tried to prevent your spouse from seeing or talking to family or friends; (8) restricted your spouse's use of the car or telephone; (9) tried to turn family, friends, or children against your spouse; (10) frightened your spouse; and (11) prevented your spouse from getting medical care that he or she needed.

By summing the maximum reports for each item, we created physical and emotional aggression scores for both husband and wife. The sample mean and standard deviation for these indices, given by couple, are as follows: (a) physical aggression ($M = 2.5$; $SD = 4.8$), and (b) emotional aggression ($M = 4.2$; $SD = 6.5$). These reports show that 43 couples had been physically aggressive in the past and had scores ranging from 1 to 22 ($M = 5.2$; $SD = 5.8$). A total of 58 couples reported emotional aggression, with scores ranging from 1 to 37 ($M = 6.6$; $SD = 7.0$). The correlation between physical and emotional aggression in the entire sample was .57. DCI scores, as a measure of background abuse witnessed by the child, are expected to be related to parents' behavior in the interactional tasks and to have both direct and indirect relations with children's behavior in the interactional task.

Dyadic Parent-Child Interaction Play Task

The dyadic parent-child play task was designed as an analog of the relatively common parent-child situation in which a parent and child are working together to accomplish a common goal in the context of a play task. Designed to be mildly frustrating and somewhat challenging, the task elicits a range of parenting styles across parent-child dyads as well as a range of positive and negative affect. According to Baumrind (Baumrind, 1991; Baumrind & Black, 1967), an important distinction is made between authoritarian parenting—that is, discouraging verbal exchanges and restricting children's autonomy—and authoritative parenting—that is, encouraging open communication and independence while firmly enforcing the rules. Research has borne out the assumption that authoritative parenting is associated with positive child outcomes, such as positive peer relationships (Dekovic & Janssens, 1992), stronger school performance and school engagement (Steinberg, Lamborn, Dornbusch, & Darling, 1992), and higher levels of social and intellectual competence (Baumrind, 1975, 1991; Dornbusch, Ritter, Leiderman, Roberts, & Fraleigh, 1987; Lamborn, Mounts, Steinberg, & Dornbusch, 1991), whereas authoritarian parenting styles are associated with negative child outcomes, such as lower grades (Dornbusch et al., 1987) and poorer self-conceptions (Lamborn et al., 1991). The purpose of this task is to examine authoritarian and authoritative parental styles, as well as children's behaviors, during the play task.

Procedures

Parents and children were videotaped while attempting to copy a black line drawing (fish, dog, or octopus) using an Etch-A-Sketch toy (Lindahl, Clements, & Markman, in press; Trickett, Susman, & Lourie, 1980). In half the families, mothers completed the task first with the children, and in the other half, fathers completed the task first.[1] The experimenter instructed the parent and child that they were to work together for 5 minutes to try to copy the design, but that each of them could use only one knob (Ghosh, Margolin, & John, 1995). One knob of the Etch-A-Sketch makes vertical lines and the other makes horizontal lines; therefore, to make curves the parent and child had to work together.

Coding System and Procedures

The parent-child interaction task was coded using a system developed specifically for this task. The coding system and procedure are discussed in greater detail in Ghosh et al. (1995).[2] The system assesses the degree to which parents display authoritarian and authoritative behaviors. Authoritarian behaviors include giving direct commands and ignoring or refusing to comply with the child's directives, whereas authoritative behaviors consist of making suggestions or asking the child's opinion when directing the child's behavior. The active participation code assesses the relative frequency with which children actively participate in the task either by actively responding to parents' directives (verbally agreeing, giving solutions, or suggesting alternatives) or by directing their parents' behavior.

In addition, the coding system measures the relative frequency of positive affect (i.e., positive feelings and emotions about the task and expressions of care, affection, praise, or goodwill toward the other participant) and negative affect (i.e., annoyance or frustration directed at the other participant, the task, or themselves) that both parents and children exhibited during the task.

Each parent-child dyad was coded by three coders who had been trained and had demonstrated knowledge of the coding system. All resulting analyses were conducted on logit transformations of the values (Ghosh et al., 1995; Mosteller & Tukey, 1977).[3] Interrater reliability was determined through an intraclass correlation coefficient (Shrout & Fleiss, 1979), which calculates reliability by comparing data from all three coders. Intraclass correlation coefficients ranged from .68 to .97. Final codes are determined by taking the average logit of all three coders.

Results

Association Between Marital Aggression and Parent-Child Interactions. The first question examined is whether parents' use of physical and emotional aggression within the marriage is related to the way parents and children behave together during the cooperative play task. Table 3.1 presents results of correlational analyses based on the father-child interactions with boys and girls. Associations are presented between

TABLE 3.1 Correlations Between Fathers' Conflict Behaviors and Fathers' and Children's Coded Behaviors

	Physical Abuse		Emotional Abuse	
	Boys[a]	Girls[b]	Boys	Girls
Fathers' behaviors				
Authoritarian	.34*	.23	.45**	.06
Authoritative	−.32*	−.15	−.37*	−.11
Negative affect	.37*	.19	.30	−.01
Positive affect	−.22	−.05	−.19	.07
Children's behaviors				
Active participation	−.39**	−.01	−.36*	.13
Negative affect	.04	.09	.11	.07
Positive affect	−.19	−.13	−.12	−.19

a. $n = 43$.
b. $n = 45$.
*$p < .05$; **$p < .01$.

fathers' physical and emotional aggression in the marriage and four adult in-task behaviors (authoritarian, authoritative, negative affect, and positive affect), as well as three child in-task behaviors (active participation, negative affect, and positive affect). The results of these analyses indicate that fathers' use of physical or emotional aggression is positively associated with their use of authoritarian behaviors and negatively with their use of authoritative behaviors during father-son interactions. The results also suggest that fathers' physical aggression in the marriage is associated positively with their use of negative affect in father-son interactions.

Fathers' physical and emotional aggression toward their wives also appears to be associated with the way boys behave during the task. Greater aggression by fathers is associated with a smaller relative frequency of active participation by boys. That is, boys living with fathers who are aggressive make relatively fewer suggestions and take a relatively less active role when interacting with the father in a play task.

As contrasted with the fathers, mothers' physical and emotional aggression in the marriage appears generally unrelated to the way they or the children behave during the mother-child play task. Mothers' aggression was not associated with their own behaviors or with sons' behaviors during the play task and was associated with only one of the girls' behaviors. Girls whose mothers exhibited physical aggression toward the father tended to be relatively less active ($r = -.37, p < .05$).

In addition, the data indicate two crossover effects, in which one parent's marital aggression is associated with the other parent's behavior during parent-child interactions. Fathers' use of physical aggression in the marriage is associated positively with mothers' use of negative affect with girls ($r = .32, p < .05$), and mothers' use of emotional aggression toward their husbands is associated positively with fathers' use of negative affect with boys ($r = .40, p < .01$).

Association Between Parenting Style and Children's Behavior as a Function of Fathers' Physical Aggression. The second question surrounding the play task examines whether the association between parents' behavior and children's behavior is different in families with physically aggressive versus nonaggressive fathers. Previously, we have found that children's active participation with their parents is positively associated with authoritative parenting and negatively associated with authoritarian parenting (Ghosh et al., 1995). The specific question to be examined here is whether this pattern is influenced by the presence or absence of fathers' aggressiveness toward the mothers.

The sample was divided into families in which the father had exhibited physical aggression or had not exhibited physical aggression based on both parents' reports on the DCI. In addition, the sample was split by child gender, yielding four groups. Table 3.2 presents correlations, for those four groups, between parents' and children's behaviors during the task. In addition to displaying which correlations are significant, Table 3.2 also indicates which correlations are of a significantly different magnitude. Correlations from the different groups were compared separately for boys and girls (boys from homes with marital aggression were compared with boys from homes with no marital aggression and girls from homes with marital aggression were compared with girls from homes with no marital aggression) using Fisher's r to z transformations to determine whether the relationship between parents' and children's behaviors is different in families having a father who is aggressive versus nonaggressive toward the wife. Matching superscripts indicate that the strength of the association is different between the two groups.

TABLE 3.2 Correlations Between Parental Behaviors and Child Behavior, by Fathers' Marital Aggression and Child Gender

	Observed Child Behaviors					
	Activity Level		Negative Affect		Positive Affect	
Observed Parent Behavior	No Marital Aggression	Marital Aggression	No Marital Aggression	Marital Aggression	No Marital Aggression	Marital Aggression
			Father-child interaction			
Authoritarian	−.47[a]	−.87***[a]	−.02	−.28	−.32	−.58*
	(−.47*)[b]	(−.81***)[b]	(.17)	(.17)	(−.01)[e]	(−.61*)[e]
Authoritative	.06[c]	.87***[c]	−.01	.45	.07	.60*
	(.18)	(.47)	(−.17)	(−.31)	(−.20)	(.46)
Negative affect	.10	.04	.62***	.61*	−.26	.10
	(−.05)	(−.36)	(.59**)	(.41)	(−.05)	(−.39)
Positive affect	−.32[d]	.79**[d]	−.33	.40	.42*	.59*
	(−.17)	(.24)	(−.12)	(−.12)	(.51**)	(.43)
			Mother-child interaction			
Authoritarian	−.65***	−.76**	.24	−.22	−.11	.49
	(−.53**)	(−.74**)	(.00)	(−.25)	(.13)	(−.18)
Authoritative	.24	.55*	.07	.40	.22	−.14
	(.48**)	(.19)	(−.13)	(.12)	(.08)	(.09)
Negative affect	−.19	−.25	.31	.19	−.15	.08
	(.07)	(−.23)	(.25)	(.27)	(−.17)	(−.33)
Positive affect	.13	−.16	−.01	−.13	.50**	.84***
	(−.14)	(.17)	(−.01)	(.13)	(.48**)	(.57*)

NOTE: Correlations between behaviors from parent-girl interactions are given in parentheses, whereas correlations for behaviors from parent-boy interactions are not in parentheses. The sample size for the groups with no marital aggression are $n = 29$ for boys and $n = 31$ for girls. The sample size for the groups with marital aggression are $n = 14$ for both boys and girls.
a., b., c., d., e. Coefficients sharing similar superscripts differ at $p < .05$.
*$p < .05$; **$p < .01$; *** $p < .001$.

With regard to the father-child interaction, several patterns characterize the relationship between fathers' and children's behavior across both groups of families. Fathers' authoritarian behaviors are associated with smaller relative frequencies of active participation on the part of both boys and girls in the physically aggressive and nonaggressive families. In addition, in both groups, there is a mirroring between parent and child in terms of the relative frequency with which positive or negative affect is displayed. That is, when fathers display high levels of negative affect, boys and girls also seem to exhibit high levels of negative affect, and when fathers display high positive affect, boys and girls also display high levels of positive affect.

Nevertheless, there are also significant differences between families with aggressive husbands versus those with nonaggressive husbands in the way that fathers' behavior is related to children's behavior. First, with respect to fathers' authoritarian behaviors, the association with less active participation noted for both groups is significantly stronger in the maritally aggressive compared to nonaggressive families, irrespective of child gender. In addition, for maritally aggressive families only, fathers' authoritarian behaviors are associated with relatively lower levels of positive affect in girls. Second, fathers' authoritative behaviors are associated with boys' behaviors only in families with marital aggression. In the maritally aggressive families, fathers' authoritative behaviors are associated with relatively more active participation and relatively more positive affect on the part of boys. Third, with respect to fathers' positive affect, there is a relationship between fathers' positive affect and boys' active participation for the maritally aggressive group only. The more maritally aggressive fathers display positive affect, the more the boys tended to participate actively in the task.

Examination of the mother-child interaction reveals no differences between groups for maritally aggressive or nonaggressive families. For both types of families, mothers' authoritarian behaviors are associated with relatively lower levels of active participation by both boys and girls. In contrast, when mothers use authoritative behaviors, boys from families with marital aggression and girls from families with no marital aggression appear to display higher relative frequencies of active participation; the relative frequency with which they exhibited this behavior, however, was not significantly different from the relative frequency exhibited by children from other groups. As with the father-child relationship, there is a mirroring of positive affect between children and mothers. Relatively higher levels of positive affect by mothers are associated with relatively higher levels of positive affect by the children.

Triadic Family Problem-Solving Discussion

In this section, we examine whether the amount of marital physical and emotional aggression relates to observed behavior of family members when both parents and child are present. Because researchers have found that parents behave differently with their child in each other's presence than in each other's absence, examining both dyadic and triadic observations is crucial to obtaining a full picture of how marital conflict is related to parent-child interaction (Gjerde, 1986; Margolin, 1981).

The purpose of this portion of the study is to examine whether parents' levels of physical and emotional aggression in the marriage relate to family members' behavior when discussing a conflictual topic together with the child. Individuals reporting higher levels of physical and emotional aggression in the marriage may be more hostile toward their spouses, more hostile and controlling toward their child, and may engage more often in cross-generational alliances, theorized to be dysfunctional in the family systems literature (Minuchin, 1974).

After independently completing various questionnaires and engaging in various other interaction tasks, mother-father-child triads were videotaped engaging in a family discussion about a child-related issue about which the parents experienced some interparental conflict. Details regarding how topics were chosen and procedures around the interaction are presented elsewhere in Gordis et al. (in press). The three-person family system had this conflictual discussion sitting around a table while eating a snack.

Coding System

The discussions were coded for parents' hostility and controlling behaviors, parent-child alliances, and three child behaviors: withdrawal, anxiety, and distraction. Hostility was created by collapsing across three behavior codes: (a) frustration-contempt (expressions of negative affect in the form of anger, contempt, or frustration toward another family member), (b) self-defense (argumentative or defensive statements made toward another person), and (c) blame (putting the responsibility for a problem on another person). Reliabilities, calculated with intraclass correlation coefficients (Shrout & Fleiss, 1979), were $r = .91$ for father-to-mother hostility, $r = .90$ for mother-to-father hostility, $r = .29$ for father-to-child hostility, and $r = .77$ for mother-to-child hostility. Controlling was created by collapsing across two codes: (a) lecture or laying down the law (moralizing at another person or asserting an inflexible rule) and (b) leading questions (asking questions to which one knew the answer or demanding a certain answer to build a case or argue a point). Father controlling child had reliability of $r = .60$, and mother controlling child had reliability of $r = .69$. Alliance with child was coded when a parent sided with the child, shared the child's position, or presented his or her perspective as being the same as the child's to the exclusion of the other parent. Alliance was a dichotomous code and had the following reliabilities: $k = .21$ for father to child and $k = .45$ for mother to child. In addition, three children's behaviors were studied: (a) Withdrawal ($r = .70$) was coded when a child made himself or herself inaccessible to the other participants or otherwise withdrew from the interaction; (b) anxiety ($r = .72$) was coded when the child seemed uncomfortable, anxious, or embarrassed during the interaction; and (c) distraction ($r = .70$) occurred when the child engaged in silly or irrelevant behavior that drew attention away from the topic of the discussion.

Further details regarding the coding system and procedures are presented in Gordis et al. (in press). All codes except alliance represent the number of minutes out of the 10-minute interaction that participants engaged in the behavior. Alliance was scored as having either occurred or not occurred across the 10-minute interaction.

Results

Correlations between parents' reported levels of marital physical aggression and family members' behavior during the observed discussion are presented in Table 3.3. Among boys, fathers' physical and emotional aggression were positively correlated with fathers' controlling behavior toward sons. In addition, mothers' emotional aggression was positively correlated with fathers' controlling behavior toward sons. Among families interacting with girls, fathers' emotional aggression was positively correlated with fathers' hostility toward mothers and also with mothers' and fathers' alliances with daughters.

In addition, parents' reports of their physical and emotional aggression were related to ratings of child behavior during the interaction. Specifically, in the boys' sample, both mothers' and fathers' physical aggression were positively correlated with boys' withdrawal and distraction. Fathers' physical aggression was also positively correlated with

TABLE 3.3 Association Between Marital Aggression and Triadic Family Interaction

| | Boys' Sample (n = 45) | | | | Girls' Sample (n = 45) | | | |
| | Physical Aggression | | Emotional Aggression | | Physical Aggression | | Emotional Aggression | |
Observed Behaviors	Fathers	Mothers	Fathers	Mothers	Fathers	Mothers	Fathers	Mothers
Fathers' behavior								
Father hostility to mother	.28	.23	.16	.28	.23	.01	.32*	-.06
Father hostility to child	.26	.22	.21	.20	.02	-.12	.14	.07
Father controlling child	.31*	.05	.38**	.36*	-.04	-.05	-.05	-.13
Father alliance with child[a]	.08	.04	.08	.11	.25	.09	.34*	.24
Mothers' behavior								
Mother hostility to father	.05	.09	.07	.07	.12	-.10	.25	-.06
Mother hostility to child	.08	.24	-.05	-.10	.22	.07	.29	.22
Mother controlling child	-.08	.06	-.16	-.12	.02	-.08	-.03	.04
Mother alliance with child[a]	-.15	-.04	-.15	-.14	.25	.18	.34*	.24
Children's behavior								
Withdrawal	.36*	.51**	.13	.45**	-.05	-.07	-.01	-.01
Anxiety	.42**	.29	.20	.05	.12	.04	-.09	-.13
Distraction	.41**	.32*	.17	-.03	.39**	.28	-.08	-.04

a. Point biserial correlations.
*p < .05; **p < .01.

53

boys' anxiety. Boys' withdrawal was also positively correlated with mothers' emotional aggression. In the girls' sample, girls' distraction was positively correlated with fathers' physical aggression.

General Discussion

The family interaction literature has recently focused on the interdependence among family subsystems (Hinde & Stevenson-Hinde, 1988). It has long been assumed that conflict in the marital relationship influences parent-child relations (Framo, 1981; Haley, 1963; Minuchin et al., 1978). Physical and emotional aggression in the marriage, presumed to be an extreme and severe manifestation of marital conflict, have also been assumed to influence the parenting relationship (Margolin, in press). An important theoretical debate, however, has been whether the negative impact of marital violence and conflict on children is due predominantly to disruption in the parent-child relations or whether there are direct effects from exposure to marital conflict (Emery et al., 1992; Fauber & Long, 1991). It has been suggested that, to further our understanding of this issue, we need to identify the specific mechanisms by which marital conflict and violence affect the parenting relationship (Fincham, Grych, & Osborne, 1994; Rutter, 1994). This study, which examines whether aggression in the marriage is associated with specific parent-child communication patterns, is one such attempt to identify mechanisms linking these two family subsystems.

The data presented here directly address the question of whether physical aggression in the marriage is associated with patterns of impaired parenting. In both the dyadic and triadic interactions, fathers' physical aggression is associated with specific patterns in fathers' interactions with their sons. Husbands' physical aggression in the marriage was associated with fathers' exhibiting more authoritarian behaviors, fewer authoritative behaviors, more negative affect in the dyadic task, and more controlling behaviors in the triadic task. These findings did not emerge when fathers interacted with their daughters, nor when mothers interacted with either sons or daughters, supporting previous research that associations between marital violence and negative parenting may be gender specific. Jouriles and colleagues (Jouriles &

LeCompte, 1991; Jouriles & Norwood, 1995) have demonstrated that child gender moderates the relationship between aggression toward the wife and aggression toward either boys or girls, with boys receiving aggression more often than girls. Although we know from other analyses that the wives' aggression is substantially different from that of the husbands'—in terms of the severity of consequences and the fear engendered in the spouse—it is still important to note that mothers' physically aggressive acts in the marital relationship are not associated with controlling, hostile, and angry behavior toward the child.

The pattern of gender specificity also characterizes the associations between parents' emotional abuse and their behaviors with respect to the children. In the dyadic task, fathers', but not mothers', emotional aggression was associated with more authoritarian and less authoritative behavior directed to sons. In the triadic task, fathers' emotional aggression was associated with controlling behaviors in the presence of their sons, whereas in the presence of their daughters, fathers' emotional aggression is associated with fathers' hostility to their wives and alliance seeking with their daughters.

The data also suggest that one parent's use of physical or emotional abuse in the marriage may be related to the way the other parent interacts with the child. Mothers' use of emotional aggression was linked to fathers' behaviors with sons, whereas fathers' use of marital aggression was associated with mothers' behaviors toward daughters during both interaction tasks. Specifically, mothers' use of emotional aggression was linked to fathers' use of negative affect with boys during the dyadic task and fathers' use of controlling behaviors toward sons during the triadic tasks. Fathers' use of physical aggression was associated with mothers' use of negative affect toward girls during the dyadic task, and fathers' use of emotional aggression was associated with more attempts by mothers to establish alliances with daughters during the triadic interaction. As these patterns suggest, one parent's aggression may be linked to the other parent's affect or to his or her attempts at intimacy or control of the child. Although directionality cannot be inferred, the possibility that one spouse's marital aggression has an impact on the other spouse's parenting style or that characteristics of parenting style affect marital conflict and aggression patterns may be an important route by which marital conflict, parenting, and child development are linked.

Data from both tasks also reveal ways that the children's behaviors are associated with aggression in the marriage. In the dyadic task, boys' active participation is lower in families in which the father is either emotionally or physically aggressive. In the triadic task, both boys' withdrawal and distraction are linked to mothers' and fathers' physical aggression, and their anxiety is linked to fathers' physical aggression. Fathers' physical aggression is also linked to girls' distraction, whereas mothers' emotional aggression is linked to boys' withdrawal. These data are consistent with the possibility that children previously exposed to more severe forms of marital aggression are sensitized to conflict and are generally stressed and reactive during interactions with their parents even during nonaggressive discussions (Davies & Cummings, 1994). Although the pathways of effects from marital aggression to children's behavior are still not entirely clear, these data show that aggression in the marriage is associated not just with parents' communication styles but with children's as well. Moreover, data reported by Gordis et al. (in press) reveal that physical marital aggression, not the parenting dimensions, account for unique variance in the children's withdrawal and anxiety, lending support to a direct effects model.

Marital conflict as a background variable not only affects overall levels of specific behaviors, such as parents' controlling or authoritarian behaviors, but also influences the relationship between parents' and children's behaviors during the interaction. Children and parents overall show a predictable emotional congruence with one another such that positive affect in one participant is associated with positive affect in the other, and likewise in the father-child interaction, negative affect in one is associated with negative affect in the other. Children exposed to their fathers' marital aggression, however, show somewhat stronger and different associations than do nonexposed children. Exposed boys and girls, for example, show less involvement when their fathers exhibit high levels of authoritarian behaviors, and exposed girls display less positive affect when their fathers exhibit high levels of authoritarian behaviors. In addition, exposed boys show more involvement when fathers use high levels of authoritative behaviors and high levels of positive affect. This closer alignment between parents' and children's behaviors during the play task for exposed children is similar to the highly reciprocal interaction pattern shown by women married to physically aggressive men (Burman, Margolin, & John, 1993). In general, there seems to be a greater contingency in the behavior of exposed children and victimized wives on the behavior of the aggressive adult male. This finding may also reflect the watchfulness and hyperawareness, particularly with respect to reading interpersonal cues of danger, said to characterize children who have been exposed to interparental abuse (Silvern, Karyl, & Landis, 1995).

Interpretation of the data presented here, however, must be viewed as speculative for two important reasons. First, the data presented here are correlational. Thus, the association between marital aggressiveness and parenting cannot be interpreted necessarily as a spillover from the marital relationship to the parenting relationship but must be viewed as bidirectional. It is also possible that stresses in the parenting relationship create strife in the marital relationship, or that nonfamilial stresses are a source of tension for both relationships. Moreover, personality characteristics as well as communication deficits in an individual could lead to aggression in the marriage as well as to a controlling, authoritarian parenting style. Bidirectional influences similarly must be considered when examining the associations between parents' behaviors and children's behaviors during the interactional tasks. Participants mutually influence each other's behaviors during interactional situations such as the play task or the triadic discussion. Second, the data are strictly cross-sectional. To better understand these mechanisms, we want to examine how relationships in one family subsystem change over time as a function of what is occurring in the other family subsystem. For example, is the onset of violence or the exacerbation of interparental conflict followed by changes in the parent-child relationship and in child adjustment?

In summary, data from these two tasks suggest that our understanding of parenting behaviors and their affect on children must be done in the context of knowledge about factors outside that parenting relationship. Knowledge about children's long-term exposure to marital violence, a background variable to current, ongoing interaction, seems to play a role in how both the adult and the child behave in the immediate interaction. More extreme forms of marital aggression appear to coexist with less extreme but potentially salient behavior patterns regarding how parents treat each other, how they treat their child, and how the child behaves when both the parent and the child are present.

Notes

1. In general, mothers and children tried to re-create a picture of a dog, and fathers and children tried to re-create a picture of an octopus. The first nine families, however, received a drawing of a fish rather than an octopus, and in two families mothers and children copied the octopus, whereas fathers and children copied the dog.

2. The complete coding system may be obtained from the third author.

3. The formula used to transform the counts was $\log(p + (1 - p))$, where p = (one count) + (start) + (total count) + (start) + (). The start = $\frac{1}{6}$. The equation can also be expressed as $\log(\text{one count} + \frac{1}{6}) - \log(\text{the other count} + \frac{1}{6})$.

4

Home Is Where the Hell Is

An Introduction to Violence Against Children From a Communication Perspective

LINDA ADE-RIDDER
ALLEN R. JONES

This chapter first provides definitions and a context for looking at child maltreatment. Second, social learning, attachment, systems, and feminist approaches are applied to the issues of child abuse and neglect. Third, the communication perspective is applied to understanding violent interactions inflicted on children by their parents. Child maltreatment is viewed as a medium of political communication; each act or threat of an act of violence is a message. These acts are not viewed as isolated incidents but are a part of a larger process and occur within multifaceted contexts. Six tenets are offered to understand this perspective before the chapter concludes with a summary of implications and possible directions for future research and clinical practice.

Chris sits alone in the living room watching his favorite television program. Mesmerized, he "forgets" about his assigned responsibilities, specifically his chores. As the program ends, Chris becomes aware that his dad will be home momentarily. A feeling of panic wells up inside as Chris cannot remember what dad told him to do. Was it clean his room?

The sounds of dad's car rumbling to a halt immobilize Chris. As dad bursts through the door, Chris first notices dad's face—sweaty, red, his brow crunched at the forehead. Dad passes his son silently, looking through him. There are no words of greeting as he is pondering work, his supervisor, the computer problems

---

AUTHORS' NOTE: As coauthors, Dr. Ade-Ridder and Mr. Jones contributed equally to this chapter.

that plagued him over the afternoon, ad infinitum. Chris is not the father's son; instead, he is an object in the way of this man getting a glass—an ottoman one pushes to the side when getting out of a chair.

Dad walks into the kitchen, his eyes drawn to the pile of unwashed dishes; at the same time, Chris remembers what he was supposed to have done. Chris slowly creeps into the hallway. Any sudden moves may set off the familiar explosion. "Get over here!" Chris freezes, looking up at the man looming over him. The father surrounds his son, glaring down at the child in judgment. "I told you to do the dishes before I got home!"

Chris, paralyzed with fear and racked with guilt, tries to decide whether to stand and get it over with or run, knowing that if he stands for his punishment, his father will hurt him. In a fit of hope, Chris runs. Dad threatens, "the longer you run, the worse it will be." Chris stops and stiffens as he feels the crack of the belt across his backside. He does not flinch, does not scream, does not shed a tear, rather he lays across the couch silently. With each blow across his buttocks and then his back, Dad's anger at Chris is increasingly lost as his frustrations with work, his boss, and life in general take over. Chris begins to cry and begs, "please stop!" but father does not respond. Chris's mother walks in and pleads for her husband to stop. Dad's forceful blow sends her across the room. "Are you questioning my authority? Who the hell do you think you are?" She sits there, her eyes meeting her son's. "I'm sorry," her eyes say. All hope of rescue gone, Chris' eyes glaze over as he tries to distance himself from the horror happening to his body. He repeats his mantra: "He won't make me hurt; he won't make me hurt; I won't let him make me hurt." Exhausted, his father finally stops. Seizing the opportunity to flee, Chris runs past his father to his room, locking the door behind him. Sobbing, he wishes his father were dead, that this chaos would stop. He wishes that he had a different family.

This story illustrates the importance of communication in the process of abuse. Problems of defining *abuse and neglect* as well as *communication* pose complex and contradictory ideas and concepts. What is punishment to one person may be abuse to another. Abusive actions and intentions are encoded, communicated messages sent by one person and received, decoded, and interpreted by others. As Cahn (1996) points out in Chapter 1 of this book, every communicated message has an intended goal by the sender and has a separate effect on the receiver. This view of communicated interactions sees them as joint ventures. Cahn describes three communication goals that can be applied to abuse: instrumental (which we define as influences of power), relational (which construct or distance a relationship through time or control), and identity oriented (the desired image a speaker wishes to convey to his or her listeners). In this situation, the father's abusive behaviors achieve all three communication goals described by Cahn: (a) he exerts control (instrumental goal) over his wife's and son's behavior—he may not be able to control what his son does when he is not present, but he has the power to enforce his will, violently if necessary; (b) he maintains an imbalance of power (relational goal) over both his wife and son and sets clear limits about how they may interact with him; and (c) he maintains his self-image (identity goal) as the rightful judge and the one responsible to "straighten his son out"—he is "king of his castle" and deserves his family's submission.

A communication perspective takes advantage of different and sometimes contradictory theories or explanations of abuse by combining them for a more holistic understanding of violence against children. As Whitchurch and Constantine (1993) illustrate, the advantage of a communication perspective over other theories is that the entire set of interrelated behaviors can be studied simultaneously rather than looking at isolated pieces one at a time.

This chapter first provides definitions and a context for looking at child maltreatment. Second, predominant explanations (theories) for understanding abuse are explored, including social learning, attachment, family systems, and feminist theories. Third, the communication perspective is applied to understanding violent interactions inflicted on children by their parents. Child maltreatment is viewed as a medium of political communication; each act or threat of an act of violence is a message. These acts are not viewed as isolated incidents but are a part of a larger process and occur within a context. Every child, family, and community experiences and adapts to violence in unique and different ways that are imaginative, meaningful, and that make sense within the environment in which they occur. Each and every voice of all involved is important to hear, including the child victims and child witnesses. Six points about violent interactions within a communication perspective are emphasized before the chapter concludes with a summary of implications and possible directions for future research and clinical practice.

Maltreatment in Context: Definition and Incidence Issues

The maltreatment of children is not a new phenomenon; what is new is the societal view that this behavior is no longer tolerable.

According to Breines and Gordon (1983), the recognition and definition of maltreatment as a problem stems from five factors: (a) the family is now thought to be in a "crisis" state; (b) there is increased permissive and child-centered parenting; (c) the resurgence of the women's movement moved women from the private shadows to a public sphere; (d) there has been increased willingness to expose one's inner self (from the 1960s and 1970s) at the same time that housing availability offers greater privacy for families; and (e) there has been a decline in religious moralism.

What is meant by abuse and neglect? Although abuse and neglect are intuitively understood, specific definitions are more difficult. Originating as the "battered child syndrome" (Kempe, Silverman, Steele, Droegemueller, & Silver, 1962), researchers have historically measured abuse in quantifiable and observable terms (e.g., broken bones, skin discolorations, bruises, handprints on bodies, or burns). Physical abuse, however, sometimes leaves no observable injuries or permanent scars. Neglect, although more difficult to diagnose and quantify, still has in its most extreme cases objective, observable consequences that can be documented (e.g., failure to thrive, death, or poor hygiene) (Ammerman & Hersen, 1990), and psychological or emotional abuse is even more difficult to quantify. Giovannoni and Becerra (1979) suggest that maltreatment includes a broad range of acts that are considered socially deviant within the context of time and place.

Cases of child maltreatment reported to official agencies exceeded 3.1 million in the United States for the year 1994; of these, over 1 million were substantiated (evidence proved that abuse or neglect or both had occurred) according to the National Committee to Prevent Child Abuse (1995). Maltreatment reporting levels increased by 50% between 1985 and 1992 allegedly due to increases in substance abuse, economic stress due to poverty, unemployment, and work concerns. In addition, greater public awareness and willingness to report child maltreatment may help account for higher incidence levels (Clearinghouse of Child Abuse Prevention, 1994). In 1994, the substantiated cases included 49% neglect, 21% physical abuse, 11% sexual abuse, 3% emotional maltreatment, and 16% classified as other (Daro & Wiese, 1995). Parental abuse or neglect was officially listed as the cause of

1,271 U.S. child fatalities in 1994, representing 48% more child deaths than in 1985 (Daro & Wiese, 1995; National Committee to Prevent Child Abuse, 1995). Children under age 5 account for 88% of the fatalities, and 46% were under age 1 (National Committee to Prevent Child Abuse, 1995).

Straus and Gelles (1990) conducted an investigation of the incidence of abuse and neglect for the U.S. population as a whole and reported that during the previous year 2.3% of parents engaged in at least one act of "abusive violence" (i.e., kicking, biting, hitting, punching, scalding, burning, or threatening with a knife or gun with a probability of injuring the child). During that same time period, 7 children in every 1,000 were injured by parents in violent acts (Straus & Gelles, 1990). Projecting their findings to all U.S. children means that in 1988, 1.5 million children under age 18 experienced abusive physical violence by a parent, and approximately 450,000 children sustained injuries (Gelles & Cornell, 1990).

Understanding what maltreatment is or how prevalent it is does not tell us how survivors define the violent event and integrate this understanding into their evolving individual and family narrative. What does the violent act communicate to the child victim? Where is his or her voice? What process does a child go through to make sense of the chaotic world in which this happens? How might this meaning reflect the distrust a child feels not only in the presence of maltreatment but also in its absence? What is the child thinking when the abuse has ceased for a day? Beneke (1982), in describing women and their experience of time and space, asserts that no place is safe because of the threat of rape. Children too are vulnerable in time and space when their homes can become their torture chambers at any time. As Beneke points out, vulnerable people experience the world differently than do those with little to fear. Learning to survive may mean giving the dominant person what he or she wants with little resistance, to be compliant, or to be silent. It may mean telling lies so that a boy or girl does not get hurt. We wonder: What do children have to do to survive? Where is the child's voice in the intervention programs and theoretical "models" that are used to define maltreatment? How are these children already speaking to us?

Theoretical Explanations of Child Maltreatment

Different theoretical explanations can be applied to better understand the dynamics of child maltreatment. We are concerned not only with the hitting moment itself, but with all the other moments and contexts leading to the strike. What are the implications of that strike? What does the hit mean for the child, and what consequences follow? Do these explanations include sociocultural factors? How? How can different theories account for the child's experience of maltreatment? We believe that four theories are particularly critical to building a communication perspective and context that is sensitive to the world of the child: social learning, attachment, family systems, and feminist theories. A summary follows of the basic concepts applied to maltreatment and how each relates to violent interactions between parent and child.

Social Learning Theory

Intergenerational transmission of abusive behavior is often explained using social learning theory (Bandura, 1969; Edleson, Eisikovitz, & Guttman, 1985). Behaviors, including communication patterns, are learned by being modeled and subsequently imitated. Chris experiences his father's outbursts and abusive behavior toward himself and his mother. This model playing out repeatedly provides many lessons: Hitting someone smaller or weaker is appropriate (Patterson, 1982); misdeeds deserve punishment, and punishment will happen; the force of an assault is unpredictable, and other adults are powerless in the face of an assault. The experience of violence in one's family of origin results in a survivor's receiving the message that violence is a viable and appropriate strategy for relating to others. Seeing others successfully get what they want by violence may cause children to recapitulate the use of violence in the families they later create (Gelles & Straus, 1979).

Physical abuse is, by itself, powerful negative reinforcement; coercion resulting in the removal of aversive stimuli additionally reinforces behavior. For example, one strategy to stop a child from crying might be to strike him, or "give him something to cry about." Although this behavior reinforces that crying in front of father results in a strike to the face (which may also be interpreted as a possible strategy for gaining attention), the father learns that to quiet his son he needs to strike his son's face. For both, learning occurs, creating a history that includes not only the present episode but expectations of what future episodes will be like. In addition, this strike asserts the dominance of the father over his son, not just in terms of physical size, but also in the assertion that he has the right to judge and deliver punishment. Thus, a closer examination of the abusive context shows that more is happening besides a hit. That hit is also an episode in an unfolding story or narrative, not just a behavior in and of itself.

Because social learning theory focuses on how behaviors are modeled without considering the larger environmental context, it has been criticized. A child sees a parent hit a sibling and learns that hitting is acceptable behavior—that is social learning. When the parent hits this particular child, however, what is the meaning that the hit has for the child within the larger context of her or his life? What repercussions might sibling or family witnesses experience after the incident? Social learning theorists are beginning to address different contexts in which behaviors occur and to look at how behavior between two people may impact others (Crosbie-Burnett & Lewis, 1993). Classic social learning theory suggests that child abuse is learned in the family of origin and repeats itself in the family of procreation, creating a cycle of violence. Wilson (1995), however, illustrates that intergenerational transmission of violence involves other inadequate communication skills and conflict negotiation styles in addition to the abusive behavior.

Attachment Theory

Attachment theory, popularized by Bowlby (1982), assumes that infants are inherently social. Infants and toddlers construct their conceptions of self through interactions with others. Bowlby (1982) and Stern (1985) define the attachment of the child to the parent in terms of the child's ability to predict the behavior of others (as well as self-behavior). This ability to anticipate what will happen in the future allows for a feeling of safety and security in relating to others, such as parents or caregivers or both. Chris's inability to predict his father's behavior at any point in time adds to his insecurity and lack of attachment to his father. A child's attention, curiosity, and cognitive-motor involvement, as well as his or her propensity to explore are all influenced by the ways in which the parent deals with the child (Stern, 1985). As such, the parent-child relationship is highly interdependent; the experiences of the child are mutually created by the child and parent(s) alike. If a parent's intended message to the child does not get his or her attention, the adult may choose other messages or may encode and send the message in a different way, including possibly intrusive or abusive means of engagement. Father's frustration that Chris failed to do as he was told results in father sending his message in a physically abusive way.

The child's ability to explore and experiment with the surrounding world depends on feeling safe and protected, a role delegated to the parent as protector. The parent can modify the amount of stimuli the infant receives or interpret a child's action for him or her or both. What type of attachment is formed when the "protector" of the child is also the "perpetrator?" Bretherton (1993) suggests that if parents provide protection and respect for the child's exploration of his or her environment, the child can develop a positive sense of self. On the other hand, if the parent is unwilling or unable to provide the necessary protection, the child may incorporate two inconsistent models of attachment. The first model imagines the parent as good and self as bad; this interpretation accepts the appropriateness of punishment for "bad" behavior. Chris was torn between his fear of his father's punishment and his feelings that he deserved it because he disobeyed his father. The second model operates at an unconscious level; in it, the parent projects his or her own feelings of rejection onto the child. Father's frustrations with work and other aspects of his life were displaced onto Chris in the beating. In this model, the child internalizes the parent's projected feelings as her or his own; that is, the child is torn between trying to maintain a sense of self while feeling self-rejection. Chris felt his father "look through him" without acknowledgment, conveying father's rejection. Chris may interpret his mother's failure to help as additional proof that he is not worth being rescued. His feelings of insecurity and rejection are likely heightened. Simultaneously, Chris feels attached to his father; it is his father, after all, who is his "protector and guide." At some level, Chris knows he can never live up to father's expectations and therefore that he is bad.

Parental attachment is fostered by the parent's accurate "reading" of and responses to his or her child's needs and behaviors. Infants whose mothers are sensitive and responsive to their signals demonstrate greater attachment and a larger communicative repertoire. In addition, children cry less and are more obedient; in effect, these infants appear to feel understood (Ainsworth, Blehar, Waters, & Wall, 1978; Crittenden, 1993). In neglectful situations, the parent may not perceive or interpret the child's cry as indicative of a need; instead, it may be interpreted as an unintentional or intentional nuisance—"just something kids do"— that may allow the parent to discount a child's crying without attentive action (Crittenden, 1993). In physically abusive situations, parents may interpret the child's cry as intentional—that is, as meant to be annoying or aimed solely at the parent (Bousha & Twentyman, 1984).

Attachment theory may be used to examine relational dynamics, but it fails to take into account the larger context or relationships or both in which any given relationship is involved. Given the emphasis on the relationship between child and caregiver (usually mother), further efforts at theorizing need to take into account social and economic factors that impact the consistency of the parent-child relationship. The child's other significant relationships (especially with father) also need to be examined and understood.

Family Systems Theory

The family may be viewed as a system of interacting individuals and relationships. It is a part of larger systems or suprasystems, and it encompasses individuals and multiple interdependent relationships or subsystems (e.g., marital or sibling subsystems). Individuals and internal subsystems are locked together by the complex interdependency of mutual needs, communication patterns, commitments, and loyalties. As such, a family is "more than the sum of its parts," and any action by one person or subsystem is thought to affect all other members of the system (Boszormenyi-Nagy & Spark, 1973; Whitchurch & Constantine, 1993). In addition, families rely on each other to balance the tasks of maintaining the family structure (status quo) while adapting to internal (developmental) and external (societal) changes.

Communication transactions are inherent to the understanding of family systems theory. Messages are continually being conveyed verbally and nonverbally in an organized process of feedback loops. Negative feedback loops serve to maintain the previously known state or homeostasis; in other words, internal system pressures attempt to re-create the status quo. Chris and mother react to father's aggression in familiar and foreseeable ways. Each communicated action serves to maintain the familiar and thus the predictability of future events; equilibrium is preserved. This view interprets the abusive action as important in maintaining the family's patterns of interaction (Bograd, 1984). Positive feedback loops incorporate new information and change accordingly with the possibility of becoming more unstable (Whitchurch & Constantine, 1993). If a neighbor hears Chris's screams and calls the authorities, who investigate the family for possible abusive behavior, this new and unexpected communicated action might force father or mother or both to alter their future actions in new and unpredictable ways.

A family systems theory explanation for child maltreatment suggests that repeated patterns of aggression become reinforced as positive feedback spiraling out of control. At the same time, the tendency toward equilibrium (negative feedback) may cause family members to engage in transactions that re-create familiar roles and patterns. Over time, these transactions define the relationship. Direct content and metamessages convey intent and may or may not be congruent with one another. Chris heard and understood father's message to do the dishes, he also clearly understood the metamessages of control through the tone of father's voice and his body language. The conflicting expectations for punishment and desire to avoid it have taught Chris to be hypervigilant—sensitive to father's moods and desires to anticipate what will happen next. It is likely that Chris does not give himself credit for this increased sensitivity to those around him, and instead blames himself for not anticipating even more perfectly, thereby avoiding an explosive incident. Chris's role as the misbehaving child deserving of punishment maintains the family's equilibrium and father's role as head of his kingdom.

Family boundaries (who is "in" and who is "out" of the system at any given time) act as barriers to regulate the flow (input and output) of information and resources into and out of the family system or subsystems. In abusive families, boundaries are thought to be overly fluid or overly rigid—that is, too few or too stringent restrictions impinge on an individual's autonomy. Rosenblatt (1994) argues that societal views and expectations provide a context for permeability; for example, he believes that because of generally sexist societal views, women may be granted less privacy in the home than men, resulting in greater frustration and anger. Abused and neglected children may be subject to similar boundary restrictions; in this case, society affords the parents primary rights to control and guide child behavior. The expectation that the family is a "haven from a heartless world" reinforces the sanctity of the nuclear family unit. In a dysfunctional family, the strong boundary may protect the family as prison rather than haven, leaving a young child few options to remain autonomous. Chris knows he cannot escape his father's wrath, and his mother is powerless to help him. Mother and Chris are allied in a subsystem to endure dad's anger and frustration; their hope that things will change is tempered by their need to maintain the delicate balance and not to do anything that would make things worse.

Feminists criticize family systems theory because it is sometimes used to "blame mother" as an accomplice and blame the victim without taking into account the power dynamics of the family or the gendered nature of much of the violence that occurs (Dell, 1988; Luepnitz, 1988). Whitchurch and Constantine (1993) argue that general systems theory does not remove responsibility from perpetrators of violence because differing levels of control or responsibility for behavior can be attributed to different members of human interactions. A feminist-systems perspective is possible if it acknowledges the gendered nature of aggression while keeping at the forefront the perpetrator's responsibility for abusive actions (Bograd, 1984). At the same time, the patriarchal context in which the family functions must be considered (Whitchurch & Constantine, 1993). Laing and Esterson (1970) express serious concern about using systemic explanations to hide individual responsibility and accountability for violent actions. An advantage of looking at child maltreatment using family systems theory is that it recognizes multiple relationships within internal and external contexts and across generations, examining not just the present episode but also the family tradition of violence.

Feminist Theory

Feminist theory posits that child maltreatment exists within a gendered society dominated by male power, particularly white, middle-class male power. The patriarchal context in which communications take place must be considered in any analysis of relationship dynamics. At every level of social analysis, feminists regard power and control as issues of gender whether the analysis be of intrafamily relationship or social policies and laws. Feminist theory has at its core a basic belief that men, those in power, subordinate women (and by implication, children); that all forms of oppression need to end; and that understanding the ways women experience life is central to understanding any and all human relationships (Osmond & Thorne, 1993). Central themes include (a) the assumption of the centrality, normality, and value of women's and girls' experiences while not excluding the experiences of men and boys; (b) gender as an organizing concept that recognizes social construction, that differences between females and males are exaggerated, and that these differences are used to perpetuate gender power inequities; (c) the importance of considering the social, cultural, and historical contexts in any relationship analysis; (d) a shared belief that there is no single notion of what constitutes a family; and (e) a commitment to social change (Osmond & Thorne, 1993). Beyond these central themes, feminist theorists differ significantly in their thinking.

Most feminist theorists have focused on issues about and for women, whereas attention to the place of children in general and girls in particular is lacking (Osmond & Thorne, 1993). Because children have historically been dominated by parents and the larger society with the concurrence of legal, religious, and social institutions, feminist theories are particularly useful for looking at child maltreatment from the victim's perspective. In instances of maltreatment, the child is subordinated by the communicated and implied messages of power and dominance of another larger, more physically and verbally capable other. The fact that the other is someone who is supposed to protect and love the child makes aggressive communication of power even more potent.

Breines and Gordon (1983) criticized scholarly work on family abuse for ignoring gender as a central construct for many years. For example, literature citing psychological explanations for child abuse tended to ignore that women want to have children, that they are the primary child caretakers, or that most women had few alternatives or socially sanctioned fulfilling roles other than motherhood. Chodorow and Contratto (1982) suggest that the role of mother has been characterized as omnipotent and either all-powerful or completely powerless. This role paints mother as solely responsible for meeting the needs of her child rather than acknowledging that the child has a life of his or her own and that father might also have an important role; this view tends to blame mother as responsible for child maltreatment when it occurs and ignores other social, cultural, or individual influences. Father clearly communicates his dominance over Chris and over his wife; yet it is likely that he views Chris's failure to have obeyed his wishes as her failure while viewing his own behavior as justified.

Women tend to be the primary parent, and child abuse is the only form of family violence in which women are as likely as men to be the assailant (Breines & Gordon, 1983). The gendered nature of parenting is culpable in abuse because when women are unable to share parental responsibilities, they have fewer options for fulfillment from other areas; at the same time, they have less power and authority. Indeed, why do men who have so little responsibility for child care abuse their children so much (Breines & Gordon, 1983)?

Feminist scholars promote the issue of gender as a basic organizing concept rather than as just another variable (Osmond & Thorne, 1993). To date, gender-focused scholarship has primarily concentrated on dimensions of power and control, ignoring other important aspects, such as race. Feminists also need to recognize that the family can be a source of strength in struggling against various forms of oppression. Most ignored is the concept of age within the context of gender. Feminist perspectives need to be applied to the special issues for the elderly and for children. Understanding the unique role of mistreated children within the context of gender is badly needed.

By generalizing men's experience to all human experience, women and children are shut off, shut out, and shut up. Feminism normalizes women's differences in experience as valid ways of knowing the world and self—in terms of relationship and connection rather than separation and status acquisition. Feminist theories suggest that the patriarchal nature of society within which abusive actions occur adds to the negative effects experienced by the abused child.

Child Maltreatment Within a Communication Perspective

Our communication perspective for understanding maltreatment incorporates aspects of the four theories discussed previously. Feminist theories that view these interactions as messages of power and control within a patriarchal context provide a backdrop of understanding for looking at the intricate relationship between parent and child. Within this context, attachment theory posits that children form their views of self through their communications with caretakers; the extent to which children can predict future behavior by their caretakers provides the safety and security needed to become autonomous. Social learning theory explains that children form lifelong communication patterns by modeling their interactions with parents and others; negative messages are learned as readily as are positive ones. Finally, family systems theory suggests that an abusive family has complex and interrelated patterns of communication between and among the members and various subsystems; each family is therefore unique. How a child responds to the communicated messages of abuse of a parent or to the silence of a nonintervening parent can best be understood by examining six tenets derived from these four theories.

Tenet 1: Violence Is Political Communication; Embedded Within Acts of Violence Are Inferences of Power and Control. Defining family violence as political communication is consistent with feminist theories that view abusive behavior within the context of our patriarchal society. Johnson (1995) describes the use of power and control within some abusive marriages as patriarchal terrorism. The desire for the man to control "his woman" is characterized by the use of multiple tactics; focus on the tactics rather than on the overall pattern misses the connection with the patriarchal roots of this behavior. Pence and Taymar (1993) offer a model that explains how men exert power over their wives to control their behavior through the use of the following: economics; coercion and threats; intimidation; emotional abuse; isolation; minimizing, denying, or blaming; children; or male privilege or all of the above. In mild forms, many of these behaviors are sanctioned by a society that grants males greater privilege and authority with respect to females. We suggest that this same model can be applied to interfamilial relationships with children who are even more helpless and vulnerable to their parents/caregivers.

As discussed previously, power is the ability of one system or individual to influence another system or individual, whereas control is the capacity to limit the influence of the other (Rosenblatt, 1994). Over time, families construct rules through the repeated use of interaction patterns and negotiation styles. These rules contain past information (history) as well as future expectations (predictions based on previous responses to information). Respect for and repetition of these patterns of rules maintain family stability. Father's verbal and nonverbal messages to Chris reflect the expectation that Chris will be bad as he has been bad before. Father's failure to acknowledge Chris in any way contributes to their shared view of the sanctioned authority of this man over his child and of the child's relative worthlessness. Mother's attempted intervention and silent withdrawal communicates her helplessness to her son and her acquiescence to her husband. Serious challenges to father's authority are prevented by both the child's and mother's instincts to survive and preserve the status quo and a predictable future. Each time a variation of the same scenario plays out, the interaction patterns and behavioral rules become more solidified.

Violence, then, is a maintenance behavior—an episode of relating in which talk is exchanged not just about an episode or situation but about the assertion or reassertion of a perpetrator's power over a victim and his or her autonomy. One model, the relational control model offered by Rogers and Farace (1975), suggests that messages can be coded into hierarchical categories that dichotomize speaker and listener as "one-up," "one-down," or "one-across." At the risk of oversimplification, violence may be seen as a one-up message in which the perpetrator asserts his or her perception of reality, as well as his or her talk, over the victim's. Father clearly is one-up relative to Chris and to his wife, whereas mother appears to be one-across with Chris as they silently endure the wrath of this man. These hierarchical positions convey much more than simple commands or rules for the moment; rather, repeated aggression and threats of aggression perpetrate messages of inadequacy, helplessness, inability to protect oneself or one's loved ones in the face of aggression, worthlessness, and servitude. Not only is his dad telling Chris who he is, Chris is being beaten closer to the image that his father wants him to be.

Goddard and Stanley (1994) take this metaphor of control a step further likening the family tradition of child abuse to a hostage situation. In their categorization, the perpetrator is seen as a terrorist who intentionally seeks to maintain control through social isolation and unpredictability. Terrorism is threatening or intentionally using violent acts to induce fear or terror in a particular person to exact allegiance or compliance (Crelinsten, 1987). The parent, doubling as captor, may lead an isolated life himself or herself, indirectly reducing the opportunities for outside social contacts or intervention (Steele & Pollack, 1974). Even more debilitating may be the avoidant socioemotional-language styles children develop through interaction with their parents as described previously. Worse yet, parents may deliberately limit peer contacts for the child through either the excessive performance of chores or the identification of the world outside of the family as "life-threatening" (Goddard & Stanley, 1994). Through this dichotomy of inside and outside world, the child is placed in a double bind. If the child talks, he or she becomes responsible for destroying the family, and if he or she does not talk, the violence continues.

Given this double bind and the child's dependency on the abusive relationship to meet many of his or her needs, the child looks to the adult-perpetrator to interpret and provide meaning to events inside and outside of the family (Goddard & Stanley, 1994). For the "captured" child, severe restrictions may not just be placed on where they can go or what they may do, but on who they are—a process Avni (1991) describes in battered wives as "mortification of the self." Goddard and Stanley describe a similar process in the child's turning to the abusing parent for meaning of chaotic events.

Tenet 2: Abusive and Neglectful Communications Have Different Intentions and Interpretations for Both Parent and Child. Parental views of their child's behavior are found to be important factors in child abuse. For example, abusive parents do not vary their discipline techniques according to their child's behavior as much as nonabusive parents do (Trickett & Kuczynski, 1986). Oldershaw, Walters, and Hall (1986) find that abusive parents are also less likely to notice and respond positively to compliant child behavior. In a study by Reid, Kavanaugh, and Baldwin (1987), abusive parents consistently rate their children as more aggressive and hyperactive, despite observers' reports that their children's behavior did not differ significantly from nonabused children. Bousha and Twentyman (1984) report that abused children were more aggressive and noncompliant than their nonabused counterparts. Oldershaw, Walters, and Hall (1989) suggest that differing definitions of aversive behavior combined with differing samples may account for the seemingly contradictory findings. Patterson (1986) argues that both results may be equally valid. Disruptive behavior, in the midst of inconsistent communications, may be functional in getting the parent's attention.

With respect to neglectful parents, Crittenden (1993) offers an information processing model based on a parent's interpretation of children's behavior. Crittenden's model for parenting action requires a perception of the child's needs, an interpretation of the child's behavior as indicative of an unfulfilled need, the selection of a particular action, and the implementation of the chosen action. In neglectful situations, the parent may not perceive or interpret the child's cry as indicative of a need; instead, it may be interpreted as an unintentional or intentional nuisance—just something kids do—that may allow the parent to discount a child's crying without attentive action. The parent may fail to choose a response due to inadequate parent education, faulty intuition, or life-stress overload. Unfortunately, no response is a response. Maltreatment may result as a selected, or even habituated, response to a child's pleas, even when a cry has been deemed significant. Therefore, abuse and neglect represent strategic responses to a child rather than parental inability to control or discipline their child (Crittenden, 1993).

Intentions or goals for discipline differ between abusive and nonabusive parents. For nonabusive parents, long-term goals characterize the strategies for disciplining their children. Abusive parents exhibit short-term goals in episodes involving moral or social sanction (Trickett & Kuczynski, 1986), and they may interpret child transgressions as challenges to parental authority against which they must retaliate to preserve an adequate self-image of "parent" (Wilson & Putnam, 1990).

In complex verbal communications when talk is reduced to efforts of control, manipulation, and information exchange, the broader definition of language, which includes nonverbal gestures, action, and silence as interpretable text, may be overlooked. Each nonverbal message also communicates something. Silence and action are interpretable events. Silence may be calm and soothing or it may foreshadow the danger of an oncoming explosion of rage. Given the proclivity for abuse survivors to be hypervigilant (Martin & Beezley, 1977), both actions and silences hold a great deal of significance for the abused. Through their constant interpretation about persons and events going on around them, abused children learn how to survive and minimize painful circumstances. Each nonverbal action conveys a meaning, which is subject to the private rules operating within the system. Father looks through Chris as he heads to the kitchen for a glass; what does his failure to recognize Chris mean to the child? That he is unimportant? That he is an object, not a son? That he is to speak only when spoken to? Chris is sensitive to his father's actions—he even follows the path of father's eyes, connecting with the sink of the dirty dishes at the same time. No words were needed for Chris to know what was coming. This child instantly "reads" his father's face and anticipates what is coming, the futility of the situation, and an inability to prevent another humiliation. From that point, the familiar script is not retrievable by any of them. The verbal and physical assaults simply confirm what had transpired in the flash of an instant.

Tenet 3: Maltreatment Is Both a Communication Event and a Process Embedded Within a Larger Context of Aversive Parent-Child Relationships. Baxter (1988) defines communication as a method to build and maintain relationships through talk—a strategy to achieve desired goals within the context of the dialectical paradoxes inherent in a relationship (autonomy and connection, novelty and predictability, and openness and closedness). Using talk, people strategically act in "scenes." Hinde (1987) views actions between people as interactions "embedded" within other relationships, contexts, and histories (relational and individual). Relational webs or networks are formed over time with situationally specific meanings and rules. A person or relationship can be understood only within the multiple contexts in which the person is involved (e.g., family, work, school, and friendships). For example, when Chris begs his father to stop the beating, is he indicating subservience to his father's will, challenging father's authority to decide when enough punishment has been meted out, simply begging for mercy, or signaling father that a certain level of punishment has been reached? Mother's pleas for her husband to stop may have similar or different meanings to her husband given the different relationship and the context of the current situation. In Chris's family, crying for a parent to "Stop!" was met with indifference and heightened anger. In another family or even at another moment in this family, the same verbal message may be instantly respected and may result in an immediate cessation of parental action.

Abuse is not just about hitting another person. Acts of physical abuse are overwhelmingly accompanied by psychological abuse (Claussen &

Crittenden, 1991). Rather than seeing the abuse as an isolated incident, Claussen and Crittenden place the hit within an environment of isolation, exploitation, inappropriate sexuality, lack of attention or affection or both, denigration of either spouse or child, and premature or bizarre discipline. In addition, physical abuse is accompanied by other aversive parent-child interactions, such as threats, shouting, negative touch, and negative nonverbals (Wolfe, 1987).

One common thread is the context of inconsistency that pervades abusive parent-child relationships. Patterson (1986) suggests that abusive parents send conflicting messages to their children due to disciplinary inconsistency. The same child behavior may be ignored at one point in time only to be severely punished at another point. Oldershaw et al. (1989) support this finding in a study showing that abusive mothers, compared with nonabusive controls, were more likely to ignore or punish child compliance. Trickett and Kuczynski (1986) report that physically abusive parents, when compared with nonabusive parents, were less likely to recall child compliance and simultaneously reported more oppositional noncompliance (child refusals to comply or displays of anger). Finally, Susman, Trickett, Iannotti, Hollenbeck, and Zahn-Waxler (1985) found that abusive parents rated themselves as more inconsistent than nonabusive parents in their disciplinary practices.

Fein's (1979) work on parental responsiveness to children's play behaviors suggests a lack of flexible role modeling by abusive parents who tend to direct their child and intervene in structured situations regardless of their child's behaviors (even when they do not differ from the play behaviors of nonabused children). Nonabusive parents demonstrate a broader range of play behaviors with their children (Kavanaugh, Youngblade, Reid, & Fagot, 1988). Abusive parents are more likely to ignore the child or focus on the child's negative behavior rather than positively engaging their child (Reid, 1986). This points to the difficulty children may have in connecting with a parent to form secure attachments.

Not surprisingly, studies looking at parental discipline styles yielded results similar to those found in play studies. Hoffman (1980) describes a difference between parents who resort to power assertion (using threats, reprimands, and punishment) versus using inductive messages (giving reasons for requiring a change in a child's behavior). Trickett and Kuczynski (1986) report that abusive mothers use more acts of punishment compared with nonabusive mothers who use reasoning or simple commands; furthermore, the abusive mothers reported feeling angry more than the nonabusive mothers. Physically abusive mothers do commit more acts of physical punishment than do nonabusive mothers; interactions between physically abusive mothers and their children, however, are not primarily characterized by negative behaviors (Reid, 1986). Furthermore, Reid goes on to conclude that the severity of the punishment tends to escalate during the incident. Given that Whipple and Webster-Stratton (1991) do not support this finding, however, it is clear that discipline styles in abusive versus nonabusive households still merit deeper scrutiny.

Tenet 4: Violent Communications Are Intentional and Instrumental: Implied or Direct Threats of Violence Are as Abusive as Violent "Incidents." How something is said is at least as important as what is said. Satir (1972) characterizes communication as having multiple messages within the same delivered speech. Messages about the relationship, the status of the speaker to the listener from the perspective of the speaker, and the desired command can all be conveyed through the same set of words in the same order (Fitzpatrick & Ritchie, 1993). Father's verbal message to Chris that "the longer you run the worse it will be" conveys not only the threat of increased violence if the child runs away but clearly establishes father's authority and right to demand strict obedience from his son.

Stets (1988), in her analysis of violent couples, found that physical abuse, although initially expressive (spontaneous emotional outburst), becomes instrumental (a means to an end) over time. The intent of violent behavior is to control another person. This model seems to be equally applicable to children as it is to the marital relationship. Abusing mothers contrasted with nonabusing mothers are more reactive to situational factors (Bauer & Twentyman, 1985), more likely to be angry while disciplining (Trickett & Kuczynski, 1986), and more likely to use more severe disciplining strategies (Reid, 1986). This does not appear to be a pattern for women alone; Margolin, John, Ghosh, and Gordis (1996) find that men who use more authoritarian strategies toward their wives are more emotionally aggressive toward their sons but not toward their daughters. What starts out as anger gotten out of hand (Belsky,

1993), with repetition and time, becomes an interactional pattern. Furthermore, the threat of repeating the pattern may induce a reaction similar to that incurred by the enactment of the pattern itself. The threat, "Wait until your father gets home," may result in a child's becoming avoidant or resistant; at the least, it becomes a barrier between father and son. Although some researchers include nonverbal threats in their definitions of abuse (Oldershaw et al., 1986), more research is needed to tease apart the evolution of instrumental violence and the role of threats in maintaining the desired control of a child.

It is not only the violence itself that is so damaging, but also the experience of living with the possibility that it could happen again. Little research has been done in this area and is badly needed. Beneke (1982) writes of the experience of the woman who is raped and her changes in experiences of time and space. No place is safe. No place is home. No noise is just a noise. Rather, noises could signify a possible intruder or a possible violation in one's home or room. Similarly, the same experiences may occur in the experience of being in constant danger and vulnerable. It seems reasonable that children experience similar feelings of vulnerability and develop hypervigilance as a defense. Goddard and Stanley (1994) suggest that these defensive strategies later get in the way of children forming meaningful adult relationships.

Tenet 5: Violent Communications Occur Within the Contexts of Family, Neighborhood, and Community. Violence does not happen within a social vacuum. All members of a family are a part of the climate in which violent behaviors occur. Children who witness family violence learn patterns of communication even if they are not the direct victim of the maltreatment. Violent interactions may leave victimized parents unavailable as they struggle with emotional fallout. Consequences, such as depression, anxiety, increased feelings of vulnerability, and terror, may leave a mother unable to empathize with her child in a time when the child needs protection (Jaffe, Hurley, & Wolfe, 1990; Margolin et al., 1996). Observing marital violence may impact how children, especially boys, relate to women. Serious repercussions may occur if a boy strongly identifies with his father and the violence successfully establishes power and control over the child's mother. McCord (1988) followed men from abusive and nonabusive homes to investigate the intergenerational transmission of antisocial behavior. She reports that men who came from physically aggressive backgrounds often interpreted the expression of violence or rage as normal or even justified.

Not only does aggression between the parent and the child shape a child's understanding of relationships, but the relationships themselves provide communication models. Margolin et al. (1996) report that fathers who are aggressive in their marital relationships take a more passive role with their sons and make fewer suggestions during play tasks. When fathers play authoritarian roles, there is much less participation with their children of either gender. Children respond most positively when fathers play authoritative roles.

Bousha and Twentyman (1984) note that neglectful parents infrequently engage with their children in any type of interpersonal actions and when they do it typically consists of such nonmatched responses as requesting and demanding. Crittenden (1993) proposes that neglectful parents may undermine the processing of information concerning feelings and emotions, in effect limiting empathy and attachment between parent and child. When information and responses are either ignored or overexaggerated, children do not have the chance to develop a more sophisticated repertoire of emotional differentiation. Should parent's nonresponsiveness persist, children will learn to cease signaling.

Societal and cultural beliefs about discipline also impact the family. Bavelock (1984) found that abusive parents strongly held the traditional belief that physical coercion was necessary—"spare the rod and spoil the child." Trickett and Susman (1988) report that abusive mothers believe in physical punishment more than do abusive fathers or nonabusive parents. Chilamkurti and Milner (1993) concur in their finding that physically abusive mothers report that physical discipline is more appropriate than do nonabusive mothers. Kelly, Grace, and Elliott (1990) point out that social class may also influence views about the appropriateness of physical discipline to deal with child transgressions.

Vondra (1990) claims that families with the economic means to move out of declining neighborhoods do so, isolating those without the means to move to better areas. The absence of public libraries, quality child care facilities, and recreational facilities in low-income neighborhoods further isolates those living there. A highly mobile neighborhood population also contributes to an inability to develop and maintain long-term relationships with peers. These factors contribute to an increase in the risk of abuse (Vondra, 1990) and may increase levels of stress. Stress and anxiety are found to be related to higher levels of abusive behavior (Milner & Chilamkurti, 1991; Whipple & Webster-Stratton, 1991).

Vondra (1990) casts the community in the role of identifying victims as well as the setting in which abuse occurs. Many other individuals and professionals may come into contact with abusive families. Daro and Wiese (1995) report that 45% of the child-maltreatment fatalities between 1992 and 1994 had current or prior contact with Child Protective Service (CPS) agencies; this is attributed to the inability of CPS agencies to investigate reports in a timely manner or deliver sufficient services to all who need them or both.

Tenet 6: The Effects of Violent Communications Must Also Be Seen Within the Context in Which They Occur: They Can Be Imaginative Adaptations and Responses to Extreme Situations. The strategies a child uses to survive in an abusive environment are learned styles of attachment and communication. Just as children with secure attachments learn to explore the world and create relationships, abused children may learn to keep to themselves, to keep quiet, or that even if they were to scream, no one would listen. Unimaginative and literal play, as well as repetition and compulsion, may be one manageable way to deal with outcomes in a controlled manner. Another major development in relationships with others might be to have someone listen to the voice of maltreated children.

Children in abusive families perform more acts of physical and verbal aggression, negative verbal messages, and noncompliance than do other children (Bousha & Twentyman, 1984). Patterson (1986) suggests that because of inconsistent discipline, children learn that aversive behavior is functional because they either get their way or stop an attack. Over time, these children learn to respond more aggressively, which elicits parental abuse that increases in severity.

Appreciation of the multiple meanings embedded in messages is important in explaining the hypervigilant scanning done by maltreated children. Problems may arise when the world becomes a place in which anything might happen, including a beating. Suspicion about a person's actions and agenda are always in question, and there is little in a child's world to explore that is not potentially hurtful. Children, through the confusing attribution of responsibility and blame, may question their own realities and motivations. Worse, they may conclude that they are at fault for other people's actions. Abused children may resort to hypervigilance as a strategy to control and evaluate situations. Martin and Beezley (1977) describe this characteristic as "frozen watchfulness," in which children scan the area and "read" the moods of those around them. Later in life, this behavior may reappear in their confusion about appropriate roles, inefficient limit setting, self-deprecating or self-destructive behavior, or impulsive or avoidant behavior or all of the above (White & Allers, 1994).

White and Allers (1994) describe the play that abused children engage in as unimaginative, literal, repetitive, and impulsive. What needs to be considered is that maltreated children may need to devote considerable energy to survival, which short-circuits their ability to be creative in traditionally recognized ways. The survival strategies these children use need to be examined for creative adaptations to the situations in which they find themselves. What does dissociation do for an abused child? What purpose does repetitive play serve? Perhaps predictability about their lives may be so difficult for these children that repetitive and literal play may be an attempt to create order and stability out of chaos.

Implications and Recommendations

Researchers, policymakers, social service providers, and clinicians need to defend women and children against victim blaming wherever and whenever it occurs, whether it be in research and theory, policy development, or therapy with survivors. Rather than regarding victims as part of a familial problem, the focus of therapy needs to examine the individual perpetrator's choice to use violence as an appropriate means to get what he or she wants. What and whom this control serves is an empirical question that needs to be investigated qualitatively. Dutton's (1988) inquiries about marital violence suggest that fears of abandonment and fantasies concerning rejection are in the heads of abusers and the abused and influence the interpersonal relationships of both. Could it be that a similar pattern exists in the violence perpetrated by adults against children?

Consideration of the contexts in which maltreatment occurs and how those are influenced by the larger patriarchal society are critical factors for researchers, clinicians, and policymakers. This includes not only listening to victims in the violent act, the society, culture, and familial traditions in which it happens, but also having perpetrators teach researchers, theorists, and clinicians what their world is like. If parents can see the other side of the fist, maybe they will be better able to empathize with their children. To attempt to put a stop to violence without a dialogue among all involved directly or indirectly is to create an atmosphere of social control that becomes an act of violence itself. In examining the communication of violence, researchers and clinicians need to be attentive to who is communicating and what, where, and how messages are sent and received.

Future research and social practice need to focus on the best interests of the child. Questions that need attention include when and how to remove children as well as what services are needed. Also important are improved communication processes among the relevant participants in the decision-making processes, including Child Protective Services staff, courts, social service providers, law enforcement, education, health providers, parents, and the child—especially the child. One important way in which to do this is to study and consider the impact of abuse and neglect from the child's perspective and through the child's voice by placing children at the center of social inquiry. Learning about maltreatment from adult survivors or parents or both is valuable but is limited by perspective and lapse of time. To talk to children and to place them in the center of social inquiry is to take them seriously, just as feminism struggles against overwhelming odds to have women taken seriously.

With shrinking resources, attention may focus more on sexual and physical abuse, yet neglect is more common and leaves lasting scars as well. Societal causes for neglect include poverty, inadequate child care, and school failures; these issues require a great deal of social action and resources (Breines & Gordon, 1983). It is much easier to place the blame and responsibility for change onto a parent or family than to support social change.

Examination of the parent-child relationship regarding abusive and neglectful communication patterns suggests that abuse is a completed communication message whereby the parent and child, verbally, nonverbally, or both signal one another; the signs are received and interpreted, and an aggressive response is given. The cues may be quite subtle or direct. For example, Chris's failure to have done the dishes may have been interpreted by his father as a willful attempt to spite his authority that is reinforced when Chris decides to run and avoid punishment. On the other hand, Chris may read hatred and disdain for him when father looks through him en route to the kitchen to get a glass. The tendency for each person to interpret behaviors and messages in a personal way may in fact be intensified in families caught up in violent patterns because of gendered role expectations (feminist theory), past history (social learning), generally low self-esteem (attachment theory), or the context in which the interactions occur (feminist and systems theory). These interaction patterns need more careful research and attention.

Parent-child communication is clearly an interactive process subject to failure at various points. The child is as much a producer of the communicated message as is the parent; this is not to imply that children are responsible for aggressive behavior directed toward them, but that the context in which the communications take place are particularly significant. The bottom line is that theorists and researchers must sort through what ends the violence is meant to achieve. Violent behavior is intentional—that is, it is meant to communicate meaning to the victim and to others. Exactly what purposes does the violence serve and for whom? Until those questions can be answered, preventative and ameliorative actions will fall short of what is needed.

Finally, we believe that there may be an additional goal of communication in abuse. We believe that the abuser may need to validate himself or herself by forcing the abused victim to match his or her perception of self. In so doing, the abusive person may avoid facing the reality of his or her own behavior. For example, a child may be beaten into conforming with the abuser's demands. This possible dynamic is worthy of future exploration.

Can any problem be more challenging or more important than child abuse and neglect? It really should not hurt to be a child. More than 1 million children in the United States each year are maltreated. For them, the cost is too high. For them, home is where the hell is.

5

Parent-to-Child
Verbal Aggression

YVONNE VISSING
WALTER BAILY

Parent-to-child verbal aggression may be the most common form of child abuse, producing serious long-term problems for children. A component of emotional maltreatment, the subject of parent-child verbal aggression has not been studied rigorously. As a result, there are few clear-cut guidelines for defining it, measuring it, or determining its exact causes or consequences. Given the frequency with which it occurs, it is important to refine the concept and develop keen insights into its conceptual base, theoretical applications, and research operationalizations. A taxonomy of parent-to-child verbal aggression is provided, along with insights into its incidence, definition, and theoretical directions for the future.

*"Sticks and stones may break my bones, but words will
never hurt me."*

This children's rhyme alleges that verbal statements cannot harm children. Parents may believe that they are better parents if they punish a child verbally instead of hitting the child. The majority of adults, however, also believe that psychological problems can result when a child is repeatedly exposed to verbal abuse. Over 70% of adults in a national study felt that repeated yelling and swearing often leads to long-term emotional problems for the child; only 7% believed the effects to be minimal. Physical punishment, in contrast, was linked to injury for a child by 40% of the American public (Daro, Abrahams, & Robson, 1988).

In contrast to the nursery rhyme, verbal aggression is defined as a verbal attack that "attempts to inflict psychological pain, thereby result-ing in the [other's] feeling less favorable about self, i.e., suffering self-concept damage" (Infante, Chandler, & Rudd, 1989, p. 164). It is a form of psychological maltreatment that, in general, "has been gaining increasing attention from researchers because it is seen as the concept that unifies and connects the cognitive, affective, and interpersonal problems that are relative to sexual abuse, physical abuse, and all forms of neglect" (Brassard, Hart, & Hardy, 1993, p. 715). Although verbal aggression and psychological maltreatment may be keys to under-standing the long-term problems associated with all forms of child abuse, parent-child verbal aggression is not well studied for several reasons. First, there is no consensus in defining what constitutes parent-to-child verbal aggression. Second, the measurement of parent-child verbal aggression has varied widely. Third, consequences of parent-child verbal aggression must be considered in light of the discrepant defini-tional and measurement issues; the result is that it is difficult to generalize about specific outcomes of verbal abuse.

Given these conceptual and measurement problems, what is needed in the study of parent-to-child verbal aggression is a clear taxonomy of verbal aggression. It could guide the development of theory, alleviating definitional and measurement problems, while providing a broader context for analysis. If verbal aggression, as part of psychological maltreatment, is responsible for countless children's trauma, then it is important to gain a clear sense of what it is, why it occurs, how it is measured, and what its consequences are.

This chapter will review what we know about verbal aggression—and what we do not. A detailed conceptual scheme is provided that will help researchers and practitioners alike to identify and measure verbal aggression and its outcomes. Possible directions for future research in the field of parent-to-child verbal aggression will also be provided.

How Much Verbal Aggression Exists?

On the one hand, parents are enjoined to avoid verbal aggression toward children. In many families, when dealing with conflict situ-ations, reasoning and discussion are the first efforts at resolution. If that does not work, yelling, scolding, or some other form of verbal punishment follow. Remarks such as "you're a bad boy!" are widely accepted as necessary. On the other hand, if verbal statements cannot motivate the child to change his or her behavior, physical means to redirect the child may occur. Physical "discipline" may range from a slap to spanking or worse and is often accompanied by verbal abuse.

How much parent-to-child verbal aggression actually exists? No one knows for sure. Most studies of incidence or prevalence of child abuse provide limited information on verbal or psychological abuse, and most are thought to drastically underestimate the extent of psychological maltreatment (Hart & Brassard, 1987; Straus & Gelles, 1990). This underrepresentation is seen in the annual analysis of cases of child abuse and neglect reported to child protective services for each state. On the basis of state data, the American Association for Protecting Children (Daro et al., 1988) estimated a rate of emotional abuse at only 0.54 per 1,000 children. Other national data, found in two incidence studies sponsored by the National Center on Child Abuse and Neglect (NCCAN), included a survey of emotional abuse that included verbal or emotional assault. These studies reported incidence rates of 2.2 (Burgdorf, 1980) and 2.8 (NCCAN, 1988) per 1,000 children. The National Committee for the Prevention of Child Abuse (1987) coined the saying, "words hit as hard as a fist," and reported a decade ago that 80,000 cases of serious emotional abuse, including verbal aggression, were reported nationwide.

These data, however, are significantly lower than what one might expect if a more stringent definition of verbal aggression were used. The *Second National Family Violence Survey* (Straus & Gelles, 1990; Vissing, Straus, Gelles, & Harrop, 1991) proposed that verbal aggression is so normative that an occasional instance of verbal inappropriateness may not be considered abuse; the issue concerns the threshold at which verbal abuse is thought to occur. In the absence of an established standard, three thresholds were computed to produce estimates of the rate and number of verbally abused children. These were

Verbal Abuse Threshold	Rate per 1,000	Estimated Number
10 or more	257	16,190,000
20 or more	138	870,000
25 or more	113	712,000

If a threshold is set at which a parent would have to be verbally aggressive toward a child 25 or more times before abuse was alleged, this would produce a rate of 113 per 1,000 children, which is 51 times greater than the NCCAN rate. If a lower threshold of 10 or more verbal incidents would be considered "abuse," then the figure jumps to 257 per 1,000 children—a rate 117 times greater than the NCCAN rate of 2.2 per 1,000. The reason for the discrepancy between the NCCAN data and the *National Family Violence Survey* data is that the NCCAN rate is restricted to cases known to human service professionals, whereas the *National Family Violence Survey* included all households with children under age 18.

In a further analysis of the continuum of symbolically aggressive words and actions explored in the *National Family Violence Survey* data, Vissing et al. (1991) found that about two of three American children are victims of verbal aggression by their parents. Parents who used verbal aggression did so an average of 12.6 times during the year of the study, and more than a third reported 11 or more such instances. Boys were subjected to somewhat more verbal aggression than girls. Children over age 6 were more likely to have been victims of verbal aggression. When children age 6 and under were the victims of verbal aggression, however, it occurred more frequently than was the case with children over age 6. Even these statistics may be significant underrepresentations of the actual phenomenon of emotional maltreatment and verbal abuse.

The criteria for which verbal aggression were used in the *National Family Violence Survey,* the National Committee for the Prevention of Child Abuse, the American Association for Protecting Children, and the National Center on Child Abuse and Neglect were all conservative measures. The actual rate of verbal aggression may be greater depending on how it is measured and defined. So what is verbal aggression?

What Exactly Is Verbal Aggression?

Conceptually, verbal aggression is a part of the larger umbrella of that which is known as emotional maltreatment or psychological abuse (Baily & Baily, 1986; Brassard et al., 1993; Garbarino & Gilliam, 1980; Hoffman, 1984; Hornung, McCullough, & Sugimoto, 1981; Murphy & O'Leary, 1989; Vissing et al., 1991). Until recently, however, it was never considered to be a major form of child abuse. As a result, few studies attempted to determine its incidence, prevalence, etiology, consequences, modes of prevention and treatment, or its legal status as abuse. Legal documentation of child abuse in general is often difficult to prove, and proving psychological abuse is even harder. The literature on verbal aggression is relatively sparse when regarded as an independent concept.

Indeed, there is no consistently held word to even describe the phenomenon. The behavior known as verbal aggression (Baron, 1977; Brown & Elliot, 1965; Golin & Romanowski, 1987; Mosher, Rose, & Grebel, 1968; Rohner, 1975; Rosenow & Bachorowski, 1984; Steinmetz, 1977; Stets, 1989; Vissing et al., 1991; Walter, LaGrone, & Atkinson, 1989) is also called verbal abuse (Gilmartin, 1985; Mulcahy, 1979; Ney, 1987; Werner, 1984; Werner & Smith, 1983), verbal attack or verbal assault (Dean, 1979; Paulson, 1983), negative verbal interaction (Downs, Miller, & Gondoli, 1987), or negative interaction (Burgess & Conger, 1977; Kavanaugh, 1982; Kavanaugh, Youngblade, Reid, & Fagot, 1988), whereas Patterson (1982) prefers to call it coercive response.

As a form of interaction that uses a variety of symbols to communicate a message, verbal aggression actually has both verbal and nonverbal components. In an attempt to provide a more general definition of verbal aggression, Vissing et al. (1991) describe it as follows:

A communication intended to cause psychological pain to another person, or a communication perceived as having that intent. The communicative act may be active or passive, and verbal or non-verbal. Examples include name calling or nasty remarks (active, verbal), slamming a door or smashing something (active, non-verbal) and stony silence or sulking (passive, non-verbal). Slamming a door or throwing an object contains a symbolic threat that can terrify the observer, who may have fears that the next object to be abused will be him or herself. (p. 225)

Aggression, in general, is the delivery of a noxious stimulus by one organism to another with the intent to harm the other and with some expectation that the stimulus will reach its target and have its intended effect (Edmunds & Kendrick, 1980). Thus, both *intent* and *outcome* are associated with aggression, which makes deciding exactly what is verbal aggression more complicated.

Verbal aggression has been defined not just by the use of other descriptors such as intent and outcome but also by types of words (insults or curses) and tone of voice (screams or yells). Other items considered to be verbal aggression include swearing at in a sexual manner and threatening to abandon the other (Downs et al., 1987); insulting, sarcasm, threatening, ridicule, name-calling, and humiliation (Paulson, 1983); and bickering, quarreling, telling someone off, making fun of someone, criticizing, humiliating, cursing, or saying thoughtless, unkind, cruel things (Rohner, 1975) that may influence the individual's emotional affect (Burgess & Conger, 1977). Walter et al. (1989) define verbal abuse as an actual or threatened attack on another person, whether it be by gesture or hostile or provocative language directed toward another person. Sometimes verbal aggression is synonymous with "saying not nice things," such as bickering, quarreling, telling someone off, making fun of someone, criticizing, or saying thoughtless, unkind, cruel things (Rohner, 1975). Verbal aggression is sometimes classified as one point of conflict among many types, measured by the Conflict Tactic Scale (Downs et al., 1987; Jorgenson, 1985; Straus, 1990).

Among two dozen verbal aggression articles, often no conceptual definition is provided. Researchers assume that everyone knows what verbal aggression is and they rely on operational definitions used to measure the items to explain the exact nature of it (Brown & Elliott, 1965; Burgess & Conger, 1977; Downs et al., 1987; Gilmartin, 1985; Golin & Romanowski, 1977; Ney, 1987; Paulson, 1983; Rosenow & Bachorowski, 1984). It is similar to Barbara Bush's quip, "I don't need to know what child abuse is: I know it when I see it." It is difficult, however, to both measure and stop verbal aggression without knowing what it is.

Underlying Assumptions About Verbal Aggression

To create a clearer definition and conceptual understanding about the nature of verbal aggression, one must first address underlying assumptions about the nature of parent-to-child verbal aggression. Six assumptions, based on our experience, knowledge, research, and data analysis in the field of parent-to-child verbal aggression, drive our work.

First, statements that could be perceived as unkind or abusive are sufficiently common to be regarded as a normative interaction pattern that exists in most cultures. The content of the message and the interpretation of the statements may vary widely among different cultures, subcultures, groups, genders, and ages. Second, just because a phenomenon happens with normative frequency does not make it socially acceptable or psychologically appropriate. This is especially true when it is part of the routine socialization of children. Third, in any communication, both the parent and the child must be present and cognizant of one another. People may think or say abusive things about another person, but such situations are not necessarily interactive unless there is personal contact in which the two parties can convey and interpret information to one another. Fourth, there is a differential power relationship that exists between parent and child. The parent has the power in the relationship and gives a multitiered message to the child. The tiers may consist of a behavioral directive, how the adult feels about the child, how the child should feel about himself or herself, and an interpretation about the nature of reality. The child, whose age, experience, and cognitive ability are less sophisticated than the adult's, is left to figure out exactly what the message means. Therein lies a wide arena for interpretation—one in which the child's interpretation is frequently seen as less accurate or valid than the one given by an adult. Fifth, a verbally aggressive statement is difficult to define and measure. It is not just what is said, it is also how it is said, why it is said, the context leading up to what is said, and the consequences of the communication. Finally, parents role model normal and acceptable social and interpersonal behavior to children. As they act, children learn. The pattern of verbal aggression therefore tends to repeat intergenerationally.

Taxonomy of Verbal Aggression

Verbal aggression is not simply a certain word used in a particular way. To build a taxonomy that can help guide both theory development and measurement, the concept of verbal aggression needs to be broken down into its subcategories. There are at least six components of verbal aggression, which include the structure of the situation, patterns of interaction, content of the communication, the process of the communication, the interpretation of the interaction, and the consequences of verbal aggression.

Structure of the Situation

Cultural Context

Cultures may vary by the degree to which one is treated in individualistic or collectivist ways (Coser, 1956; Fry, 1993; Leach, 1964; Mulcahy, 1979; Semin & Rubini, 1990). According to Durkheim (cited in Fisher & Chon, 1989), the individual psyche is itself a sacred object—an expression of one's place in the social collectivity. What is considered abuse at the individual level is culturally determined, and what is considered abusive in one culture may not be regarded as such in another. Therefore, verbal aggression must be considered in its specific cultural context:

1. Individualistic verbal abuse includes psychological properties involving the ascription of negative intellectual abilities, such as being stupid, a cretin, an imbecile; physical features, such as being ugly or fat; civil conduct, such as a person being ill-bred or having poor manners; or wishing ill health—that is, "I wish you would die," get hit by a car, and the like. The abusive impact of these statements may vary from one culture to another.

2. In collectivist cultures in which the focus is on the person as a part of a distinct group, verbal abuse will involve relational references and an insult will be hurled not just at a person, but it will also be directed to their entire kin or group. Collectivist insults include insults referring to group membership (i.e., a drunken Irishman), expressing incestuous relationships or familial sexual insults (i.e., your sister is a whore), and bad wishes for the family.

3. Verbal aggression may become socially sanctioned through both visual and auditory media as seen in messages delivered on TV, at the movies, in advertisements, in popular music, or on public-access computer mail services. Common acceptance of verbal aggression makes it more dif-

ficult to decide whether a statement is verbally aggressive, socially acceptable, or inappropriate (Atkin & Greenberg, 1977; Dominick, Richman, & Wurtzel, 1979; Tan & Scruggs, 1980).

4. Verbal aggression in the United States has become very individualistic and personal. Middle-class people are more likely to engage in an individualistic culture as opposed to a more collective culture shared by lower-class people. Some ethnic or subgroups within the dominant culture may hold different normative standards of what is defined as verbally abusive.

Power Differential Between Parent and Child

Parents have physical power, intellectual power, social power, and emotional power over children. It is not a level playing field, and parents have all of the advantages to identify situations of conflict, promote communication around them, interpret the interaction, and develop resolution strategies that best promote what they think is best.

Where the Communication Occurs

Conversations that take place in one's home will likely be different from interactions that occur at the restaurant, at the market, or in another person's home. It is likely that "truer" communications occur behind closed doors at home. This is largely due to the presence of others who could witness the parent-child contact.

Who Is Present During the Interaction

Who is present during the interaction can influence what is said and how the situation is interpreted. Are the parent and child alone in their interaction, in which no one else can hear what each says to the other? Are there other children involved directly or standing around within earshot? Are other family members present? The presence of a spouse, grandmother, or uncle may alter what is said. Are there "outsiders" to the family witnessing the interaction? Strangers on the street who are merely passing by can also serve to be an audience to parent-child interactions.

Relationship Structure Between Parents

Some parents regularly spar verbally in front of the children, whereas others do not. Couples and families develop their own way of interacting with one another, and some of these methods expose children to physical, emotional, and verbal aggression. Sometimes the conflict is so great that families break apart; other times, families stay intact and remain abusive to one another. Even in cases of conflict that can lead to parental separation and divorce, children may find themselves exposed to verbal aggression. Parents may continue to be hostile and verbally aggressive toward the other parent even when that parent no longer resides in the household. Children in this situation learn that divorce does not necessarily resolve their parents' interpersonal conflict (Radovanovic, 1993).

Patterns of Interaction

Patterns of Interaction Stability

These include one's cultural context, the parent-child historical pattern for resolving conflict, learned interaction and problem-solving behaviors, and the number of times the dyad has experienced the interaction. Whether the abuse happened before or if it is the first time may influence whether a situation is perceived as abusive.

Patterns of Interaction Dynamics

Interactions change, as do their interpretation, because of the dynamic nature of communication. Specific factors that promote change include the following:

> Aging may be a factor in deciding if an interaction is abusive—children who were too young or isolated to identify that they were not being talked to like other children may come to identify that they are being verbally abused. As children age, they may reevaluate times in which they thought that their parents were verbally aggressive and find that they did not understand the full nature of the interaction.
>
> Accommodation—if a child hears verbal abuse often it may have two different types of effects. One effect will be that the negative words no

longer mean anything—some children have "resilient" or "hardy" characteristics and appear to go relatively unscathed by exposure to abusive episodes (Garmzy & Tellegren, 1984; Kobosa, 1982; Werner, 1984). On the other hand, hearing verbally aggressive words day after day can chip away at any positive self-image that a child may hold; over time, the verbal attacks whittle down the child into a person who carries out the parent's negative prophecy (Cooley, 1922; Rosenthal & Jacobson, 1968; Thomas, 1931).

Verbal aggression can be used as a dynamic means of coping with events that appear stressful or beyond one's personal grasp. Parenting, although rewarding, is fraught with stress, and managing daily household activities, finances, transportation, errands, employment, and adequately caring for the plethora of children's needs can become overwhelming. Verbal aggression may not be a response to any particular act but a response to an accumulation of stress (Cox, 1994; Dietrich, Berkowitz, Kadushin, & McGloin, 1990).

Content of Communication

Stimulus-directed statements are aimed at specific behavioral change, such as "clean your room" or "don't do that." Learning the rules of social and emotional conduct necessarily involves redirecting and controlling children's behavior, and it is a fundamental part of their socialization (Leavitt & Power, 1989). Spontaneously directing a child in a loud voice to "stop that now" may not be verbally aggressive; the child, however, may be embarrassed and cry when given the order. The child may be reacting not just to the content but also to the way the directive was delivered.

Diffuse statements provide a general assessment of the child's worth. Statements such as those found by the National Committee for the Prevention of Child Abuse include "you're no good," "you disgust me," "get outta here, I am sick of looking at your face," "you're more trouble than you're worth," "why don't you go and find some other place to live," and the ultimate, "I wish you were never born."

Combined Messages

Sometimes parents combine stimulus-directed and diffuse statements, turning what could be benign interactions into malignant ones.

Statements that could positively redirect behavior become humiliating when the parent equates a negative deed with a negative doer. Examples such as "you didn't watch your little sister closely and she got hurt because you were so irresponsible," "you didn't water the plant and made it die," "hey stupid—don't you know how to listen?," and "you're pathetic, you can't do anything right," all show the linkage of an action with personal degradation.

Role of Parental Intention

Parents can make statements in which they definitely intend to cause a child emotional distress or hurt. Sometimes parents say things in ignorance that hurt a child's feelings, but the child may experience hurt irrespective of the parent's intent (Rohner, 1975).

Parental Hostility

The presence of verbal hostility is frequently regarded as a requisite for verbal aggression, and hostility is a negative affect expressed in both the style and the content of speech (Brown & Elliott, 1965; Buss & Durkee, 1957; Golin & Romanowski, 1977; Mosher et al., 1968).

Process of Communication

Although content is obviously an important part of the communication, how the content is conveyed also is critically important to the actual meaning and subsequent interpretation of the message. The old saw, "it is not so much what you say but how you say it," certainly holds true in the study of verbal aggression.

Tone can be calm, excited, joyful, agitated, depressed, or angry. The words can be said at different volumes—from soft to loud, from a whisper to a yell, shout, holler, or scream. The timing of the verbal attack during the course of the conversation is also important. Does the verbal aggression build up slowly over a lengthy course of conversation or is there a sudden outburst that appears to come out of nowhere? An incremental progression from a rational, calm conversation into a heated argument will undoubtedly be perceived differently by the child than would an unexpected outburst.

Verbally aggressive statements range from those that are clearly abusive (e.g., "Get away from me, you stupid bitch, I hate you, you are no good for anything.") to statements whose abusive nature is unclear (e.g., "Well, that was *another* of your shrewd moves, wasn't it, Mr. Smarty?"). Although one's interpretation of a statement may rely on the tone, timing, observers, parent-child relationship, and situational context, we found that there is a range of potentially aggressive statements that can be used to help determine if certain words are indeed verbally aggressive. Each category of comment, from statements that are questionably abusive to comments that are clearly abusive, will be described below.

Distracting Comments. These are statements made that are inappropriate given the context of the current communication-situation. Such comments take the focus away from the current communication and into a different topic that has nothing to do with the current one. Examples: "Your best friend just got arrested for drunk driving? Any son of a bitch who drinks and drives deserves what he gets. I think those alcohol companies . . . " or "You're having problems at school? When I was in school I did . . . " The parent fails to address the child's real issue and takes the conversation in a direction that has absolutely no relevance to the interaction that the child initiated. If this reaction occurs regularly, it can shut the door on a child's attempt to engage the parent in future meaningful conversations.

Jokes and Teasing. Although jokes are funny to the speaker, they are seldom humorous to the recipient. Children become the target for an adult's attempt to "joke" or "tease" by making fun of the child for some aspect of his or her behavior, appearance, or ability. The child does not know if the tease is meant to be funny or cutting and is hence put in a difficult response situation. If the child gets upset by the joke, it only becomes fuel for additional teasing. If the child accepts a painful interpretation of the joke, it can reinforce a negative self-image. If the child laughs it off and really thinks the joke is funny, then no abuse is perceived. Therefore, the actual meaning of jokes, like distracting comments, is ambiguous. Example: "Look at those ugly zits on your face! Aw, don't get upset, I was only teasing you. It's just a little zit."

Sarcasm. Sarcasm, like the previous two categories, is also an ambiguous type of communication. It may focus on irony but also centers on contempt, mockery, ridicule, scorn, and derision. Adults may dismiss sarcastic statements when children are offended by them, or they may blame the listener for being offended. As a result, children feel uncomfortable because the rules of interpretation are not clear. Examples: "You couldn't really mean to say such a thing, could you?" "I just love it when you spill milk all over the counter."

Blaming, Belittling, Ridiculing, Making Fun of, and Criticizing. Children developmentally do not have the same physical, cognitive, experiential, or social abilities as adults—they should not and cannot. Parents who expect that children should be able to do something in the same way as would an adult are likely to have unreal expectations that will pose them to denigrate the child's performance. Also, children go through developmentally appropriate periods when they are learning to walk, lose teeth, have baby fat, acne, are clumsy, or have other physical characteristics that are convenient for some people to ridicule. Belittling the child for innate characteristics or behaviors will be taken personally by the child, and it is likely that the child will feel a sense of failure and low self-esteem. Examples: to a child who tasted sand—"Why didn't you eat your breakfast? Only pigs eat dirt!"; a child does not want to share a toy—"No one likes you because you are so selfish" (Paulson, 1983).

Disparaging Terms, Insults, Name-Calling, and Derogatory Comments. Children learn "not nice" names early in life and can be upset when they are equated with animals (ass or pig), body excretion (shit or asshole), or part of sexual anatomy (cunt or boob) (Leach, 1964).

Bickering, Arguing, and Quarreling. In the heat of a disagreement, unkind words will likely be said; the verbal abuse content in this type of verbal statement will consist not just of the words but especially the tone and volume. Example: "I hate you!!!"

Cursing. Verbal aggression occurs when a parent uses words as a form of blasphemy or profanity. There is wide variability regarding the degree of offensiveness of curse words. For instance, someone saying "Oh, God" or "Jesus Christ!" may be seen as indicating surprise or emphasizing a point; someone else may regard the speaker as "taking the Lord's name in vain." Common swear words, including reference to bodily functions, may be used as a regular part of one person's language, whereas another individual may become terribly offended by the use of such words. Therefore, although there is a normative prescription against cursing, there are also many groups who are not offended by the use of such words.

Threats. Threats are frequently regarded as a form of verbal aggression because the threat conveys intimidation and danger and hazard or peril. Examples: "If you continue to do that, I will beat your butt" or "You will never see tomorrow if you don't leave me alone."

Humiliation, Cruel Statements, and Total Verbal Attack. These statements are intended to cause psychological distress and are often inflicted using words that the parent knows will be emotionally devastating to the child. Everyone has an Achilles' heel, and parents know exactly where their children's most vulnerable parts lie. Example: "You lousy little son of a bitch, you fuck everything up and I just can't stand being anywhere around you and neither can anyone else in this family. Just get the hell out of here!"

Nonverbal Statements of Communication

Although *verbal aggression* or *verbal abuse* is the term most frequently used to discuss dysfunctional communication, there are nonverbal parts to any communication. Therefore, it is important to include the range of nonverbal aspects of interaction that are routinely used and discuss how they influence whether an interaction is perceived as abusive.

Failure to Respond. Sometimes a parent will react to a child's conversation with a stony silence, ignoring that a comment was even made. If a child presses the parent to talk, the parent may directly refuse to talk about something that the child perceives to be important. Babies can be crying, and the parent sits reading a newspaper or watching TV instead of getting up to address the child's needs. In other cases, the parent may actually turn his head or eyes in the other direction or walk away. Other forms of failure to respond include sulking and pouting—conveying that there is a problem that one refuses to discuss. This can create frustration for others who know there is a problem but the person will not talk. The most severe form of failure to respond is abandonment.

Facial Expressions. It may be easy to control what one says but harder to control facial expressions. Even when one tries, fleeting looks pass across one's face that give the observer a message about what the person really thinks or feels. Facial expressions abound but include frowns, scowls, sticking out one's tongue, eye rolls, tics, lip biting, and so on.

Gestures. Body language also influences the interaction's meaning. Crossing arms across the chest is a sign of keeping away, hands are used to convey that someone is "coocoo," fingers are used to "flip the bird," and a fist is banged on tables or waved in the air.

Objectify Interaction. In communication, parents may slam doors, break or kick objects, hit the dog, cut the ears off of the bunny, angrily toss out the child's favorite toy, or otherwise use nonhuman violence to give a message to the child that if the child's behavior is displeasing bad things can happen to the child also.

Direct and Indirect Verbal Aggression

In the process of communication, the message may be conveyed directly (both verbally and nonverbally) to the child or indirectly through nonverbal or ambiguously worded verbal communication. Such communication may be called active and passive, respectively.

Interpretation of Communication

In most interactions, the exact meaning is negotiated. Some communications are ambiguous, whereas others are very clear. In parent-to-child interactions, the child must ask, "Do I really understand what the message is?" It is dependent on

1. Symmetry. If both the sender and the receiver understand the content and intent of the communication, there is agreement or symmetry.
2. Asymmetry. The interaction is asymmetric when the sender and receiver do not agree on the intent and content of the communication.
3. Degree of ambiguity. Communications may be unclear in their content, there may be conflicting nonverbal messages, or there may be tone or volume aspects that do not agree with the verbal message.
4. Intentional changing of the message. In some cases, the parent gives off a meaning that the child accurately interprets but then says that the child was incorrect when the message receives adverse attention from others.

Consequences

What is the effect of parent-to-child verbal aggression? Little is known about the long-term effects of psychological abuse despite recent advances in the area of childhood victimization. Although there is wide consensus that child victims of verbal maltreatment are at risk for future social and psychological maladjustment, conspicuously few controlled, well-designed empirical studies that examine this problem exist (Briere & Runtz, 1988; Lamphear, 1985). Many studies combine verbal abuse with other types of physical and emotional maltreatment, which makes it difficult to ascertain exactly what are the effects of verbal abuse as an independent factor (Bousha & Twentyman, 1984; Brown, 1984; Egeland, Sroufe, & Erickson, 1984; Gilmartin, 1985; Ney, 1987; Vissing et al., 1991). When the few studies that focus on just verbal abuse are analyzed, methodological problems exist, including retrospective studies in which adults are asked to reflect on childhood experiences of verbal abuse or the use of nonrepresentative samples (Briere & Runtz, 1988; Downs et al., 1987; Ney, 1987).

The literature, irrespective of definition or methodology, alleges that parent-to-child verbal aggression and its umbrella of psychological maltreatment are responsible for a variety of potentially serious and lifelong psychosocial problems (Bousha & Twentyman, 1984; Ney, 1987). As Steele (1986) wrote,

> We do not know nearly enough about the long-term effects of maltreatment during the early formative years of life . . . through observing some

of the immediate effects of maltreatment on the . . . young child and comparing them with the histories given by adults of their early maltreatment and the observations of their adult behavior, we can make reasonably reliable connections between these two stages of life. (p. 283)

To facilitate research, one may wish to consider the following effects of verbal aggression that have been identified in previous studies:

a. Short-term effects—for example, hurt feelings or termination of a specific behavior
b. Long-term effects—for example, poor self-image, inability to parent, and violence (Lemert, 1972; Ney et al., 1987; Scheff, 1984)
c. Intergenerational parenting effects—that is, because of the abuse experienced as a child, one is unable to adequately parent one's own children (Burgess & Conger, 1977; Garbarino & Gilliam, 1980; Gelles, 1973; Jorgenson, 1985; Kavanaugh et al., 1988; Nagaraja, 1984; Patterson, 1982; Patterson & Bank, 1988; Steinmetz, 1977)
d. Personal hardiness factors—for example, some children are more resilient than others and do not seem to be adversely affected by actions that may be detrimental to other children (Garmzy & Tellegren, 1984; Kobosa, 1982; Werner, 1984; Werner & Smith, 1982)
e. Psychological problems—for example, poor self-esteem issues and dysfunctional coping mechanisms (Berger & Luckmann, 1967; Bousha & Twentyman, 1984; Carter, 1994; Cooley, 1922; Dean, 1979; Firestone, 1993; Harris & Olthof, 1982; Mead, 1962; Ney et al., 1986, 1987; Pollak & Thoits, 1989; Rohner, 1975; Spinetta & Rigler, 1972; Yates, 1982)
f. Developmental problems—for example, regression of sleep, toileting, and speaking (Allen & Oliver, 1982; Friedrich & Boriskin, 1976; Martinez-Roig, Domingo-Salvany, & Llorens-Terol, 1983)
g. Social problems—for example, delinquency and violence (Bousha & Twentyman, 1984; Ney et al., 1986, 1987; Patterson & Bank, 1988; Radovanovic, 1993; Savin-Williams, 1994; Vissing et al., 1991; Wolfe & Mosk, 1983)
h. Interaction-communication problems—introversion, extroversion, or inability to adequately express one's own feelings (Burgess & Conger, 1977; Camras & Rappaport, 1993; Crittenden, 1992; Gilmartin, 1985; Kinard, 1978; Leffler, 1986; Miller & Sperry, 1987; Oates, Forrest, & Peacock, 1985; Vissing et al., 1991)
i. Experience of other forms of child abuse—for example, physical and emotional abuse (Bousha & Twentyman, 1984; Brown, 1984; Egeland

et al., 1984; Gilmartin, 1985; Hirshi, 1969; Lytton, 1979; Ney, 1987; Vissing et al., 1991)

j. Substance abuse (Downs et al., 1987; Savin-Williams, 1994)

Although the exact effects of parent-to-child verbal aggression are unclear, the previous list does provide a good guide for future research.

Directions for Future Research

The taxonomy provided here can guide a variety of theoretically based research questions that should help identify key elements in the creation, maintenance, treatment, and prevention of parent-to-child verbal aggression. Take into consideration just a few potential questions for investigation.

For instance, under what conditions do certain types of interaction patterns take place? What is the difference in outcome for children who experience a single, a few, or multiple verbal aggressive interactions with their parents? Does one event have more or less trauma than multiple episodes? Is verbal aggression a precursor to physical aggression? If the child has experienced other types of abuse, will a verbally aggressive episode have a different meaning than for a child who has never experienced abuse? What is the impact on children who, although not personally abused, witness the abuse of others? To what degree will these children wonder "Am I next?"

What are predictors of verbal aggression? In what circumstances do learning and accommodation take place? Does ambiguity increase the chances of statements being seen as verbally abusive? Do verbal statements provide more clarity than nonverbal cues?

What does the presence of observers do to alter the normal parent-child interaction? There may be a theater effect in which the parent may become more dramatic and verbally aggressive when others are present to "prove" that they are keeping their children "in line." Conversely, there may be a tendency to curb interactions and not be as verbally aggressive as one may normally be when people are trying to meet the standards of others whom the parent believes will disapprove of the verbally aggressive statements.

Is it the diffuse quality of the statement that turns a statement into an aggressive one? How do different types of content get perceived as verbally aggressive—is it primarily by words or by other means of communication? As Baron (1977) wrote,

> It is essential to determine whether, and to what extent, subjects actually accept the suggestion that their verbal comments or evaluations can harm the victim. Only to the degree that they attach credence to such statements can it be argued that aggression has occurred. (p. 47)

Interpretation of episodes would prove to be a fruitful area of investigation.

What are the outcomes of verbal aggression? Is there a relationship between type of abuse and its consequence? What is the relationship between parental intent and consequence on the child? Should verbal aggression—or emotional maltreatment—be defined as abusive whether or not it has any observable negative consequences on the child? The child may not show signs or effects of the abuse, so is the behavior still abusive? Child responses vary dramatically to situations and interactions. Although some children may not be bothered, others will be. Some are very sensitive and will suffer intensely and immediately. Other children do not show any impairment for a long time. Are verbally abusive words kept in some memory bank in the brain to be retrieved years later? Because of invisible scarring, the child may experience trauma not at the time of the abuse but years later. The consequences of the abuse may become serious years later when the child grows into adulthood and may be seen in interactions with others. Although we feel that abuse is abuse irrespective of consequences, this would be an important area for further inquiry (Edmunds & Kendrick, 1980). From this view, both intent and outcome are associated with aggression.

One tentative model for assessing this relationship would be to study the relationship between parental intent to be verbally aggressive compared with the child's perception of whether or not the interaction was abusive. With the use of even dichotomous variables (see Figure 5.1), one can begin to develop both theoretical understanding and quantitative data analysis of the parent-to-child verbally aggressive interactions.

Parental Intent to Be Aggressive

		Yes	No
Child's Perception of Aggression	Yes	Definite aggression	Perceived aggression
	No	Intended, not perceived	No aggression

Figure 5.1. Relationship Between Parental Intent and Child's Perception of Outcome

What causes parents to become intentionally verbally aggressive toward their children? What are other interaction alternatives that could be substituted? How would a parent learn different interaction skills?

These questions, and countless others, can be developed through the use of this preliminary taxonomy. Certainly, as good research accumulates, the taxonomy will be altered so that a better understanding about verbal aggression is ultimately created.

Conclusions

Strong arguments are to be made in support of verbal aggression receiving more attention. The inability of traditional child abuse measures—even those that measure physical injury—to predict degree of developmental dysfunction suggest that we need to depend less on information on the severity of injury and more on measures of process and psychological maltreatment (Brassard et al., 1993; Crittenden, 1992; Egeland et al., 1984). According to Garbarino and Gilliam (1980), child abuse is not simply less than optimal child rearing. It is a pattern of behavior that drastically violates moral, interpersonal, and scientific norms concerning child care. It is critical to understand more about how the pattern of verbal aggression is created, maintained, and altered.

Children who are verbally accosted for who they are as individuals—who have their physical, psychological, cognitive, and behavioral characteristics attacked—will likely experience a host of long-term problems. These problems are just now being identified. Because the normative child-rearing practices in Western cultures have "pathogenic properties and effects" that often create personal suffering, limitation, and maladjustment of children, according to Firestone (1993), parents are free to engage in any and all forms of interaction—including saying almost anything they want—with children up to a point at which a clear and present danger to the child's welfare arises.

In the opinion of many experts, the point at which intervention can occur is set far too high. Adults must be held accountable for behavior that is developmentally damaging. Just as it is inexcusable for a parent to maintain that he or she was simply disciplining a child by burning him with cigarettes, it is no adequate defense to argue that one is only toughening the child when engaging in verbally and emotionally destructive behavior.

As parents, it is an essential part of one's role to adequately socialize a child and prepare him or her for life. McClellend (1973) argues that social competence includes successful performance in communication skills—a child must be able to accurately receive and transmit messages verbally. If parents fail to socialize a child to become a competent adult and do not prepare him or her for what will be demanded of him or her throughout life, is that a form of abuse?

Human society and interpersonal solidarity are created, maintained, and renewed by routine human interactions (Fisher & Chon, 1989). Although the expression of negative emotions appears to be culturally universal and innate (Ekman & Friesco, 1982; Izard, Huebner, Risser, McGinnes, & Doughtery, 1980), evidence suggests that socialization, through a child's primary relationships and emotional understandings, affects the child's abilities to identify his or her own and other's emotional experiences, to control his or her own affective displays (Pollak & Thoits, 1989), and to form relationships with others (Leavitt & Power, 1989). When emotional distance exists between children and their caregivers, it is difficult for children to develop healthy relationships (Berger & Luckmann, 1967; Cooley, 1922). Parents have great power over the construction of a child's emotional reality; many seem more concerned with how children behave instead of how children feel, and they can transform children into "nonpersons" by denying the legitimacy of the child's emotions (Goffman, 1959).

This is not to say that children should not be disciplined; indeed, we are arguing that it is essential for parents to be conscious of their active and critical role in guiding and socializing children. Parents need to create an interpersonal infrastructure that will create normative patterns of communication that will enhance a child's socially responsible and psychologically healthy behaviors. Adults who say unkind things to "punish" their children must recognize that punishment is a form of retaliation that does not seek to redirect behavior, as is the focus of guidance or discipline (Dreikurs, 1964; Gordon, 1970).

The messages that parents give to their children must be further explored in a rigorous, scientific way to (a) identify the key determinants of verbal aggression; (b) understand the relationship between the factors that influence the presence of verbal aggression; (c) determine the short- and long-term effects of verbal aggression; and (d) develop prevention, education, and treatment programs that will help parents to become more effective in their role in socializing happy, healthy, socially productive citizens. Practitioners cannot provide useful information to parents without having the etiological and theoretical understandings that can be generated from good research. Parents, practitioners, and researchers, as active partners in this process, can work together to prevent verbal aggression and other forms of psychological maltreatment.

6

Communication Patterns in Families of Adolescent Sex Offenders

SANDRA M. STITH
GARY H. BISCHOF

In this chapter, we review the limited literature on communication within families of adolescent sexual offenders. We then detail a study conducted to increase our knowledge of parent-adolescent communication and communication regarding sexuality in families of adolescent sex offenders. This study compares adolescent sex offenders' perceptions of their families with the perceptions of other non-sexual-offending delinquents and with a normative sample of adolescents using the Parent-Adolescent Communication Scale and the Family Sex Communication Quotient. We conclude with implications for understanding and treating families of adolescent sexual offenders and suggestions for future research are offered.

In normal development, a child's dependency needs for empathic care, closeness, intimacy, and a sense of self follow a separate line from that of sexuality, although the two coexist and in some ways interact. . . . Throughout the life cycle of healthy persons, sexuality and intimacy can be expressed together or separately. Intimacy may occur in relationships that are not sexual, and sexuality can be expressed without intimacy. Ideally, both occur together in romantic relationships and can be enjoyed together although they do not replace each other. For some, however, there may be a merging of the desires or drives during childhood with sexuality being used to replace the ability to be truly empathic and intimate and to establish a sense of self and identify. . . . Pedophilic behavior in both adolescent and adult life may be the attempt to satisfy through sexual activity the emptiness and yearning left over from the bleak early years. . . . Sexually exploitive behaviors reflect a basic

inability to be empathic, appreciative of, and caring for another human being,
a deficit that is a residue from early years of unempathic care.
—Steele and Ryan (1991, p. 101)

Nicky Jones, a 14-year-old boy, had been in family therapy at our university-based family therapy clinic with his grandmother (his primary caregiver) for 10 months when she came to the session distraught over discovering that Nicky had sexually abused his 7-year-old cousin. Nicky's grandmother originally sought family therapy to help Nicky deal with his temper and to help her adjust to single parenting an adolescent grandson. Mrs. Jones was committed to doing a better job parenting her grandson than she had done parenting Nicky's father, who had abandoned him and his alcoholic mother. When Nicky's mother decided she could not care for Nicky, Mrs. Jones, with a mixture of love and trepidation, agreed to take on the challenge. Now it looked as though she had once again failed. She needed to know what happened and how to understand the factors that might have led to this offense. During the 2 years she had been primary caregiver for Nicky, she had tried to keep their communication channel open and to be available to him when he needed to talk. She needed to know if she had been responsible for his offense. She believed, like Monastersky and Smith (1985), that the family is often a crucial influence in the development or elicitation of the offending behavior. Along with these authors, however, she did not understand how this occurs. To help her understand Nicky's behavior, she spent many hours at the library reading research that examined various dynamics associated with adolescent sexual offending. This chapter presents results from a study that was designed to assist Mrs. Jones and others in understanding communication patterns in families of adolescent sex offenders.

An adolescent sex offender is defined as a "youth from puberty to the legal age of majority who commits any sexual act with a person of any age, against the victim's will, without consent, or in an aggressive, exploitative or threatening manner" (Ryan, 1986, p. 126). Sexual offenses by adolescents include noncontact offenses, such as exhibitionism or voyeurism; contact offenses, such as fondling, that often involve deception or coercion; and completed penetration as in the case of violent rape done with a deadly weapon. When younger children are victims, an age difference of 5 years between the adolescent and the victim, or the presence of any form of coercion or intimidation are generally thought to constitute a sexual offense (Groth & Loredo, 1981). Adolescent sex offenses are a significant problem in the United States. As many as 20% of all rapes and 30% to 50% of all cases of child sexual abuse are perpetrated by adolescents (Davis & Leitenberg, 1987). Studies of adult sexual offenders (Abel, Mittleman, & Becker, 1984; Becker & Abel, 1985) indicate that about half of adult offenders report that their first sexual offense occurred as an adolescent, and often, offenses escalated in frequency and severity over time. These alarming findings have led to increased efforts in the identification and treatment of adolescent sexual offenders and to the recognition of this group of offenders as a distinct juvenile justice problem and clinical population.

Understanding overall patterns of communication and communication about sexuality in families of adolescent sex offenders should be of interest to practitioners developing specialized treatment programs for this group or providing family therapy for these families or both. Families of adolescent offenders are frequently involved in treatment, and findings from this study are likely to enhance services to these families. In residential treatment facilities, adolescent sexual offenders and other juvenile delinquents are frequently placed together, but most experts advocate offense-specific treatment for sexual offenders (Knopp, 1985). Professionals in the sex offender field claim that adolescent sexual offenders are unique and distinct from other delinquent and nondelinquent adolescents (Knopp, 1985; O'Brien, 1985).

For domestic violence researchers, results from this study may help clarify whether, and in what ways, the family communication patterns of adolescent sexual offenders differ from the family communication patterns of other juvenile delinquents and from a normative adolescent population. Findings may also promote continued development of theories on factors that may lead adolescents to commit sexual offenses and help foster early identification of at-risk families. In addition, results of this study of family communication in families of adolescent sex offenders should be useful to researchers who are interested in understanding abusive family relationships.

This chapter will first provide an overview of research regarding adolescent sex offenders and particularly research on communication in these families. Then, a study will be described and results presented that compare families of adolescent sex offenders with families of other adolescent offenders and with a normative sample of families. Finally, suggestions will be made for clinical application of these findings and for future research.

Review of Literature

Sexual offenses are perpetrated by juveniles of all ethnic, religious, and geographic groups in approximate proportion to these characteristics in the general population (Ryan, 1991). Although 70% of adolescent sex offenders are living in two-parent homes at the time of discovery, over half report some parental loss, such as divorce, illness, or death of a parent or permanent or temporary separations due to placements or hospitalization of child or parent. Most adolescent sex offenders have at least average grades, although a significant number have been identified with special problems, such as learning disabilities. The range of social characteristics includes every type of youngster from star athlete to social outcast. Fewer than 5% have been previously identified as suffering mental illness or psychosis, although there may be an over-representation of emotional-behavioral disorders and affective or attention-deficit disorders. As Ryan (1991) wrote,

> Only about 30 percent have been involved in nonsexual delinquent or antisocial behaviors that might support a diagnosis of conduct disorder or antisocial personality. The remaining 65 percent appear to manifest their paraphilia without other observable personality or behavioral characteristics setting them apart from their peer groups. (p. 6)

Although research has mushroomed in the past 15 years, it has primarily been concerned with individual characteristics of offenders and offenses. Information is sparse about the family environments in which these offenders live. Many studies are limited by small sample size and geographical bias. Studies including normal control groups are sparse (Davis & Leitenberg, 1987). Clinical impressions abound, but little scientific research has been conducted to confirm or disclaim these impressions. This is especially true of research on the family environments of these adolescents, although there is conjecture on how the family influences the commission of an offense. For example, one study (Kaplan,

Becker, & Cunningham-Rathner, 1988) surveyed 27 parents of adolescent incest perpetrators and found these parents underreported physical and sexual abuse of their sons, had a high incidence of being sexually abused themselves, and a high rate of denial of their sons' offenses. These parents generally failed to educate their children about sex.

It is unclear how, if at all, the family communication patterns of adolescent sexual offenders differ from family communication patterns of juvenile delinquents who have committed either violent or nonviolent offenses or from patterns in families of normal adolescents because few studies compare these groups or include a representative sample of nonoffenders as a comparison group. Two previously published articles that have used the same database as the current study (Bischof, Stith, & Whitney, 1995; Bischof, Stith, & Wilson, 1992) compared factors related to family environment among these three groups (violent juvenile offenders, nonviolent juvenile offenders, and adolescent sex offenders) and included a normative sample for comparison. Bischof et al. (1992) used FACES-III (Olson, 1986) to assess adolescents' perception of family adaptability and cohesion. They found that families of sex offenders are characterized by greater family cohesion when compared with other delinquents but that sex offenders perceive their families as less cohesive than do members of normative families. No significant differences between the groups were found for family adaptability. This study indicated that although adolescent sex offenders perceived their families as more helpful and supportive than did violent delinquents, they viewed their families as less helpful compared with adolescents from a normative sample of families.

Bischof et al. (1995) used the Family Environment Scale (Moos & Moos, 1986) to examine family environments. They found that families of juvenile delinquents (including families of adolescent sex offenders) were less cohesive, less expressive, more controlling, less intellectual-cultural oriented, and less active-recreational oriented than were families in the normative sample. No differences were found on four variables (i.e., conflict, achievement orientation, moral-religious emphasis, and organization). No significant differences were found among the three categories of delinquents. Therefore, a pattern has begun to be developed that indicates that the groups of offenders are more alike in their family environment than they are different but that there seem to be some important differences between families of adolescent offenders and families of normative samples. No study has specifically examined family communication patterns of families of adolescent offenders and compared them with families of other adolescents. This study aims to fill this gap.

Parent-Adolescent Communication

Communication between adolescents and parents seems to be a reliable indicator of the quality of the relationship. Galvin and Brommel (1986) define communication as a symbolic, transactional process in which participants both affect and are affected by the interaction. Communication affects the way family members relate, and family relationships affect the communication that occurs. Satir (1972) believed that good family communication is the largest single factor determining kinds of relationships family members have with others. The significance of effective communication between family members has been recognized by therapists, researchers, and family life educators. Olson (1976) discussed the important diagnostic function of communication patterns as indicators of the quality of relationships. This strong association between communication and the quality of a relationship is the basis on which communication will be examined in this study. That is, communication is seen as an indicator of the relationship between an adolescent and his or her mother or father or both.

The association between parent-child communication and general juvenile delinquency has been examined. Several reviews of the literature (McGaha & Fournier, 1988; Thornburg, 1986; Tolan, Cromwell, & Brasswell, 1986) report relationships between aspects of family communication and juvenile delinquency. In communicating with their children, parents of delinquents have difficulty establishing consistent rules and expectations, are less likely to praise children or show interest in their activities, often disagree, and give conflicting directives to children. Family communication is often defensive, lacking focus, or dominated by one family member. Communication is further characterized by difficulty resolving conflicts, an unwillingness to compromise, and a greater proportion of communication was misperceived.

Parent-child communication has not been studied for adolescent sex offenders, but the father appears to play a significant role in the etiology of adolescent sexual offenses. A generally poor relationship between father and son, if there is a relationship at all, is a common thread among adolescent sex offenders (O'Brien, 1985). From on-site interviews at treatment programs across the country, Knopp (1982, 1985) reported that none of the offenders claimed to have a warm, close, nurturing relationship with their fathers. Instead, fathers seemed to be either abusive or physically or emotionally absent from these young people. In comparing adolescent sex offenders and a matched group of non-sexual-offending delinquents (Awad, Saunders, & Levene, 1985), fathers of adolescent sex offenders were found to be more rejecting and were nearly twice as lax in providing parental control as fathers of the general delinquents. Mothers of the two groups of boys scored very similarly across measures of parent-child interaction. O'Brien (1985) postulates that a poor father-son relationship may have a profound impact on sexuality, sex roles, parenting, and attitudes toward women. He recommends examining father-son relationships among other juvenile delinquents and among nonoffending teens to determine whether these initial indications are indeed unique to adolescent sex offenders.

Parent-Adolescent Communication About Sexuality

Peers have remained the major source of information about sexuality for adolescents for several eras (Walters & Walters, 1983). Adolescents in several studies, however, report a preference for parents as the primary source of sexual information (Handelsman, Cabral, & Weisfeld, 1987). The relationship between parent-adolescent communication about sexuality and responsible sexual behavior appears unclear. Although Walters and Walters (1983) report that adolescents who talk with their parents about sex begin having sexual intercourse later than those who do not discuss sex with parents, Handelsman and colleagues found that the presence of open parent-child communication did not seem to influence sexual activity but did influence contraceptive use. Furthermore, a study that assessed adolescents' sexual self-disclosure to parents (Papini, Farmer, Clark, & Snell, 1988) found that disclosure was strongly associated with adolescent perception of the openness and adaptiveness of the family context and that teens generally disclosed more to the same-sex parent.

Clinicians working with adolescent sex offenders suggest that sexual knowledge of these youth is lacking and that sexual myths and misinformation abound in this population (O'Brien, 1985), but virtually no studies have addressed how these offenders gain information about sexuality or how much they have communicated with their parents about sexuality. This study is designed to fill that gap in the literature as well.

In this study, we chose to compare communication patterns of families of adolescent sexual offenders with families of non-sexual-offending juvenile delinquents who committed nonviolent offenses and with non-sexual-offending delinquents who committed violent offenses for several reasons. First, we wanted to know if the communication patterns that were uncovered were specific to sexual-offending delinquents or were more generally related to delinquent behavior. Next, to determine if communication patterns differed if the delinquent behavior was violent versus nonviolent, we further divided the delinquent non-sexual-offending group into violent and nonviolent categories. Finally, because it was important to determine if the communication patterns in families of sexual-offending delinquents were different from the patterns observed in families that had not been identified through delinquent behaviors, we selected instruments that had been normed on a sample that was not identified as offenders. Thus, we chose the groups of participants to assess whether family communication differs as a function of the type of offense or whether it is being an offender per se that is important in understanding family communication patterns.

Methods

Participants

Questionnaires were distributed to 109 adolescent males in various outpatient and residential programs; 105 questionnaires were returned (96.3%). Participants were adolescent males, ages 12 to 18, who were grouped as follows: (a) adolescent sexual offenders ($n = 39$) who self-reported having committed child sexual molestation or who were involved in treatment programs designated for identified adolescent sexual offenders; (b) non-sexual-offending juvenile delinquents ($n = 25$) who self-reported committing violent offenses (e.g., homicide, manslaughter, robbery, or aggravated assault); and (c) non-sexual-offending juvenile delinquents ($n = 41$) who self-reported committing nonviolent offenses, such as property offenses, nonviolent crimes against persons, status offenses, or substance abuse violations. A non-delinquent control group was not included in this study, but both measures used in this study have been normed to the general population of adolescent families and these norms were compared to scores by the study groups. Participants were not paid but were encouraged to participate as a way to help other young people and society in general.

Measures

The Parent-Adolescent Communication Scale (PAC) (Barnes & Olson, 1982) was used to assess the quality of various features of parent-adolescent communication. Norms were developed for this measure from a subgroup of a larger randomly stratified sample of 1,140 intact families (Barnes & Olson, 1985). This subgroup consisted of all the families who were at the adolescent or launching stage of the family life cycle and had an adolescent child who participated in the study ($n = 426$). Other than being intact families, no other criteria were used for excluding families from this sample. Barnes and Olson (1985) wrote,

> These families appeared to be rather "normal" and without serious problems. The vast majority of the parents had never been divorced (96%), and only 8% had ever received individual, marital or family therapy. The adolescent participants ranged from 12 to 20 years of age, with a mean of 16.4 years. Data were collected from 214 male and 212 female adolescents. They were generally good students. About half of the teens reported working part-time jobs. Several analyses were completed to test for sex differences attributable to the sex of the adolescent. The findings clearly demonstrated no sex differences between adolescent males and adolescent females in how they perceived their communication with their mothers or fathers. (p. 10)

The 20-item questionnaire has both a parent and an adolescent version. The adolescent version used in this study contains each of the 20 items twice—once in reference to mothers and once in reference to fathers. Items are worded both positively and negatively. An example of a positive item is "I can discuss my beliefs with my mother/father without feeling restrained or embarrassed." An example of a negative item is "I don't think I can tell my mother/father how I really feel about some things." This instrument yields two subscale scores. The Openness of Parent-Adolescent Communication subscale assesses the quality of information exchange between adolescents and their parents. The Problems in Parent-Adolescent Communication subscale identifies barriers to parent-adolescent communication. The PAC subscales have high reliability (Cronbach's alpha: openness = .87, problems = .78) (Papini, Farmer, Clark, Micka, & Barnett, 1990). Separate scores were tallied for adolescents' perceptions of their communication with mothers and fathers in this study.

The Family Sex Communication Quotient Scale (FSCQ) (Warren & Neer, 1986) was designed as a diagnostic measure of family orientation toward sexual communication, with a focus on communication between parents and children. A normative sample was obtained from 93 male and 94 female undergraduates enrolled in a basic communication theory course. Students were requested to complete a questionnaire on family sex communication prior to a course lecture on family communication. Participants were told to complete the questionnaire with family in mind as whoever raised them. Respondents answered the questions retrospectively how their parents communicated as they were growing up.

The Family Sex Communication Quotient Scale assesses communication comfort, communication information, and value of communication about sexual issues between parents and children. The communication comfort dimension measures the perceived degree of openness with which sex is discussed in the family (e.g., "I feel free to ask my parents about sex."). The information dimension measures perception of the amount of sexual information learned and shared during family discussions (e.g., "My parents have given me very little information about sex."). The value dimension measures the perceived overall importance of the family role in sexual learning (e.g., "The home should be a primary place for learning about sex."). All items yield significant correlations with the summed FSCQ score, and dimension-to-dimension correlations provided strong evidence (.82-.93) for the internal consistency of the FSCQ with all three dimensions.

Procedure

A paper-and-pencil self-report survey was administered to adolescent participants by a research investigator or treatment professional. Programs-facilities participating in the study signed a statement of participation, indicating their understanding of the purpose and procedures of the study. Both the youth and the parents, guardians, or custodians gave their written permission and informed consent for the youth to participate in the study.

Results

Demographic Factors

There was a significant difference in age among the three groups ($F = 6.41, p = .002$); mean age for the adolescent sexual offender group was 15.39, whereas mean age for violent and nonviolent juvenile delinquents was 16.16 and 16.34, respectively. Although difference in age was statistically significant, the groups fall within the same developmental range of middle adolescence. There were no significant differences in race among the three groups (73% white, 16% black, 3% Latino, 3% Asian, 5% other for entire sample).

Participants came predominantly from the Washington, D.C. metropolitan area. Level of family income differed significantly between the three groups ($F = 4.44, p = .01$). Mean family income was $38,400, $41,000, and $52,000 for adolescent sexual offenders, violent juvenile delinquents, and nonviolent delinquents, respectively. The majority of fathers (74%) and mothers (71%) were employed full-time. Mothers most frequently worked in service occupations (33%) or in technical or clerical work (32%). Fathers worked primarily in service or military occupations (26%) and in administration, engineering, or scientific endeavors (19%). There were no significant differences among the groups for parents' employment level or occupation.

In summary, adolescent sexual offenders were slightly younger than both violent and nonviolent delinquents, but there were no significant differences in race, parental employment, or occupation. Nonviolent delinquents in this study tended to come from families with higher incomes.

Parent-Adolescent Communication

Although three aspects of communication were assessed (open communication, problems in communication, and overall quality of communication), normative data were available only for overall quality of communication. Analysis of variances (ANOVAs) revealed no significant differences between groups of offenders on open communication with mother or with father (Table 6.1). Adolescent sex offenders and nonviolent delinquents scored significantly lower than the normative sample of adolescents on overall father-adolescent communication ($F = 8.38$, $df = 4$, $p < .01$). All three study sample groups also scored lower on overall communication with mothers when compared to the normed sample of adolescents ($F = 5.52$, $df = 3$, $p = .001$). No other differences between groups were found for measures of parent-adolescent communication.

As illustrated in Table 6.2, using paired t tests, adolescent sex offenders were found to score higher on measures of open communication ($t = 2.90$, $df = 31$, $p = .0007$) and overall communication ($t = 2.18$, $df = 31$, $p = .04$) with their mothers than with their fathers, but there was no significant difference between adolescent sex offenders' problems in communication with mothers and with their fathers. In contrast, violent delinquents did not differ on any measures of communication between mothers and fathers, and nonviolent delinquents differed significantly only on the measure of open communication ($t = 2.24$, $df = 32$, $p = .03$) with their mothers and with their fathers, reporting more open communication with their mothers.

Parent-Adolescent Communication About Sexuality

Adolescent sex offenders were found to value the role of the family in sex education more highly than did nonviolent juvenile delinquents ($F = 6.15$, $df = 2$, $p = .003$) but did not differ from violent delinquents (Table 6.1). There were no significant differences between adolescent sex offenders, nonviolent juvenile delinquents, or violent juvenile delinquents regarding their comfort about sexual communication with

TABLE 6.1 Analysis of Variance With Duncan Procedure for Parent-Adolescent Communication and Family Sex

Variable	I Adolescent Sexual Offender	II Violent Juvenile Delinquent	III Nonviolent Juvenile Delinquent	IV Normative Adolescents	F Ratio
Parent-adolescent communication	n = 36 (w/mo.) n = 32 (w/fa.)	n = 22 (w/mo.) n = 21 (w/fa.)	n = 40 (w/mo.) n = 33 (w/fa.)	n = 426	
Open communication					
Mother	33.69	31.18	31.65	36.03[a]	0.65
Father	28.97	29.86	27.33	33.35[a]	0.41
Problems in communication					
Mother	27.44	28.82	29.13	30.56[a]	0.54
Father	26.31	29.62	28.09	30.47[a]	1.42
Overall communication					
Mother	61.31[IV]	60.16[IV]	60.94[IV]	66.58[I,II,III]	5.52**
Father	55.28[IV]	59.37	55.42[IV]	63.82[I,II]	8.38**
	n = 35	n = 25	n = 38	n = 187	
Family sex communication					
Comfort	17.46	17.32	15.24	NA	1.85
Information	17.23	16.68	15.13	NA	2.28
Value	20.06[III]	17.92	16.32[I]	NA	6.15*
Total score	54.74[III]	51.92	46.68[I,IV]	54.08[III]	3.41*

NOTE: Roman numerals indicate location of significant differences between groups.
a. Although group means were available for the subscales of the Parent-Adolescent Communication Scale, they were not able to be entered in the ANOVA analyses because other statistical information (i.e., standard deviations) could not be obtained, thus F ratios for these PAC subscales pertain to the study groups only.
*p < .05; **p < .001.

parents or regarding the amount of information about sexuality obtained from parents.

Normative data were available only for overall parent-adolescent communication about sexuality. Using an ANOVA, significant differences between groups were found (F = 3.41, df = 3, p = .02). Adolescent sex offenders and the normative sample of adolescents scored higher than nonviolent delinquents. Violent delinquents did not significantly differ from any of the groups on this measure. Mean scores for adolescent sex offenders (54.74) and the normative sample of adolescents (54.08) were very similar.

TABLE 6.2 Paired *t* Tests Comparing Adolescents' Communication With Mothers and Fathers on the Parent-Adolescent Communication Scale

Type of Communication	ASO		VJD		NVJD		Normative	
	Mean	t Value	Mean	t Value	Mean	t Value	Mean	t Value
Openness—mother	33.84		31.16		31.64		36.03	
		2.90*		0.35		2.24*		5.08**
Openness—father	28.97		30.05		27.33		33.35	
Problems—mother	27.47		28.21		29.30		30.56	
		0.78		−0.81		0.84		0.20
Problems—father	26.31		30.10		28.09		30.47	
Overall—mother	61.31		59.37		60.94		66.58	
		2.18*		−0.15		1.73		3.28*
Overall—father	55.28		60.16		55.42		63.82	

*p = .05; **p = .001.,

Discussion

Parent-adolescent communication was assessed for communication with both mothers and fathers. Parent-adolescent communication for families of adolescent sex offenders had not been considered in previous research. Three aspects of communication were evaluated: open communication (positive aspects), problems in communication (negative aspects), and overall quality of communication. Adolescent sex offenders and nonviolent delinquents reported significantly less overall father-adolescent communication than did the normative sample of adolescents. No differences existed between scores of violent delinquents and any of the other groups of adolescents with regard to father-adolescent communication. All three groups of offenders reported less overall communication with mothers when compared to the normative sample of adolescents. Thus, there was little difference in parent-adolescent communication among the three study groups, but all three groups of adolescent offenders reported less overall communication with their mothers and their fathers than did the normative sample of adolescents.

Clinical impressions (Eddy, 1990) have suggested adolescent sex offenders have poor relationships with both mothers and fathers. Because adolescent sex offenders scored significantly lower than the normative sample of adolescents on overall communication with both mothers and fathers, this finding may be viewed as support for these impressions. It is possible that this lack of positive overall communication with parents may be a factor in the development of pedophilic behavior. As discussed in the quote by Steele and Ryan (1991), which was used to introduce this chapter, pedophilic behavior

> may be the attempt to satisfy through sexual activity the emptiness and yearning left over from the bleak early years. . . . Sexually exploitive behaviors reflect a basic inability to be empathic, appreciative of, and caring for another human being, a deficit that is a residue from early years of unempathic care. (p. 101)

Because this lack of overall communication with parents also occurred in families of other offenders, whereas communication deficits may influence the development of delinquent behaviors, other factors operate to determine the development of sexually deviant behavior.

Our clinical impressions and previous research (O'Brien, 1985; Knopp, 1982, 1985) also suggest that adolescent sex offenders have poor or nonexistent relationships with their fathers and tend to identify more with their mothers. We found that adolescent sex offenders had more open communication and better overall communication with their mothers than with their fathers, thus lending some support to the clinical impressions. It should be noted, however, that adolescents in the normative sample also report a greater degree of openness and higher overall quality of communication with their mothers (Barnes & Olson, 1982, 1985; Olson et al., 1983). Therefore, differences between communication with mothers and fathers for adolescent sex offenders are not necessarily specific to that population but rather may be indicative of normal differences between adolescents' perception of communication with mothers and fathers. It was also noted in this study, however, that adolescent sex offenders' overall communication with fathers was significantly poorer than that reported by the normative adolescent sample. These results highlight concerns about the importance of the father-son relationship mentioned previously. If O'Brien is correct in his hypothesis that a poor father-son relationship may have a profound impact on sexuality, sex roles, parenting, and attitudes toward women, these results only increase this concern.

Parent-Adolescent Communication About Sexuality

Although previous research (O'Brien, 1985) has suggested that adolescent sexual offenders lack information about sexuality, we found that they tended to value the importance of the role of the family in sexual learning more highly than did nonviolent delinquents. Due to the higher score on this subscale, they also scored higher than nonviolent delinquents on the total score for family sex communication. There were no significant differences between groups in adolescents' ratings of the frequency of sex communication with mothers or fathers or in the level of comfortability they have discussing sexuality with parents.

The finding that adolescent sex offenders value the family's role in sex education more highly than other offenders and the lack of differences in parent-adolescent communication about sexuality between groups may have resulted from the treatment received by the adolescent sex offenders. Participants in this study were all involved in treatment programs and most of the adolescent sex offenders were being treated in programs specifically designed for this population. The amount of time that the adolescent had been involved in treatment was not assessed, but many had been in treatment for several months. Sex education and family discussions about sexuality are included in many sex offender treatment programs.

We were especially interested in the fact that adolescent sex offenders value the role of the family in sex education more than other groups of offenders. This finding could be due to the adolescents' recognition that they received an inadequate amount of information about sexuality from parents and that they desired much more. Adolescent sex offenders may be more aware of the need for parent-adolescent sex communication and their valuing the role of family may be an expression of a desire for more communication about sexuality.

Future studies should collect data prior to or at the onset of treatment to assess the family's role in sex education so results are not biased by the effects of treatment. This would help clarify the significance of the quantity and quality of family sex education in the etiology of sexual offenses by adolescents. There may be a considerable amount of overt and covert communication about sexuality in families of adolescent sex offenders, but this communication may be inappropriate and of a poor quality.

Limitations and Future Research Suggestions

Participants in this study were voluntary and self-selected and therefore are not necessarily representative of the delinquent populations included here. Parental-guardian permission first had to be obtained, and then adolescents decided if they would participate after learning what would be required. Participants came from programs-facilities that agreed to cooperate with the study. Non-sexual-offending delinquents came primarily from four residential programs, and all but one was involved in a residential program. Adolescent sex offenders were closely divided between outpatients and residents. Placement in residential care often comes only after other less restrictive alternatives have been exhausted, and frequently severe family dysfunction is a criterion for out of home placement. Future studies should include offenders from various levels of outpatient and residential treatment or control for placement setting.

Information in this study was obtained from the adolescent only. Future work should include data from parents also. In addition, data were obtained from adolescent retrospective self-reports. Participants were asked to report on conditions at the time of their offense. In some cases, a long period of time had passed since the offense, inviting the possibility of treatment effect or inaccurate recall of prior family conditions. For a more accurate and complete perspective of the family environment, information should be obtained early in the assessment or screening process and should include the perceptions of several family members. It is recommended that family instruments be included routinely in assessment, as families are frequently involved in treatment. The limitations inherent in collecting data on family communication through survey instruments are also important to note. Future research using observational techniques could enhance our understanding of family communication patterns. A more comprehensive understanding of the family context would prove valuable in treatment planning and intervention design.

Detailed information about offenses and offense history was not obtained in this study. Future studies should attempt to differentiate family characteristics and environments among various types of adolescent sexual offenders. Indeed, Bera (1985) found little difference between families of adolescent sexual offenders and normal adolescent families in general, but significant differences emerged between various types of adolescent sexual offenders classified according to offenses and offense patterns.

Clinical Implications

Given the fact that delinquent adolescents perceive that their families have less positive parent-adolescent communication, one implication of this study is that focusing on family relationships to improve communication may be useful. Previous research (Papini et al., 1990) has indicated that emotional self-disclosure among family members may be lowest when families are perceived as being closed to communication and that moderate amounts of self-disclosure are associated with individual mental health (Carpenter, 1987; Stiles, 1987). Families who are closed to communication may be at high risk for subsequent dysfunction given the relationship between self-disclosure and mental health. Papini and colleagues suggest that one suitable strategy for helping families adapt to normal changes brought on by the child's transition to adolescence may be to focus on patterns of self-disclosure. Rather than attempting to treat adolescents individually, clinicians should direct efforts toward changing the ways adolescents and their parents relate to and communicate with one another. This may not be easy because poor communication patterns may be exacerbated by the offense, the stigma attached to sexual offenses, and by involvement with an adversarial legal system.

Results of this study offer particular concern regarding the importance of the father-son relationship. Therapists should encourage the development of more open channels between fathers and sons. Fathers may be given tasks to complete with their sons that would enhance their connection and assist them in developing warmer relationships. When fathers are absent or unavailable, efforts should be made to include positive male role models from the adolescent's context, such as a coach or an uncle.

Also, according to research reviewed by Harnett and Misch (1993), lack of sexual knowledge is an important factor that decreases the likelihood that the adolescent sexual abuser will form close relationships with members of both sexes. Without the experience of close relationships, the adolescent sex offender will be less likely to engage in socially accepted sexual experimentation that could enable him to develop a sexual identity that is not deviant. The adolescent sex offenders in this study recognized the value of parents providing sex education to their children. We do not know whether this recognition came before or after the offense, but we recognize the importance of these offenders' perspective and encourage treatment or prevention programs or both to include sex education and especially sex education that includes parents in the process.

Summary

Gilgun's (1988) qualitative research with adult sexual offenders points to the lack of a "confidant" (someone in whom to confide personal matters) as a significant variable in the early childhood experiences of sex offenders. That confidant may be the factor that helps the young person deal with distressing experiences and helps him learn to trust. She also found that these offenders report a sense of isolation throughout their childhood. This study, which demonstrated that families of adolescent sex offenders have less positive overall communication than families of a normative sample of adolescents, points to the importance of open ongoing communication within families. "Interaction is the sine qua non of relationships; it is through communicative action that persons initiate, define, maintain, and terminate their social bonds" (Baxter, 1985, p. 245). Sexually exploitive behavior may be an end result of a deficit in positive interaction within the family in a child's early years.

7

Communication and Violence in Courtship Relationships

COLLEEN M. CAREY
PAUL A. MONGEAU

This chapter focuses on the role of communication in the perpetration and inhibition of courtship violence. Specifically, this study investigates the ability of several communication variables to predict the occurrence of verbal and physical aggression in dating relationships. An important part of this study is to test Infante, Chandler, and Rudd's (1989) Communication Skills Deficiency Model of Interpersonal Violence (CSDM). Participants were selected from 228 university students. Results from the 147 participants currently involved in dating relationships provide partial support for the CSDM as verbal aggressiveness is a consistent predictor of both verbal and physical aggression. Coping strategies and social support also successfully predicted both verbal and physical aggression. Implications for the perpetration and control of courtship violence are discussed.

Makepeace's (1981) seminal study helped focus considerable research attention on courtship violence. Many of these studies focused specifically on the prevalence of violence in dating[1] relationships (see for example, Allbritten & Bogal-Allbritten, 1985; Laner, 1983; Matthews, 1984; Pirog-Good & Stets, 1989). Several of these studies have been particularly enlightening. Bergman (1992) discovered one

AUTHORS' NOTE: The present data were collected as part of Colleen Carey's Senior Honors Thesis study directed by Paul Mongeau. The authors thank Ann Frymier for her assistance on the honors thesis, Steve Duck for his helpful comments on an earlier version of this manuscript, Lee Cahn for his help in improving the book chapter, and Sally Lloyd for her help at all stages of this project's life.

127

of four females had experienced severe physical or sexual violence or both in high school dating relationships. Makepeace determined that a majority of college students had personally known someone involved in a violent courtship relationship. Stets and Henderson (1991) used a nationwide representative sample and found that 30% of respondents reported using or receiving physical aggression, whereas nearly 90% reported using or receiving verbal aggression.

In summarizing these incidence studies, Sugarman and Hotaling (1989a) found that levels of involvement (i.e., initiating or receiving violence) ranged across studies from 9% to 66%, with an overall mean of 31% (quite consistent with results of Stets & Henderson, 1991). These data indicate that approximately one third of all high school and college students have experienced violence within the context of a dating relationship. A problem that affects one third of our nation's adolescents deserves serious attention. As social scientists have become more aware of the courtship violence problem (e.g., Aizenman & Kelley, 1988; Henton, Cate, Koval, Lloyd, & Christopher, 1983; Lloyd, 1991; Makepeace, 1981), they realized how important it is to spend additional time investigating the phenomenon.

This investigation's primary goal is to examine how communication influences courtship violence. This is an important goal because communication between partners (e.g., conflict management) is frequently cited as a potential predictor of interpersonal violence. In addition, communication factors, such as argumentativeness, verbal aggressiveness, negotiation skills, coping strategies, and social support systems, have been found to predict the occurrence of violence in courtship relationships (e.g., Bird, Stith, & Schladale, 1991; Caulfield & Riggs, 1992; Infante, Chandler, & Rudd, 1989; Lloyd & Emery, 1994; Stets & Henderson, 1991). An important part of this goal is to test the Communication Skills Deficiency Model developed by Infante et al. (1989) on a sample of couples in the courtship stage of relationship development. Such findings should be of interest to therapists as well as researchers interested in interpersonal violence and dating relationships.

Defining Courtship Violence

Sugarman and Hotaling (1989a) report that researchers have had a difficult time developing consistent conceptual and operational definitions of courtship violence. These difficulties appear to center on trying to define the terms *courtship* and *violence* both separately and as a unit. Courtship, as defined by Cate and Lloyd (1992), includes dating relationships that lead to marriage as well as those that end before marriage. The term *dating* refers to couples engaging in mutually rewarding activities that may lead to future interaction, emotional commitment, or sexual intimacy or all three (Sugarman & Hotaling, 1989a).

The term *violence* has many definitions (see Chapter 1). For example, the term violence can be defined as the intentional or unintentional occurrence of an act or threat of aggression by one person or group of persons on another person or group of persons. The operational definition of the term violence, then, includes the frequency with which individuals engage in or threaten violent behaviors within a specific time period. Violent behaviors include pushing, shoving, slapping, kicking, biting, hitting, hitting with a fist, hitting with an object, beating, use of a weapon, threatening any of these behaviors, or verbal assault or all of the above (Straus, 1979).

Sugarman and Hotaling (1989a) claim that dating violence typically occurs when one member of a dating couple commits or threatens to commit an act of violence toward their dating partner. Therefore, courtship violence is the perpetration or threat of an act of physical aggression (e.g., pushing, hitting, shoving, kicking, etc.) or verbal aggression (e.g., swearing, insulting, character attacks, etc.) by one person toward their partner with the intent of causing some degree of physical, psychological, or emotional harm or all three. This violent behavior must occur within a dyadic courtship relationship that explores the possibility of romantic interest by engaging in mutually rewarding activities that may lead to future interaction, commitment, sexual intimacy, or marriage or all four. This definition is broad enough to include heterosexual, gay male, and lesbian relationships from the first date through to cohabitation or engagement or both, but it excludes marital relationships.

Communication Variables and Courtship Violence

The primary goal of this investigation is to explore the ability of communication variables to predict the occurrence of verbal and physical aggression in college dating relationships. An important part of this goal is to test the Communication Skills Deficiency Model of Interpersonal Violence (i.e., CSDM; Infante et al., 1989; Infante, Riddle, Horvath, & Tumlin, 1992). It is important to consider communication variables and models of courtship violence because they clearly indicate "that when violence occurs it is not an isolated event in people's lives, but is embedded firmly in the process of interpersonal communication which people use to regulate their lives" (Infante et al., 1989, p. 174). Moreover, because communication variables have frequently been cited as predictors of interpersonal violence (e.g., Bird et al., 1991; Caulfield & Riggs, 1992; Infante et al., 1989; Lloyd & Emery, 1994), research in this area has the potential to discover more effective methods of predicting, dealing with, and potentially avoiding violence in dating relationships.

Several researchers have linked communication skill deficiencies to marital violence (DeTurck, 1987; Infante et al., 1989, 1992). The most complete explication of this link comes in Infante et al.'s (1989) CSDM. Developed from the aggression literature, the CSDM is built on the assumption that destructive forms of communication (e.g., verbally attacking the partner) are likely to lead to physical violence, whereas constructive forms of communication (e.g., discussing issues) should reduce the likelihood that conflict will escalate into physical aggression. Infante, Sabourin, Rudd, and Shannon (1990) argue that an inability to argue an issue can instigate violence. Without positive verbal skills, the victim of a verbally aggressive attack can defend himself or herself with a physical attack. As a consequence, two individual difference characteristics, verbal aggressiveness and argumentativeness, play central roles in the CSDM.

Argumentativeness

Infante, Sabourin, et al. (1990) define *argumentativeness* as an individual difference characteristic representing the extent to which a person is willing and able to effectively present, attack, and defend issues. Although the term *argument* frequently conjures up images of negative interpersonal events, the term argumentativeness refers to a preference to engage in positive methods of discussing controversial issues or disagreements. Specifically, argumentativeness represents the extent to which an individual enjoys arguing issues on controversial topics. Infante, Sabourin, et al. reported that low argumentative individuals possess fewer argumentative skills and a lower desire to argue issues than their highly argumentative counterparts.

Verbal Aggressiveness

It is important to differentiate verbal aggressiveness from verbal aggression. Infante and Wigley (1986) define the term *verbal aggression* as an exchange of messages between two individuals in which one person attacks the self-concept of the other in an attempt to hurt them psychologically. Common forms of verbal aggression include character attacks, background attacks, competence attacks, physical appearance attacks, maledictions, teasing, ridicule, threats, and profanity. On the other hand, the term *verbal aggressiveness* refers to an individual difference characteristic representing the extent to which an individual engages in verbally aggressive behaviors. That is, verbal aggressiveness is a trait possessed by individuals who engage in communication behaviors that attack other people rather than issues.

Building on Infante and Wigley (1986), Infante et al. (1992) distinguished between high- and low-verbal-aggressiveness individuals in three ways. First, high-verbal-aggressiveness individuals engage more frequently in competence attacks, teasing, swearing, and nonverbal emblems. These characteristics are particularly important because Infante, Sabourin, et al. (1990) indicate that use of swearing, competence attacks, and threats differentiate physically violent from nonviolent confrontations as well. Second, high-verbal-aggressiveness individuals believe that competence attacks, physical appearance attacks, and threats are less hurtful than do low-verbal-aggressiveness individuals. Third, high-verbal-aggressiveness individuals attribute their verbally aggressive behaviors differently than do low-verbal-aggressiveness individuals. High-verbal-aggressiveness individuals claim that their verbal aggression reflects an attempt to appear tough, to be mean to (or show disdain for or both) the message target or as their inability to keep a rational discussion from generating into a verbal fight.

Infante et al. (1992) note that the expression of negative emotions (e.g., anger) and reciprocity of verbal aggression are frequently found in the verbally aggressive behavior from both high- and low-verbal-aggressiveness individuals. Reciprocity of verbal aggression is a key factor in both verbal aggression (e.g., Infante, Sabourin, et al., 1990) and physical violence (e.g., O'Keefe, Brockopp, & Chew, 1986; Stets & Henderson, 1991). Therefore, Infante et al. (1992) contend that frustration, anticipated positive consequences, and the presence of verbal-aggression cues from one's partner may spark verbally aggressive behavior. That is, if any of these indicators occur within a disagreement, verbal aggression may result.

The CSDM and Courtship Violence

Infante et al. (1989) proposed that individuals who are low in argumentativeness will be more likely to be involved in violent relationships because they will be more likely to verbally attack their partner rather than their partner's stance on the issue at hand. As a consequence, the CSDM predicts that argumentativeness is negatively correlated, and verbal aggressiveness positively correlated, with the perpetration of both verbal and physical aggression. There are a number of forces, however, involved in the escalation of verbal aggression into physical violence (Infante et al., 1989).

The CSDM also predicts that verbal aggression often serves as a catalyst for physical aggression (Infante et al., 1989). Therefore, verbal aggression is a necessary, but not sufficient, condition for physical violence. An interesting aspect of the catalyst concept is that "a reaction can be blocked if the catalyst is controlled, even though the other ingredients are in place for a reaction" (Infante et al., 1989, p. 166). Therefore, the CSDM presumes that violence might be prevented if individuals are taught to attack issues rather than the personality and other personal characteristics of their partners.

Infante and colleagues (1989, 1990) have generated important data on the role of verbal aggressiveness and argumentativeness in the perpetration of interpersonal violence. Bird et al. (1991) investigated how other personal and communication factors (specifically, negotiation styles, coping strategies, and social support) influence interpersonal violence. The role of these variables in courtship violence will also be investigated in the present study.

Negotiation Styles

According to Bird et al. (1991), "negotiation styles" are methods used by one partner in an attempt to control their partner's behavior despite the partner's opposition. Bird et al. argue that negotiation strategies are relevant to interpersonal violence, as violent partners may lack positive negotiation skills (i.e., they may not know how to communicate in a nonthreatening manner). This is consistent with the CSDM's assumption that low-argumentative individuals may be unable to effectively verbally defend themselves and their ideas in a conflict (Infante et al., 1992).

Bird et al. (1991) found that college students involved in violent relationships who rely on negative negotiation tactics, such as communicating negative affect or being particularly disagreeable, are significantly more likely to use confrontation and blame. Couples who resort to violence in their dating relationships are also significantly more likely to use indirect, one-way negotiation styles that do not require their partner's cooperation (Bird et al., 1991).

Coping Strategies

According to Makepeace (1981), violence is more likely to occur in a relationship when dating partners perceive problems in the relationship to be threatening and beyond their coping abilities. As a consequence, Bird et al. (1991) suggested that it is important for researchers to investigate how relational partners cope with stress in their relationships and in their lives. They found that couples involved in violent dating relationships are more likely to engage in confrontive coping strategies, characterized by expressing anger and blame, as well as attempting to change the partner. Bird et al. also reported that violent dating couples will cope with relational problems by swearing, using insults, and avoiding the problem more often than nonviolent dating couples.

Bird et al. (1991) suggest that when individuals convince themselves that violence is a form of love or a normal behavior to cope with its occurrence, they may not concern themselves with stopping the violence or ending the relationship. Bird et al.'s contention reflects the need for concern associated with our society's overromanticized notions of courtship behavior (e.g., Lloyd, 1991).

Social Support

A final important factor relevant to courtship violence is social support. *Social support* is a term used to refer to the interpersonal relationships that individuals maintain with others in which they may feel free to express their own and listen to others' concerns and provide and receive information, feedback, advice, assistance, comfort, and care. Bird et al. (1991) indicate that individuals with strong social support systems may be more likely to communicate about issues involving conflict in their dating relationships. In their study, Bird et al. found that individuals who talk about their relationship conflicts with others (e.g., their dating partner, parents, friends, or coworkers) are less likely to be in violent relationships. Therefore, strong social networks may be essential for encouraging open communication about relational problems or provide partners with a "vent" for their frustrations created by the relationship or both.

Sex Differences

Significant sex differences exist in several of the variables discussed thus far. For example, several researchers have found that women often receive more positive social support than do men (e.g., Olson & Schultz, 1994). Many women also use different coping strategies in response to stressful situations than do men (e.g., Ptacek, Smith, & Dodge, 1994). Moreover, many men have been found to be higher on both argumentativeness (Roach, 1992) and verbal aggressiveness (Sallinen-Kuparinen, Thompson, & Klopf, 1991; see, however, Burgoon, 1991). Finally, women tend to engage in more verbal and physical aggression in dating relationships (e.g., Clark, Beckett, Wells, & Dungee-Anderson, 1994; Pedersen & Thomas, 1992).

Moreover, several of these variables have different impacts on a variety of outcomes. For example, Acitelli and Antonucci (1994) found that social support correlated more strongly with marital satisfaction for women than for men in general. Moreover, Riggs, O'Leary, and Breslin (1990) found that correlates of courtship violence differed for men and for women. As a consequence, it is important not only to look for sex differences in all variables under consideration but also to investigate the extent to which the predictors of verbal and physical aggression differ for men and women.

Summary and Hypotheses

Further investigation into the area of courtship violence from a communication perspective has great potential for increasing our understanding of the dynamics of interpersonal violence. Such investigations may also be useful in designing interventions aimed at preventing violence. Tests of the CSDM (e.g., Infante et al., 1989, 1992) have focused exclusively on married couples. Bird et al. (1991), on the other hand, have investigated the role of other communication factors in courtship relationships. The present investigation extends this previous work in interpersonal violence by testing how communication factors outlined in the CSDM and other research (especially Bird et al.) inhibit or promote violence in courtship relationships. This literature review suggests the following hypotheses and research questions:

> Hypothesis 1: Argumentativeness, the use of positive negotiation styles and coping strategies, and the existence of positive social support are negatively related to the occurrence of verbal and physical aggression.
> Hypothesis 2: Verbal aggressiveness, the use of negative negotiation styles and coping strategies, and the existence of negative or poor social systems are positively related to the occurrence of verbal and physical aggression.
> Research Question 1: Do predictor variables, the frequency of verbal or physical aggression, or both differ between men and women?
> Research Question 2: Do the predictors of verbal and physical aggression differ between men and women?

To test these hypotheses and to answer these research questions, a questionnaire study was performed involving college students currently involved in dating relationships. Regression determined the extent to which predictors were related to verbal or physical aggression or both and the extent to which these predictors differ for men and women.

Method

Participants

Two hundred twenty-eight undergraduate students (143 females, 62.7%; 83 males, 36.4%; and 2 individuals who did not indicate their sex, 0.9%) from two introductory communication classes at a midsized midwestern university volunteered for the present study. All analyses are based on the 147 participants (93 females, 63.3%; 54 males, 36.7%) who indicated that they were currently involved in a dating relationship. Of these 147 participants, over half (i.e., 53.1) were sophomores. Participants' average age was 19.5 years old, whereas their partners were reported to be slightly older ($M = 20.1$).

Procedures[2]

One partner in a dating relationship performed in the study. Participants performed in the study in a classroom, however, outside their regularly scheduled class. A single experimenter led experimental sessions of 10 to 25 participants. Instructions indicated that participants were to think of their current (or most recent) dating relationship while completing all scales. The questionnaire generally took participants 25 to 30 minutes to complete.

Instrumentation

All participants completed a battery of the following six self-report questionnaires. The order of scales was identical for all participants.

Argumentativeness. The Argumentativeness Scale (Infante & Rancer, 1982) consists of 20 items (e.g., "While in an argument, I worry that the person I am arguing with will form a negative impression of me."), each accompanied by a five-interval Likert-type response scale ranging from "almost never true" to "almost always true." This scale was found to be reliable (Cronbach's alpha = .88).

Verbal Aggressiveness. The Verbal Aggressiveness Scale (Infante & Wigley, 1986) also consists of 20 items (e.g., "I am extremely careful to avoid attacking individuals' intelligence when I attack their ideas."), each accompanied by a five-interval Likert-type response scale ranging from "almost never true" to "almost always true." Participants rated both their own and their partner's verbal aggressiveness. Both the ratings of self verbal aggressiveness (Cronbach's alpha = .87) and partner verbal aggressiveness (Cronbach's alpha = .92) were reliable.

Coping Strategies. The Ways of Coping Inventory (Folkman, Lazarus, Dunkel-Schetter, DeLongis, & Gruen, 1986) contains 50 items, each accompanied by a four-interval Likert-type response scale ranging from "does not apply/was not used" to "used a great deal." This scale is composed of eight subscales: confrontive coping (e.g., "Stood my ground and fought for what I wanted"; Cronbach's alpha = .37), distancing (e.g., "Made light of the situation; refused to get too serious about it"; Cronbach's alpha = .64), self-controlling (e.g., "I tried to keep my feelings to myself"; Cronbach's alpha = .47), seeking social support (e.g., "Talked to someone to find out more about the situation"; Cronbach's alpha = .66), accepting responsibility (e.g., "Criticized or lectured myself"; Cronbach's alpha = .50), escape-avoidance (e.g., "Wished that the situation would go away or somehow just be over with"; Cronbach's alpha = .63), planful problem solving (e.g., "I knew what had to be done, so I doubled my efforts to make things work"; Cronbach's alpha = .70), and positive reappraisal (e.g., "Changed or grew as a person in a good way"; Cronbach's alpha = .73).

Several of these subscales exhibited unacceptably low reliability. Removing one item from both the planful problem-solving and distancing scales increased these scales' reliability. The reliabilities for the confrontive coping, self-controlling, and accepting responsibility subscales are admittedly low; removing scale items, however, would not improve reliability.

Social Support. Levels of social support were measured with a scale developed by R. Milardo (1984). This scale contains 25 items, each accompanied by a nine-item Likert-type response scale ranging from "once a day or more" to "don't know/can't estimate." The scale is composed of two factors: positive social support (17 items; e.g., "Comforted you by showing some affection"; Cronbach's alpha = .89) and negative social support (8 items; e.g., "Refused to listen to your side of things"; Cronbach's alpha = .77).

Conflict Tactics-Behaviors. Frequency of both verbal and physical aggression was measured with Straus's (1979) Conflict Tactics Scale (CTS). This scale contains 19 items describing a range of behaviors. Each behavior was accompanied by several items, including a dichotomous response scale indicating whether the behavior was performed in the relationship in the past 6 months. These behaviors were divided into four dimensions: CTS verbal reasoning (3 items; Cronbach's alpha = .51), CTS verbal aggression-coercion (5 items; Cronbach's alpha = .84), CTS physical aggression-threat (7 items; Cronbach's alpha = .82), and CTS severe violence (4 items; Cronbach's alpha was not computable because there was no variation in these items). Each behavior was also accompanied by a single item measuring how frequently each behavior was performed in the relationship. Responses to the frequency item included once, 3 to 5 times, 6 to 10 times, 11 to 20 times, and more than 20 times. If a participant indicated that he or she had not experienced a particular behavior in his or her dating relationship, the frequency was coded as zero. This adaptation of scoring the CTS produced a single measure of the frequency of violence that sums the extent to which participants were a victim or perpetrator or both of each subscale of behavior. Thus, our use of the term *experienced violence* refers to all three possibilities—victim, perpetrator, and mutual violence. Finally, participants were asked whether each behavior was performed by the self, the partner, or both.

Relational Characteristics. Participants also completed a series of items concerning their relationship. Items tapped the length of the relationship, whether participants considered their relationship a long-distance relationship, what percentage of the time were they unable to see their partner because of physical distance, and whether they considered their relationship to be violent.

Results

Relational Characteristics

Individuals in the 147 intact relationships had been dating, on average, for just over 1 year. Nearly one half (48.6%) of the participants indicated that they were in a long-distance relationship. Participants spent an average of 35.8% of their time away from their partner solely because of physical distance. Finally, only 2 of the 147 participants (1.4%) considered their relationship to be violent.

Incidence of Courtship Violence

Incidence of courtship violence was the percentage of the participants who had experienced at least one behavior in the CTS verbal aggression-coercion, CTS physical aggression-threat, or CTS severe violence subscales. The vast majority (i.e., 91.8%) of participants report having experienced CTS verbal aggression-coercion. Just over 1 in 3 participants (i.e., 35.4%) reported having experienced CTS physical violence-threat. None of the 147 participants involved in current dating relationships reported experiencing CTS severe violence. As a consequence, these behaviors were excluded from any further analyses. Clearly, as the violent nature of the behavior increased, frequencies of those behaviors decreased.

Sex Differences

A series of t tests determined which variables contained significant sex differences. Three variables differed significantly ($p < .05$) between men and women. The strongest difference occurred on ratings of one's own verbal aggressiveness (Infante & Wigley, 1986). Males ($M = 2.69$) tended to rate themselves as being significantly more verbally aggressive than did females ($M = 2.28$), $t(145) = 4.47$, $p < .001$. Second, females ($M = 3.62$) tended to report significantly higher levels of positive social support (higher numbers indicate lower levels of social support) than did males ($M = 4.45$), $t(145) = 4.03$, $p < .001$. Finally, females ($M = 1.81$) were significantly more likely to report seeking social support as a coping strategy than were males ($M = 1.63$), $t(145) = -2.33$; $p < .05$.

For the CTS verbal aggression-coercion subscale, almost exactly half (i.e., 50.2%) of the reported behaviors were mutually enacted. If behaviors are mutually enacted, no sex differences can exist. As a consequence, sex differences in aggressive behaviors reported here focus on those behaviors enacted by only one partner.

Females were found to engage in significantly more CTS verbal aggression-coercion than males, χ^2 (1) = 73.31, p < .001. This sex difference was most markedly true for the item "cried." Men seem to rarely cry alone. Women were also more likely than men to have "sulked/refused to talk" and "stomped out of the room."

Only a little more than a quarter (i.e., 26.4%) of CTS physical aggression-threat behaviors were mutually enacted. Of those behaviors enacted by only one partner, males and females tended to exhibit similar levels of CTS physical aggression-threat, χ^2 (1) < 1.0. The lack of a significant sex difference was due in part to low frequencies on several items. Moreover, the nature of the sex differences varied across CTS physically aggression-coercion behaviors. The only item on the entire CTS in which men's behavior far exceeded women's was "throw/smash/hit/kick something." Women, on the other hand, were more likely to "slap" their partner, "hit/try to hit with something," and "threaten to hit/throw something" than were men.

Predictors of Courtship Violence

Multiple regression procedures were used to determine which variables predicted the frequency of courtship violence experienced by participants in the 6 months prior to completing the study. CTS verbal aggression-coercion and CTS physical aggression-threat subscales served as dependent variables. Predictors of CTS verbal aggression-coercion included verbal aggressiveness, argumentativeness, the eight coping strategies, negative and positive social support, and the CTS verbal reasoning subscale. Predictors of CTS physical aggression-threat included all the same variables with the inclusion of the frequency of CTS verbal aggression-coercion. Regression analyses were performed separately for male and female participants. A .10 level of significance was used in all analyses. This rather liberal choice was made because breaking the sample into males and females creates relatively small subgroups. As a consequence, using the traditional level of significance (i.e., .05) might cause us to miss important, but relatively small, relationships.

CTS Verbal Aggression-Coercion. Results from multiple regression analyses on the frequency of CTS verbal aggression-coercion broken down by participant sex are presented in Table 7.1. The strongest predictor of CTS verbal aggression-coercion for both male and female participants was the CTS verbal reasoning subscale. As the frequency of CTS verbal reasoning increased, so did the frequency of CTS verbal aggression-coercion. Ratings of one's own and the partner's verbal aggressiveness (Infante & Wigley, 1986) also significantly predicted CTS verbal aggression-coercion for both males and females. As scores on Infante and Wigley's verbal aggressiveness scale increased, so did the reported frequency of CTS verbal aggression-coercion. The coping strategy of confrontive coping was a significant predictor of CTS verbal aggression-coercion for males, whereas the coping strategies of escape-avoidance and planful problem solving were significant predictors for women. Confrontive coping and planful problem solving were negatively related, whereas escape was positively related to CTS verbal aggression-coercion.

CTS Physical Aggression-Threat. Results from multiple regression analyses on the frequency of CTS physical aggression-threat for both men and women are presented in Table 7.2. The frequency of CTS verbal aggression-coercion was the strongest predictor of CTS physical aggression-threat for both males and females. As CTS verbal aggression-coercion increased, so did CTS physical aggression-threat. The only other significant predictor of CTS physical aggression-threat for males was negative social support. Increased negative social support was associated with increased physical aggression. For women, three coping strategies (i.e., escape-avoidance, planful problem solving, and distancing) and ratings of one's own verbal aggressiveness (as measured by Infante & Wigley's, 1986, scale) were also significant predictors. The use of all three coping strategies and self verbal aggressiveness were positively related to the frequency of physical violence.

TABLE 7.1 Predictors of Verbal Aggression-Coercion Subscale of the Conflict
Tactics Scale Broken Down by Participant Sex

Predictor	b	t	$p <$
For male participants			
CTS verbal reasoning	.50	4.60	.001
Self verbal aggressiveness	.36	3.02	.01
Partner verbal aggressiveness	.35	2.91	.01
Coping: Confrontive coping	−.23	−1.75	.10
$R^2 = .62$; Adjusted $R^2 = .48$			
For female participants			
CTS verbal reasoning	.52	6.05	.001
Self verbal aggressiveness	.23	2.30	.05
Coping: Escape	.20	1.80	.10
Coping: Planful problem solving	−.17	−1.67	.10
Partner verbal aggressiveness	.15	1.68	.10
$R^2 = .52$; Adjusted $R^2 = .44$			

Discussion

The primary goal of this study was to determine the role of communication variables in the perpetration or inhibition of courtship violence in a college student sample. An important part of this goal was to test factors relevant to Infante et al.'s (1989) Communication Skills Deficiency Model of Interpersonal Violence in a nonclinical, college student population. The CSDM argues that violence in interpersonal settings is a function of relational partners' relative ability to effectively respond in a conflict situation. Participants who lack argumentative skills (i.e., the ability to develop arguments that attack issues rather than people) presumably feel frustration in a conflict situation. When faced with a partner's verbally aggressive messages (i.e., those attacking people not issues), individuals are likely to respond in kind (i.e., with either a verbally or a physically aggressive move). As a consequence, argumentativeness is predicted to be negatively related to verbal and physical aggression, whereas verbal aggressiveness is predicted to be positively related to such acts.

TABLE 7.2 Predictors of Physical Aggression Subscale of the Conflict Tactics Scale
Broken Down by Participant Sex

Predictor	b	t	p <
For male participants			
CTS verbal aggression–coercion	.59	3.05	.01
Negative social support	.32	2.21	.05
R^2 = .46; Adjusted R^2 = .24			
For female participants			
CTS verbal aggression–coercion	.67	6.05	.001
Coping: Escape-avoidance	.28	2.55	.01
Coping: Planful problem solving	.23	2.23	.05
Coping: Distancing	–.17	–1.68	.10
Self verbal aggressiveness	.16	1.69	.10
R^2 = .55; Adjusted R^2 = .46			

Incidence of Courtship Violence

The incidence of violence reported in this sample is quite consistent
with that of previous investigations (see especially Stets & Henderson,
1991; Sugarman & Hotaling, 1989a). Nearly all (91.8%) participants
had experienced CTS verbal aggression-coercion in their current dating
relationships, whereas just over one third (i.e., 35.4%) experienced CTS
physical aggression-threat. None of the participants reported severe
physical violence in their relationships. As a consequence, as the severity
of the aggression increased, frequencies declined (see, e.g., Riggs et al.,
1990).

Sex Differences

Several of the variables in this investigation differed between men
and women. It is interesting that more females sought social support as
a coping strategy than did men. Moreover, women also tended to report
receiving more positive support than males. These data are consistent
with previous investigations (e.g., Olson & Schultz, 1994; Ptacek et al.,
1994) and suggest that women in this sample may have a better

developed social support system than do the males. Many women, then, appear to have a greater opportunity to talk about relational issues outside the bounds of their dating relationship.

Males tended to rate themselves as more verbally aggressive (as measured by Infante & Wigley's, 1986, scale) than females. This result is consistent with other investigations (Sallinen-Kuparinen et al., 1991) and may help explain how men are able to maintain their dominance in interpersonal interactions, especially in cross-sex interactions. This finding seems inconsistent, however, in light of the finding that women engage in more CTS verbal aggression-coercion than do men. This apparent contradiction is partially answered by investigating the particular CTS verbal aggressive-coercion behaviors in which sex difference occurred. Women exceeded men in crying, sulking (or refusing to talk), and in stomping out of the room. These behaviors are similar in that they are indirect means of dealing with conflict. These reported behaviors, perhaps because they are indirect means of communicating negative emotions, may be considered more acceptable for women to perform than for men. Although these behaviors may express emotions, they do not deal with issues. As a consequence, it is questionable whether these behaviors should even be considered verbally aggressive.

Women are often socialized to be nice, caring, compassionate individuals and to always think about the other person's feelings. It appears that some men do not have such compunction and are more likely to say what they think without considering the effect it may have on the individual with whom they are communicating. This parallels Infante and Wigley's (1986) finding that high verbally aggressive individuals perceive verbally aggressive messages as being less harmful than low verbally aggressive individuals (Infante & Wigley, 1986).

Predicting Courtship Violence

Verbal Aggression and Courtship Violence. Predictors of verbal and physical aggression were consistent with the CSDM's predictions when it came to Infante and Wigley's (1986) concept of verbal aggressiveness. Participants' own and their partners' level of verbal aggressiveness was positively related to CTS verbal aggression-coercion for both men and women. Moreover, verbal aggressiveness was positively related to CTS physical aggression-threat for women (but not for men). Perhaps men's direct verbal aggression will be met with an indirect response, whereas women, in the same situation, may find their partner acting in a verbally or physically aggressive manner. Together, these data serve as additional partial validation for the verbal aggressiveness scale (Infante & Wigley, 1986; particularly those linking the trait of verbal aggressiveness to the behavior of verbal aggression).

Data from the present investigation are also consistent with the CSDM in that the frequency of CTS verbal aggression-coercion in the relationship was the strongest predictor of CTS physical aggression threat for both men and women. These data were consistent with Infante et al.'s (1992) results indicating that attacks on the partner's sexual ability, job, and success were particularly likely to generate a physically violent response. These results are also consistent with the CSDM's assumption that verbal aggression can often escalate to physical aggression (Infante et al., 1989).

Argumentativeness and Courtship Violence. The CSDM did not fair as well in the present investigation when it came to argumentativeness. Argumentativeness did not significantly predict either CTS verbal aggression-coercion or CTS physical aggression-threat. Perhaps argumentativeness is not as strong a predictor of the frequency of aggression as we hypothesized, or perhaps it is a better predictor with other non-college-student samples. Infante, Wall, Leap, and Danielson (1984), however, report that in argumentative contexts highly argumentativeness individuals may receive the most verbally aggressive messages. Although highly argumentative individuals may generally avoid attacking the other person's characteristics, it may become increasingly difficult to argue effectively in the face of a series of highly verbally aggressive messages. Future research needs to be conducted to determine the true extent of the influence that argumentativeness has on the occurrence of verbal and physical aggression.

Coping and Courtship Violence. Several coping strategies were significant predictors of verbal or physical aggression or both. The coping strategy of escape-avoidance significantly predicted the occurrence of both verbal aggression-coercion and physical aggression-threat for women. This is consistent with Bird et al.'s (1991) finding that couples who attempt to avoid problems tend to experience greater physical violence. That is, when individuals avoid conflict, the conflict does not necessarily go away. That escape-avoidance predicts verbal aggression for females is consistent with those verbally aggressive behaviors more likely to be performed by women. Crying, sulking, and stomping out of the room may express emotion, but they do not deal directly with the conflict.

If the conflict is not resolved, it may continue to upset the individual who perceives it to be problematic. When individuals typically avoid conflict in their relationships, eventually they may reach the breaking point, lose control, and let all of their anger and frustration out at once. In these situations, verbal and physical aggression may be more likely to occur.

The coping strategy of distancing was found to be inversely related to the frequency of physical aggression-threat for women. That is, the more an individual tries to distance herself from a conflict, the less frequently she is likely to experience physical aggression. This appears to be contradictory with the escape-avoidance finding. Although avoidance implies that the individual tries to actively avoid dealing with the conflict, distancing involves a particular means of dealing with stressful situations. Specifically, distancing involves trying to make light of the problem to try to cut it down to size.

This conceptualization of distancing is consistent with Makepeace's (1981) suggestion that physical aggression is more likely to occur when dating partners perceive problems to be threatening and beyond their coping abilities. If individuals can learn to put problems in perspective, they will not feel as though problems are beyond their coping abilities, will be more likely to deal with these problems, and will therefore be less likely to use verbal or physical aggression. Similarly, if couples can be taught to distance themselves from threatening problems, perhaps they will be better able to step back and analyze or diffuse a conflict situation rather than resort to physical violence.

Results concerning other coping strategies are not as easily explained. For women, planful problem solving was negatively related to verbal aggression but positively related to physical aggression. It is unclear why these relationships might go in opposite directions. Perhaps women's plans might allow them to avoid conflict (and verbal aggression) but not alleviate the conflict. Over time, however, the conflict does not go away, leading to a larger conflict, including physical aggression. In addition, confrontive coping is negatively related to verbal aggression for males, whereas Bird et al. (1991) found the opposite. These relationships are all rather small (i.e., $p < .10$) and may be due to sampling error.

Social Support and Courtship Violence. Negative social support was found to be positively related to the frequency of physical aggression-threat—only for men, however. That is, as the amount of negative social support received increased, the individual was more likely to experience physical aggression in his or her dating relationship. Men apparently tend to seek less social support as a coping strategy and receive less social support than do women. This is consistent with Bird et al.'s (1991) findings that physical aggression may be more likely to occur when individuals lack strong social support systems. It is important to note, however, that positive social support was unrelated to either verbal or physical aggression. Perhaps, this seeming contradiction indicates that it is not necessarily positive social support that is predictive of healthier communication patterns, but that it is simply the absence of negative social support that is important in preventing physical aggression. Regardless, future research needs to be conducted to determine the exact relationship between social support (both positive and negative) and verbal and physical aggression.

Conflict and Courtship Violence. Finally, the CTS verbal reasoning subscale was the strongest predictor of the frequency of CTS verbal aggression-coercion for both men and women. The CTS verbal reasoning subscale presumably consists of positive behaviors that are reported to occur in the course of relational conflict (e.g., discussing an issue calmly or bringing in a third party to back up their side). It is not clear why these positive behaviors would strongly predict the frequency of verbal aggression, although they might not be as positive as has been thought.

The CTS verbal reasoning subscale may reflect the frequency of conflicts or disagreements that a couple has experienced. The more disagreements a couple engages in, the more likely it is that conflict will escalate to verbal aggression (Straus, Gelles, & Steinmetz, 1980). It appears that one of the specific circumstances in which verbal aggression is a catalyst for physical aggression may be simply the number of conflicts experienced. If this is the case, then it is crucial to teach individuals how to effectively manage conflict in their relationships.

Summary, Limitations, and Suggestions for Future Research

Planalp (1993) argues that researchers need to learn how to convert unhealthy communication patterns into healthy ones. The study of communication variables in courtship violence certainly attempts to fulfill this call. This study extends previous work in the area of interpersonal violence by increasing our understanding of communication patterns in courtship violence. Specifically, these results extend Infante et al.'s (1989) Communication Skills Deficiency Model of Interpersonal Violence to a nonclinical, college student population.

The present data, however, are only partially consistent with Infante et al.'s (1989) CSDM. Consistent with the CSDM, verbal aggressiveness for both the self and the partner predicted the frequency of verbal aggression experienced in the relationship. Moreover, the frequency of verbal aggression in a relationship was the strongest predictor of physical aggression. Inconsistent with the CSDM, argumentativeness was not found to inhibit either verbal or physical aggression in current dating relationships.

These and earlier data imply that verbal aggression is experienced in nearly all courtship relationships; rates of physical aggression, however, are much lower. The CSDM (Infante et al., 1989) asserts that verbally aggressive behaviors serve as a catalyst for physical aggression (Infante et al., 1989). The present data are certainly consistent with this assertion; it is also clear, however, that not all verbal aggression results in physical aggression. One intriguing question, then, is to consider when verbal aggression will (and when it will not) spark a physically violent episode.

Although coping strategies significantly predicted both verbal and physical aggression, measurement of these variables was hindered by some very low reliabilities. Measurement problems associated with several of these coping strategies represent a limitation of the present study. Alternative measures of coping strategies should be sought. Hobfoll, Dunahoo, Ben-Porath, and Monnier (1994), for example, developed a measure based on their dual-axis model of coping. The axes include both activity (i.e., active-passive) and social (i.e., prosocial-antisocial) dimensions. Hobfoll et al. claim that this conceptualization should tap sex differences (particularly using one's social support system as a coping strategy) more effectively than existing measures. As a consequence, this new scale may work well in the courtship violence context.

Future research should attempt to generalize this model to non-college-student populations. The present study used college students. It is unclear the extent to which these results generalize to older and younger groups that vary in the extent and quality of their academic background. Students at the school where the research was performed have strong academic records. Perhaps argumentativeness was unrelated to physical and verbal aggression because of the participants' verbal skill. Regional differences should also be investigated as there is no guarantee that midwestern college students will react in the same ways as students from other parts of the United States (e.g., Andersen, Lustig, & Andersen, 1987). The use of a broader sample including nonstudents—particularly individuals without college educations—should be investigated.

Researchers also need to consider whether samples should be randomly selected from the population. Random selection increases external validity; it, however, typically reduces sample size. The balance between increased sample size and generalizability should be weighed.

The CSDM is also a transactional model—that is, dating violence is an interpersonal rather than a personal issue. In other words, the CSDM predicts that it is the combination of both partners' argumentativeness and verbal aggression that creates violence-prone dating relationships. Verbal aggression, in certain circumstances, can serve to escalate an otherwise verbal argument into a conflict characterized by physical violence. As a consequence, research that involves both partners is necessary (see also Makepeace, 1986). It would be ideal to have both partners' responses to scales to further test the CSDM in a college dating context. Moreover, it would be interesting to observe how couples engage in conflict behaviors (e.g., as performed by Courtright, Millar, Rogers, & Bagarozzi, 1990) to determine how actual behaviors relate to questionnaire responses.

Another limitation to this study is the fact that the CTS physical violence subscale is not normally distributed; instead, it is positively skewed. Statistical tests, such as multiple regression, assume a normal distribution. Therefore, conclusions drawn from analyses on this variable should be taken with some caution.

The issue of intent is also important to the definition of courtship violence. That is, courtship violence must be inflicted with the intention of harming the relational partner for some reason, purpose, or goal (see Chapter 1). Little of the existing research, however, has considered the goal, or intent, behind aggressive verbal or violent physical responses. If we can learn more about the psychological state existing within a verbally aggressive or physically violent individual immediately preceding the verbally aggressive or physically violent behavior, we will be better able to understand and control motivations for this type of behavior. Thus, once we comprehend the extent to which each factor influences this phenomenon, we will be better able to understand and control the process of courtship violence as a whole.

It is important that people be educated about the negative impact of verbally aggressive messages. Across several investigations (Infante et al., 1989, 1990, 1992) verbal aggressiveness plays an important role in the development and perpetration of interpersonal violence. In addition to education, people need to be provided with some means of avoiding verbally aggressive strategies and tactics in conflict contexts.

Notes

1. The terms *courtship* and *dating* will be used interchangeably. Dating is the informal term used to refer to the relationship type studied in the present investigation. Individuals may not consider themselves engaging in courtship because it is often interpreted as an old-fashioned idea or directly linked with a desire for marriage or both. Courtship, however, is a social science term and will be used whenever possible.

2. Participation partially fulfilled a research requirement for two introductory speech communication classes. This study's procedures were approved by both the Departmental and the University Committee on the Use of Human Subjects in Research. Each participant initially read and signed an informed consent form. Participants were assured of anonymity and asked to answer questions as honestly and as accurately as possible. Due to the sensitive nature of the questionnaire, the experimenter encouraged participants to ask any questions they might have, to skip any question or section of the questionnaire that upset them, and to stop participating at any time (without consequence) if they so desired. Debriefing occurred in writing and participants were given the telephone numbers for several local counseling centers.

8

The Ties That Bind Women to Violent Premarital Relationships

Processes of Seduction and Entrapment

KAREN H. ROSEN

Premarital relationships can become intimate relationship contexts in which love and violence coexist. This chapter describes processes that led young women to maintain their premarital relationships despite damage to them physically and emotionally. Analysis of qualitative interview data provided by 22 women who survived violent premarital relationships revealed intrapersonal and interpersonal themes of seduction and entrapment. These include romantic fantasies and romantic fusion, survival tactics, cognitive dissonance, roller coaster relationships, traumatic bonding, Romeo and Juliet effects, and peer-family collusion.

I can remember the night I finally knew that I made the decision [to leave the relationship]. I can remember gasping for breath. I was talking to my girlfriend, saying "I feel like I'm going to die." I was really scared. I didn't know who I was. Because I was in this situation for so long, I had no idea what life was like outside all that craziness before that. I was scared of what life offered, what was out there. It was like I was in a big ocean and there was one little piece of wood out in the ocean. I've got to get to the wood. And I hung on to it and every day I wanted to go back.

This young woman's description of her experience as she made and followed through with the decision to leave her abusive boyfriend illustrates how powerful the forces to remain in a premarital relationship, even an abusive one, can be. For 5½ years after the abuse began, Alexandra (a pseudonym) held on to her relationship almost as if it

151

represented life itself. For Alexandra and for many other young women, abuse within a premarital relationship does not necessarily mean the relationship will end. Indeed, nearly 40% of the victims of dating violence continue their relationships despite suffering abuse (Henton, Cate, Koval, Lloyd, & Christopher, 1983). Premarital violence is a serious social problem that affects more than 30% of the young people in the United States who date (Sugarman & Hotaling, 1989a). Although much is known about its precursors, correlates, prevalence, and conse-quences (e.g., Arias, Samios, & O'Leary 1987; Burke, Stets, & Pirog-Good, 1989; Follingstad, Wright, Lloyd, & Sebastian, 1991), it is a complex phenomenon that remains largely an enigma after a decade of scholarly investigation. Premarital violence, also referred to here as dating violence or premarital abuse, is being defined as using or threat-ening to use physical force or restraint with the perceived intent of causing pain or injury to one's dating partner (see Chapter 1, this volume). Although women can also behave aggressively toward their male partners, the focus of this chapter is on violence against women within heterosexual dating relationships.

Because of the prevalence of dating violence and its link to a number of psychological and psychosocial symptoms (Graham & Rawlings, 1991), helping professionals from a variety of disciplines and in a variety of settings need to be prepared to assist young women who are entangled in this kind of destructive relationship. This study was conducted to provide information for helping professionals in the trenches who develop and deliver intervention and prevention strategies aimed at empowering young women. It was also conducted to enhance our theoretical understanding of abuse and to identify issues for future research.

The phenomenon of abusive relationships that remain intact has been studied primarily from the perspective of married women. For a married woman, there are often a multitude of factors to consider when making the decision to stay with or leave an abusive husband, some of which are interrelated and difficult to weigh. One component that influences a wife's decision to stay or leave her abusive partner is the cognitive judgment she makes about the abuse. That is, a victim may see her abuse as her own fault, as an aberrant event that will not be repeated, or as part of an otherwise acceptable relationship that compares posi-tively with the relationships of others (Ferraro & Johnson, 1983;

Herbert, Silver, & Ellard, 1991; Mills, 1985). Another component of her decision to remain in an abusive marital relationship is the strength of her emotional attachment to her partner (Strube & Barbour, 1983, 1984). In addition to these two components, a critical third component relates to practical matters, such as child care arrangements, financial support, and legal commitments (Johnson, 1992; Strube & Barbour, 1983, 1984). When making the decision to stay with or leave their abusive husbands, married women often need to consider how they will support themselves, what effect leaving will have on their children, and whether they can or are willing to dissolve their legal contract.

Although there are certainly similarities between marital abuse and premarital abuse, many of the barriers to leaving experienced by abused wives do not apply to women in premarital relationships. Thus, we need to look specifically at premarital relationships to understand why some women who are abused by their dating partners remain in their relationships in the absence of legal, financial, or familial ties. The ties that bind them to their relationships are not as concrete, but they are equally as powerful. Examining why women stay with their abusive premarital partners presents the opportunity to study entrapment processes that are free of some of the encumbrances of marriage.

Researchers have established that, as with abused wives, psychological commitment plays a role in women's decisions to remain in abusive premarital relationships (Lloyd, Koval, & Pittman, 1987). Young women, in effect, can become trapped by their attraction, continuing commitment, and their great investment even after it becomes costly to continue the relationship. In addition, women's decisions to stay with or to leave their abusive premarital partners have also been shown to relate to whether they see themselves as having acceptable alternative partners, their sex role attitudes, and their perceptions of the effect of abuse on the relationship (Henton et al., 1983; O'Keefe, Brockopp, & Chew, 1986). In general, women who think they have acceptable alternatives, who have egalitarian sex role attitudes, and who do not view violence as a sign of love are more likely to leave abusive premarital relationships than women who do not share these beliefs.

Previous investigations provide some understanding of why a woman might choose to stay in an abusive premarital relationship; how she becomes entrapped, however, is not well understood. The question, "why does she stay?" implies a simplistic explanation for what is a complex process. Although we have begun to learn something about the complex processes involved in how women develop a readiness to leave abusive relationships (Rosen & Stith, 1995), little attention has been paid to studying the processes that solidify a woman's commitment to a relationship that is clearly harmful. This is largely due to the fact that much of the previous research on premarital abuse has been survey research that is not well suited to collecting such information (Sugarman & Hotaling, 1989a). In this study, I attempt to develop an understanding of events, interactions, feelings, and beliefs that were involved in women's decisions to maintain abusive premarital relationships. How does a woman's premarital relationship become so important that she chooses to remain with her partner despite the reality of violence and the risk to herself? I have looked at communication-related processes of entrapment as they occurred over the course of women's abusive premarital relationships. The purpose of this study is to examine women's initial seduction into dating relationships that became abusive and the forces that tended to galvanize their commitment to these relationships despite the onset of abuse.

This study was informed by feminist thinking regarding research for and about women (see Thompson, 1992). It seeks to "unpack" complex, intimate relationships in which women are subordinated and intimidated by the men in their lives and in which the politics of patriarchy became replicated in the politics of personal relationships. I sought not only to understand women's behavior but also to understand the meaning they make of their own and their partners' behavior. This effort to understand how young women became entrapped in abusive premarital relationships was not undertaken to "blame the victim" but rather to offer an explanation that addresses some of the complexity—an explanation that will be freeing to women who think "I must be crazy" to do this. Participants in this study were viewed as the knowers; the researcher was viewed as the one who wanted to be educated. In addition to the information participants provided during the interview process, they were given an opportunity to read and to respond to the researcher's preliminary interpretations. Finally, I use the "voices" of participants to illustrate processes described using their own words transcribed verbatim from their interviews (all names used are pseudonyms). A brief description of the research design and methods is followed by the presentation of results.

Method

Research Design

A qualitative research design sacrifices traditionally generalizable results to make possible a holistic study of complex processes within intimate relationships, including interactions, meanings, and context. This research design is ideal for capturing the subjective experience of violence, the complexities of violent relationships, and the multifaceted realities of informants (Eisikovits & Peled, 1990). Through the interaction between researcher and informants during the interview process, aspects of violence that have become ordinary and taken for granted can be rediscovered and become part of their shared awareness. Naturalistic inquiry enables "the knower and the known to explore their mutual realities and the ways in which they were created" (Eisikovits & Peled, 1990, p. 6).

Procedures

Participants were recruited through newspaper advertisements, flyers reaching the general public as well as university students, and referrals from clinical colleagues. Recruitment efforts were directed toward young women who had been in or were currently in serious dating relationships in which violence had been inflicted more than once. Twenty-two women participated in this study. Twelve women were interviewed once and 10 women were selected to be interviewed in more depth (two or three interviews each). Data collection and analysis were integrated and decisions about whom to select for in-depth study were made in part on the basis of their availability and in part according to the tenets of theoretical sampling outlined by Strauss and Corbin (1990). Initial interviews varied from 1 to 3 hours; subsequent interviews tended to be more intense, varying from 2 to 4 hours. With the permission of participants, all interviews were audiotaped and transcribed. The interviewer asked questions about participants' expectations for their relationships, how their relationships began, circumstances surrounding violent incidents, how they responded to and made sense of the violence, and what role family and friends played throughout the process. Interviews were semistructured to provide ample opportunity for a dialogue to develop between interviewer and participant.

As discussed previously, informants were given the opportunity to participate in the analysis process by reading and commenting on written summaries of initial interpretations of their stories (Thompson, 1992; Yin, 1989). Twelve participants provided feedback after reviewing their summary, which was incorporated into the results where appropriate. Other tactics for achieving trustworthiness included cross-coding transcript material (Yin, 1989) and regular discussions with colleagues to critically question analyses and to consider rival explanations (Marshall & Rossman, 1989).

Participants

The 22 women who participated in this study ranged in age from 16 to 32 years old when they began their violent dating relationships (mean age is 21 years old) and from 18½ to 38 years old when they were interviewed for this study. Relationships lasted from 10 months to 9 years and the violence lasted from 3 months to 8 years. All but 2 of the women had ended their relationships prior to participating in the study, 10 of the women cohabited with their abusive partners, 2 married their abusive dating partners after violence had become a pattern in their relationships (both were divorced when they participated in the study), and 1 gave birth to her abusive boyfriend's child. Data relevant to seductive and entrapment processes provided by the 2 women who married their partners and the 1 woman who had her partner's baby were included in the study unless they specifically related to their marital or parental status.

The physical abuse ranged from moderate (e.g., pushing, shoving, holding down, grabbing, or pinching) to severe (e.g., punching, choking, being thrown down, or being hit with an object). All the women reported experiencing verbal and emotional abuse—for example, constant criticism, name-calling, yelling, destruction of property, and threats of harm. In addition to physical trauma (e.g., black eyes, bruises, permanent nerve damage, broken bones, and cuts), the women reported a variety of psychological symptoms, including anger and resentment, reduced academic or work productivity, or both, nightmares, startle responses, distrust of men and intimate relationships, lowered self-esteem, feeling out of control and "crazy," and homicidal or suicidal ideations or both.

Participants' families of origin ranged from lower-middle-class to upper-middle-class. Most participants, however, saw themselves as growing up in middle-class families. One participant was African American, the remainder were white. Fifteen participants grew up in intact families, 3 were raised primarily by single mothers, 3 grew up in remarried families, and 1 was raised primarily by her grandparents. Seventeen women reported that they neither witnessed nor received physical abuse during childhood and 17 had not been physically abused in prior dating relationships.

Analysis

A modified version of the constant comparative method of data analysis (Glaser & Strauss, 1967; Strauss & Corbin, 1990) was used to identify patterns of meaning from the transcribed accounts of the women's experiences with dating violence. Each transcript was read twice and then, through open coding, segments were named, or coded, and placed in as many categories as possible. Higher-level categories— that is, conceptualizations from a broader perspective—emerged as lower-level codes were grouped according to their similarities or differences from other codes. Finally, categories were related to each other to develop constructs that were grounded in the data. Open coding was accomplished with the assistance of Ethnograph (Seidel, Kjolseth, & Seymour, 1988)—a computer program designed for the analysis of text-based data. Theoretical insights that emerged during the data collection and analysis process or through discussions with colleagues were recorded into a written log. This log became a record of insights into the data about interrelationships between various codes and categories and guided the iterative process of data collection and analysis. This written log, composed of various levels of theoretical memos, was sorted and became the foundation for the final analysis and synthesis of the data.

Results

This study confirms the notion hypothesized by others that becoming a battered woman is a process just as leaving a violent relationship is a process (Kirkwood, 1993; Mills, 1985). In this study, seduction and entrapment processes emerged as forces that tended to draw women into their relationships and to keep them there. Forces that tended to disentangle them from their relationships as well as other themes that emerged from this study are reported elsewhere (see Rosen, 1992; Rosen & Stith, 1995).

It is important to provide a context within which to place the women's seduction and entrapment. At the onset of their relationships, vulnerable young women entered relationships that, for varying lengths of time, seemed to be dreams come true. Eventually, conflicts, usually related to issues of closeness and distance or power and control or both, began to mar otherwise blissful relationships and to escalate to emotional and then to physical abuse. Despite the pain, shock, and confusion that resulted from experiencing abuse at the hands of their lovers, however, the women held to the belief that they needed to maintain their relationships. As relationships unfolded, a number of processes tended to strengthen the connection between partners. Over time, most of the women seemed to build a readiness to leave through "disentanglement processes" that culminated in shifts in thinking from the position "I need this relationship" to "I need to get out of this relationship." These shifts in thinking were soon followed by the dissolution of the relationship. The following sections are devoted to describing how women initially became inducted into their relationships (processes of seduction) and then, once committed, processes that served to further entrap them despite the onset of abuse (processes of entrapment).

Processes of Seduction

Processes of seduction are the forces that initially pulled these women into their relationships making them dependent and more likely to tolerate abuse once it began. They came to believe "I am because I am in this relationship and I cannot walk away." Romantic fantasies and romantic fusion are two themes central to the women's initial seduction. Enticed by romantic fantasies, these women became locked into fused relationships with their boyfriends. Their fusion marked the beginning of their loss of independence and sense of self as separate from their boyfriends.

Romantic Fantasies

The two romantic fantasies identified in the women's stories were so named for their similarities to popular fairy tales—*Cinderella* and *Beauty and the Beast* fantasies. Some young women actually thought of their boyfriends, particularly at the beginning of their relationship, as a Prince Charming. The women had romantic images or illusions about what their relationships could do for them or for their boyfriends. These relationship expectations were in part based in reality and in part myth. That is, the women were indeed happy, but they could not sustain this bliss over the long haul nor magically erase the difficulties they were facing in their own lives.

As in a study conducted by Mills (1985), most of the women in this study were vulnerable prior to beginning their relationships (see Rosen, 1992, for a detailed discussion of participants' vulnerabilities). Some were situationally vulnerable (recovering from recent stressful life events) and some chronically vulnerable (evidence of being victimized in a series of relationships, including in their families of origin). These vulnerabilities seemed to open the door for the women to become seduced by romantic fantasies and to cling to their relationships for comfort. Indeed, it has been argued that all women in this society, to some degree, are vulnerable to such seduction because of societal messages to cling to relationships at all costs (Lloyd, 1991; Smith, 1984).

Cinderella Fantasy. The Cinderella fantasy refers to the illusion that a man can transform a woman's life, erase her insecurities, protect her from her fears, or save her from her problems or all four. When a woman's boyfriend appealed to, addressed, or seemed to mend a woman's unique vulnerability, she became seduced by what we call the Cinderella fantasy. The reality aspect of this fantasy is that a sensitive, caring partner can positively influence a woman's feelings about herself, her approach to life, or her ability to cope with stressful life events. This realistic potential for healing, however, became a delusion when women placed too high an expectation on how much their partner could rescue them from or when they held on to the image of their boyfriend as Prince Charming despite his behavior reflecting the opposite. The Cinderella fantasy may include some or all of the following components: the woman's extreme dependency on her partner, her sense that she and her partner will live "happily ever after," and her sense of being swept away or saved by the love of a princelike man.

Case Examples

Fred was princelike to Alexandra, not because he was handsome, rich, or particularly adept socially but because he met a specific need of hers—he treated her like a queen. Alexandra felt discounted and devalued by significant others in her life to the point where she almost felt invisible. The following was her unique vulnerability:

> I was a kind person and people took advantage of me. . . . It's not just with men . . . it seems like it's a pattern with me. I end up choosing men who end up being like my father, who don't listen to me, who don't give me any kind of emotional support. . . . I was constantly searching to be real, for somebody to recognize me.

What made Fred so special to Alexandra was that, in contrast to other men in her life, Fred did far more than simply recognize Alexandra—he idolized her. This made Alexandra feel very good, which she talks about in the following quote:

> He put me on a pedestal. Basically at the very, very, beginning, I can hardly remember but I can remember he talked about me as being some sort of queen or something. . . . I can remember him telling some friends of mine that I deserved somebody better. . . . I was fragile. In his words, I was breakable. . . . I was like special. I was very special to him. Just in the way he used to talk, I was going to break. He used to make me really feel good. . . . I can remember it was like floating on a cloud. . . . I had never had anybody like that.

Cory shed some light on how seductive a romanticized image can be even after the man's behavior shows that he is not a Prince Charming. Unlike most of the other women studied, Cory did not seem particularly vulnerable to or in need of a Prince Charming when she met Carl at age 17. She did feel, however, that she was subject to some magical thinking about her boyfriend Carl. She had a romanticized notion of a man and a relationship that she was hoping to fulfill someday:

> I always had the notion [a romantic image] and was looking for someone who filled it. In other words, I wanted to be in a monogamous relationship and I wanted to get married and have somebody to go to dances with and have roses and all of that business. You know, I was looking for that man.

Cory became ensnared because she believed that Carl was the man of her dreams and therefore they would live happily ever after like her image directed. When his behavior became abusive, it was not the real man that was so difficult to let go of but rather the dream that he represented. Although at some level she decided that she needed to give him up after the first severely abusive incident, Cory had difficulty convincing herself:

> I was not at peace with the concept of having to let Carl go. But it was more of the idea of Carl. Carl was the first person I was ever with [sexually]. Carl was the person I was engaged to. It wasn't the Carl who just pulled the trick [choking her] out in the parking lot. It was the notion of Carl. . . . I wanted the notion [the fantasy], but I couldn't stand him.

Even though Roy had become physically and emotionally abusive to Meg prior to their engagement, her fantasy image of Roy was strong enough to carry her into marriage with him. She was loyal to the illusion that Roy was Mr. Right:

> I think I had begun to realize [by the honeymoon] that the marriage never should have taken place; that we got married for all the wrong reasons. He was supposed to be my knight in shining armor. The first guy I dated; if I didn't make it with him, there wasn't going to be anyone else.

Beauty and the Beast Fantasy. In contrast to being seduced by the man's power to be the woman's Prince Charming, often a woman was touched by and drawn to her boyfriend's vulnerability; in some cases, they almost became kindred souls due to their common pain. Thus, the woman would become seduced by the illusion that she had the power to transform, heal, her man as in *Beauty and the Beast*. Women seduced by this fantasy seemed to be under the illusion that they could be the ones who could save their boyfriends from their insecurities or mold them into kind and sensitive partners. In part, this version of reality seems to lend itself to the woman's excusing her boyfriend's "beastliness" or at least understanding it at some level.

Case Examples

Alexandra not only fell in love with Fred not only because he made her feel like a fairy princess but also because, like her, he too was vulnerable. He had a gentle, almost meek nature, and in a way she felt sorry for him because he was insecure. She saw a scared little boy in him and he appealed to the part of her who liked to care for others. He gave her the opportunity to think that she could play a significant role in his transformation. Alexandra's voice softened as she talked about how Fred was as vulnerable as she:

> It breaks my heart sometimes to think that what happened in his family made him that way, too. So there were two broken people, probably looking for the same thing and not getting it . . . There was a part of me inside that just really saw this little boy who was frightened, and afraid, and didn't like himself. And I was like a mother in a sense. I was going to make it better. Fix it for him.

Tess described herself as being very protective and loyal to her friends, particularly those who were vulnerable. Given this aspect of her nature, it is easy to understand that although she was convinced that she needed Matt, she was also drawn to his vulnerability.

She believed it was her role to make things better for him. Later in the relationship, the sense that Matt was vulnerable somehow seemed to soften her view of his abusive behavior. In the following, Tess describes how she tried to build Matt's ego when she could:

> When I met him, he didn't have any kind of ego. He was always very self-conscious. He'd make everyone else laugh but underneath it he was hiding the fact that he was really insecure and depressed about how things were. Just had a very fragile ego. And I was very big on building

that up, trying to make him feel good about how he looked and what he did at school, stuff like that. I always tried really hard to do that and, at the same time, he sucked away mine.

Similarly, Adele was one who developed a reputation in her family as a person who liked to bring home stray dogs and heal them. She could easily see the connection between this earlier role and her attraction to Clint. It also fueled her determination, and her illusion, that her love could heal him:

> He was a bully that I was willing to tame. . . . He had been hurt somewhere along the way and I knew that. And I thought that if I gave him everything that I had that we could live in bliss forever.

Romantic Fusion

Marks (1986) used the term *romantic fusion* to describe couples in which "the partnership itself becomes each partner's all-consuming passion and interest" (p. 102). Romantic fusion seemed to characterize most of the relationships described by participants in this study. The women described relationships in which their needs (including safety and security) and self-interests became subsumed by and, to some degree, synonymous with their relationships. These relationships often became intense quickly. During the early months of the relationship, partners tended to become fused to each other as if their separateness had disappeared. Couples constantly did things together, talked together, or thought about each other and the majority of their energy was spent devoted to the partner and the relationship.

Case Examples

Alexandra enjoyed the bliss of fusion for nearly a year before abusive arguments began to mar her happiness. During this period, she and Fred spent a lot of time alone together and Fred was very open, attentive, and kind:

> We were real close, at the beginning. And he was happy with me and I was happy with him. . . . We would go to this pond that I told you about and he'd tell me about things when he was a little boy and he would

share with me about his feelings. . . . I want, I need people to share with me who they are and Fred did that.

Tess emphasized the amount of time she and Matt spent together. When she and Matt began dating exclusively, Tess radically changed from a young girl who spent a lot of time doing things with her friends to one who was constantly with her boyfriend:

> I mean it was crazy, the amount of time we spent together. . . . I'd pick him up from his house, we'd go to school. We'd spend break together, lunch together; and then, my senior year, I had sixth period where I was teacher's aide, but I hardly ever had to do anything, so we'd spend that whole hour together. Then we'd spend all this time until 6, 7, or 8 o'clock at night together. Twelve hours later we are back together again.

These women began their relationships in romantic bliss. Romantic fantasies and romantic fusion were seductive processes—that is, initial inductions to relationships in which women's sense of self became subordinated to their boyfriends and their relationships. This powerful initial seduction made it more likely that the women would tolerate abuse when it began—first as emotional abuse and then as physical abuse (see Kirkwood, 1993, for a rich description of how emotional abuse insidiously increases a woman's tolerance for physical abuse).

Entrapment Processes

As their fused relationships continued, inevitable differences and disagreements presented challenges to couples' abilities to tolerate differences and negotiate conflicts. Now I turn to a discussion of entrapment processes that seemed to bind the women to their relationships, still further, despite the onset of abuse. The entrapment processes identified include survival tactics, cognitive dissonance, roller-coaster relationships, traumatic bonding, Romeo and Juliet effects, and peer or family collusion.

Survival Tactics

The women in this study showed considerable creativity and strength in coping with relationship events. Many of the women developed very effective ways of reducing their emotional stress—some were healthy and some were not. For example, one woman wrote poetry, danced, and took long walks with her dog to help herself calm down. Another woman took up weight lifting; another tracked her relationship and expressed her feelings in a daily journal, and others read self-help books or actually sought counseling from a professional or the informal counsel of friends. Some of the women admitted to using alcohol or drugs to relieve the stress they were experiencing and a few women hit or yelled back, which made their situation worse. Some of the coping strategies women used to deal with the abuse and to maintain their relationships served to further entrap them in their unhealthy relationships. These "survival tactics" were used to manage abuse-related emotional stress, to contain or stop the violence, or to improve the relationship or all three. The belief that the relationship must be maintained drove the development and use of survival tactics. These system-maintaining coping strategies were named survival tactics because so many of the women in this study remarked that they did not cope, they just survived. For them, the idea of coping represented a sense of being in control and consciously making choices; survival meant doing what was necessary to go on. Sometimes their efforts to cope became part of a vicious cycle in which the solution they applied to the problem made the problem worse or led to the creation of a new problem (see Fisch, Weakland, & Segal, 1982, for a more complete discussion of vicious cycles). In this chapter, I focus on these coping behaviors and the role they played in the women's entrapment.

Avoidance Strategies. These survival tactics included what Lazarus and Folkman (1984) called emotion-focused avoidance strategies that limit the negative emotional impact of abuse—for example, minimizing the seriousness of the incident, forgetting about the incident, or denying that an incident is abusive. The use of avoidance strategies was often evident in the ways women described the violence, such as "He choked me, but not very hard." Jackie offered an even more overt example of avoidance. She related that during most of her 4-year struggle to survive her partner's abuse (during which she suffered permanent hearing loss in one ear due to a ruptured eardrum), she did not think of herself as an abused woman. In fact, during our interview she read passages from her diary pertaining to violent arguments that did not mention her assault but only described the content of their arguments and how they made up afterward. Apparently, one of her ways to deal with the trauma of abuse and to preserve her relationship was to focus on the positive aspects and to ignore the abusive aspects. Although this tactic reduced abuse-related emotional stress, it allowed the danger to go unacknowledged and her fantasies about the relationship to go unchallenged. Thus, she could legitimately maintain her commitment to the relationship.

Illusions of Control. Illusions of control repeatedly surfaced in the women's descriptions of their experiences with dating violence and how they coped with it. This term was used by Lazarus and Folkman (1984) to describe a phenomenon that stems from people's need to feel in control of their environment, which leads to their unrealistic expectations of controlling situations that are uncontrollable. Although the women often felt powerless, paradoxically, they also believed that they could control their boyfriend's behavior whether it was his abusive behavior or the way they got along in general. Illusions of control were often linked to self-blame and the beauty and the beast fantasy. That is, women who believed they held the key to "fixing" the man or the relationship tended to blame themselves when it did not work. Furthermore, women who were attracted to men in part because their vulnerabilities touched them were also likely to blame themselves for failing to find the "key" to his healing.

Illusions of control were part of the web of entrapment because they kept hope alive. The hope was based on the notion that if they persevered, they would eventually make the relationship work. As long as the women continued to think there was hope, they tended to stick with the relationship rather than consider other options. Illusions of control kept alive the hope that things would change until absolutely all avenues had been exhausted. This finding supports the work of Denzin (1984) who also found a strong link between women's beliefs that they can change the situation themselves, their hope that things will change, and their choosing to stay in violent relationships.

Case Example

Alexandra was abused by Fred for more than 5 years. During most of that time, she blamed herself for what was happening and believed that she had the power to fix what was wrong between them. She tried to improve her relationship in a number of ways, including meeting his sexual needs even when the act was distasteful to her, bringing him little gifts, writing him little notes, and trying not to confront him about his neglect of her or other things that made her unhappy. The link between Alexandra's illusions about her ability to make things work and her self-blame is illustrated in the following quote:

> I blamed myself always. I must have done something wrong. . . . I can make it better. It's obviously my behavior. Maybe I can do this. Maybe I can do that. I constantly felt like I was walking on eggshells, trying to fix it.

As long as she believed that she had the power to fix what was wrong between her and Fred, Alexandra did not want to give up trying.

Placation. Sometimes survival tactics became part of a vicious cycle in which the women's attempt to improve the situation, in the long run, made it worse or added another strand to the web of entrapment. For example, Tess learned that one way to avoid trouble with Matt when things got tense between them was to have sex with him. Although this usually worked, it had a negative impact on Tess' sense of self-esteem because it went against her belief that sex is an expression of love. The less she liked herself, the less likely she was to think that she deserved a better relationship. Another strategy that Tess developed to avoid Matt's wrath also backfired. She tried to figure out what Matt wanted her to say or do in a given situation and gave him the response she thought he was looking for rather than an honest response. When Matt figured out what Tess was doing, he became angry and decided he could not trust her no matter what she said, which led to frequent abusive harangues.

Isolation. To survive, the women often isolated themselves from family and friends. Although sometimes the boyfriend would try to drive a wedge between the woman and her family or friends, often the isolation was self-imposed. This tactic was used to save face because the women felt ashamed for allowing themselves to be in the situation they were in, to avoid having to explain themselves, or to preserve their family's image of their boyfriend because they were convinced that he would eventually become part of the family.

Case Example

Like many of the young women who participated in this study, Debbie was reluctant to seek help and support from friends and family because of humiliation, embarrassment, and the fear that they would try to make her leave her boyfriend:

> I didn't want them to know a whole lot because they would probably tell me what I already knew, that I shouldn't be in that relationship so I wouldn't tell them a whole lot. . . . So I would just sit with my friends a lot of times and really be alienated.

Unfortunately, her alienation from family and friends meant that Dan was Debbie's only source of information about herself and her relationship. When she cut herself off from others, she deprived herself of resources that could bolster her self-esteem or enhance her perspective on her relationship.

Cognitive Dissonance

Festinger (1957) used the term *cognitive dissonance* to refer to the discrepancies between what one expects from a given situation and what one actually encounters. To avoid this uncomfortable predicament, individuals will do what they can to reduce the dissonance or to avoid information that would likely increase the dissonance. The women in this study experienced cognitive dissonance when the men they were devoted to began to abuse them and continued to abuse them despite confessions of love and promises not to abuse them again. When faced with the dichotomous positions, "he loves me" and "he hits me," women tended to focus on the "he loves me" position and to discount or explain away (it's my fault, he was drunk, or he didn't mean it) the opposing position. For some, this ambiguity led to a state of confusion about the meaning of violence and to a suspension of critical judgment or a paralysis in action or both similar to those described in discussions of the classical double-bind experience (Bateson, Jackson, Haley, & Weakland, 1981). Nielson (1989) asserts that this kind of internal dissonance resulting from abuse is often accompanied by feelings of "going crazy" and leading to the tendency to "solve" the dilemma by polarizing (e.g., I am to blame, he is good). Indeed, many of the women in this study reported feeling crazy and paralyzed by the mixed messages from their boyfriends. Thus, these mixed messages contributed to the women's entrapment not only through their effects on the women's emotional state but also in their tendency to foster ineffective coping strategies.

Roller-Coaster Relationships

In the essence of the women's stories and how they were told was the sense of relationships that took on a life of their own with a powerful force of their own. The reification of an out-of-control relationship and concomitant swings from one extreme to another were powerful components of the cycle of violence. With each recurring cycle of tension-explosion-contrition (Walker, 1979), the women experienced shifts in emotional extremes. One extreme was happiness and hopefulness so strong that it could wipe out the memory of even the worst abusive incident and the other was the depths of despair and humiliation following yet another abusive incident. The happiness extreme, of course, occurred during the contrition phase when boyfriends were once again the princes with whom they fell in love, in which the women temporarily felt a bit of power in their relationship, and in which partners regained emotional closeness. The despair preceded and followed abusive incidents when tensions were building and when violence was repeated. The constant relational shifts and emotional extremes sent women scrambling to maintain their balance and meant that the women focused on their relationships as the driving force in their lives, often to the exclusion of other interests and certainly to the exclusion of objectively reflecting on their relationships and their options. Although these are components of fusion, they are qualitatively different than the blissful fusion described previously. Some women stated that as a result of surviving years of this ordeal, they no longer knew who they were. It was as if they missed large portions of their development. Some believed they became "addicted" to the emotional roller coaster and found that new relationships paled in comparison. In a sense, they had become entrapped in a lived experience in which the bizarre became commonplace and in which their lives revolved around episodes of violence or threats of violence.

Traumatic Bonding

Dutton and Painter (1981) used the term *traumatic bonding* to refer to a mutual need-fulfilling process between the abuser and the abused in an intermittently abusive, imbalanced relationship. According to Dutton and Painter, the abused person bonds with and becomes dependent on the kind and warm side of the abuser, whereas the abuser's needs for power are satisfied by the abused person. The stories of the women in this study lead to a slightly different sense of traumatic bonding. For the women in this study, their sense of increased bonding with their partner came from surviving common trauma (abusive incidents or severe arguments) together. Abusive incidents were traumatic for the women in this study and often for their partners as well. The experience of surviving this trauma as a couple seemed to deepen couple bonds. For some couples, this bonding became deeper as more and more traumas were survived.

Case Examples

For Debbie, as time passed each physically abusive incident was a traumatic event and, paradoxically, a glue that kept the relationship together. The more traumatic experiences she and Dan survived together, the more they were inclined to cling to each other:

> It almost made me feel like with every incident, when I look back, it seems like I felt closer to him. I mean almost like, maybe not closer, but almost like we were, you know, more or less in the situation and it was getting so deep that we weren't going to be able to get out of it. It was just making us stay together.

This bonding was so strong for Tess that although it was almost 2 years since she and Matt had broken up, she still felt a special love for him. She likens it to surviving a concentration camp experience with another person:

> To this day, I'll still say I'm not in love with him, but I love him. I love him not because he is a good person, not because of anything he did for me. . . . It's purely because we both survived it. It's like two people being in a concentration camp. They may never like this person the entire time they are there. They might have fought with them and hated them the entire time. But once they got out of it, they cared a great deal about each other only because they both survived it.

Romeo and Juliet Effect

The *Romeo and Juliet effect* was first coined by Driscoll, Davis, and Lipetz (1972) to describe situations in which romantic love was intensified by parental opposition and interference. Several women maintained relationships that were openly contested by their families or were purposely kept secret from their families. For these women, in addition to other commitment components, their relationships seemed to represent an opportunity to break away from their families—to, in effect, attain pseudo-autonomy. Their boyfriends were usually young men they knew their family would not accept. The drama of their situation was often palpable as they told their stories. For some women, this "you and me against the world" extended to friends as well. When the Romeo and Juliet effect was part of the entrapment process, the boundaries around the relationship became even more closed than might ordinarily occur. Closing boundaries around their relationships led to the women's increased isolation making them more vulnerable to their boyfriends and dependent on them for validating their sense of self and defining their relationship, thus strengthening the ties that bound them to their boyfriends.

Adele was attracted to Clint in part because he was a renegade biker—very different from her friends and her family. Being with him catapulted her into a different world than the one she had known growing up. In the following quote, Adele talks about clinging defiantly to her relationship despite his abuse and the disapproval of her family and friends:

> My parents couldn't stand him. They were like, where did you find him? I was very defiant. I was like, well I love him and you have to accept him because I do. . . . All my friends were like, what are you doing? I couldn't bring him to parties, or if I was invited to other places he just didn't fit in. I guess the way I felt about it was that I wanted to prove them wrong, and I had a stronger desire to stay with him because they couldn't be right.

Peer or Family Collusion

Sometimes, family and friends tried to be helpful primarily by listening or telling the woman to leave. In contrast, sometimes friends or family members actually colluded with the violence or the violent relationship. Peer or family collusion refers to the phenomenon in which friends or family members of the abused woman "see" the abuse, yet fail to see it or fail to register a response that communicates a clear message to the woman that abuse is not acceptable. Family or friends may inadvertently collude with the violence by accepting the woman's minimizations or denials without question, by witnessing or learning about the abuse and not expressing outrage or concern, by keeping the abuse secret, or by directly aligning with or failing to censor the abuser. Sometimes these responses seemed to stem from a general tendency to deny things that were difficult to manage—a tendency that was historically part of the family's way of coping with stressful events. Sometimes, these responses seemed to stem from a belief system that did not place abusive behavior clearly within a category of unacceptable behavior. These responses from friends or family were subtle but powerful messages to the women that violence is acceptable. They reinforced the women's tendency to deny the impact of abuse or to downplay their own needs. These responses served to add one more strand to the invisible web that ensnared the women in relationships that were destructive.

Case Examples

Although Alexandra defended Fred to her parents, a part of her seemed to be crying out for them to see how much pain she was in—to tell her that Fred's behavior was unacceptable and that she did not deserve to be treated that way. In the following quote, Alexandra talks about how hurt she was that her parents did not "see":

> I had a black eye, a big black eye. It was obvious. You couldn't miss it and I covered it up with makeup as well as I could. They made me eat dinner with them. So I would just keep my head hung. My dad never noticed. So there was a lot of hurt there. I felt so hurt that people didn't notice. But my mom one day told me, "What's the matter?" and "Why wouldn't I look at anybody?" And I said "nothing's wrong," you know, whatever. And she noticed and she was angry but they never just really talked about it. So my mother kept it quiet probably because she didn't want my father to know. I had no help anywhere. Nobody could see that I was hurting. Because I can remember that I was frantic, you know, somebody tell me that I'm not going crazy. That its okay to feel this way. That I don't deserve this.

Alexandra desperately needed confirmation from her family or friends that her situation with Fred was unacceptable and undeserved and instead she got a subtle confirmation that she was indeed "invisible" and perhaps going crazy.

Debbie's and Dan's friends also colluded with the violence. One evening, Dan put an end to their festivities when he beat her up. She remembers meeting their friends in the hall of the hotel where they were celebrating New Year's eve covered with blood and visibly shaken while the police took Dan away:

> [They] saw Dan get taken away and they were mad at me. . . . They were all just kind of in the hall, just quiet, just kind of looking at me. I had thought that at least somebody would say something or help me, you know, take me home. I ended up having to call my brother to come get me.

Her friends' failure to be helpful or to show caring increased Debbie's humiliation and affirmed her sense that somehow what happened was her fault. Furthermore, when Debbie and Dan went out with these friends after this incident, it was never mentioned. It was as if it never happened.

Tess got covert messages from her parents, her grandparents, and her friends that provided an affirming climate for the continuing survival of her abusive relationship with Matt. Most of the young people in her group seemed to tacitly accept abusive behavior as something that happens between people. There was no sense of outrage or efforts to intervene even when they saw or suspected abuse. In fact, Tess was, in an odd way, rewarded by her friends for being able to survive abuse:

> Part of being in the kind of subculture that we were in, when stuff like that [abuse] happened, it was something that you bragged about. . . . They were like badges of honor: "Oh you're tough, you're cool, you can take whatever bad comes your way."

Summary and Discussion

From the women in this study, we see how relationships that begin romantically can become destructive traps for the women involved. The women interviewed became entrapped by powerful processes pulling them toward their partners and away from their own self-interests. Feeling that they had to maintain their relationships, these women developed a set of survival tactics that allowed them to endure until they developed a readiness to leave. Kirkwood (1993) used the term *spiraling inward* to describe what I call processes of entrapment in which the abuser has increasing control and the term *spiraling outward* to describe what I call processes of disentanglement in which the abuser's control decreases. Spiraling inward and outward seems an appropriate metaphor for the processes described by the women in this study as well.

When examining physical aggression within romantic relationships, it is important to consider the social context within which those relationships exist (Lloyd & Emery, 1994). Sociocultural messages that prepare women to be dependent on the security of their intimate relationships and to view themselves as having primary responsibility for the smooth operation of those relationships make women vulnerable in their relationships with men (Smith, 1984). Furthermore, courtship themes that mirror the hierarchical social order and media's idealization of the power of love relationships are additional contextually based messages that make women vulnerable to tolerating abuse and maintaining their relationships at all costs (Henton et al., 1983; Lloyd, 1991).

Although contextual processes influence and shape violence against women, the violence is produced and experienced in the lives of interacting individuals (Denzin, 1984). At this level of examination, a communication perspective is useful in understanding violent relationships as Cahn discusses in Chapter 1 of this book. With stars in her eyes and beliefs about love in her heart, a woman can fall in love with a man and a dream. In a sense, the effect of initial interactions leads the woman to think that this man fulfills her relationship and her identity goals. For Alexandra, who had little sense of self other than what was reflected through the eyes of others, Fred provided her the identity of a princess. As the relationship progresses, the woman may hang onto this dream. She may struggle to survive and to make her relationship work despite significant pain and confusion. As testimony to the strength of her commitment, her actions (survival tactics) are purposive and functional reflecting the instrumental dimension of communication. The influences of her boyfriend's mixed messages (I love you and I hit you), perhaps reflecting a conflict between the young man's relational and instrumental goals, and the mixed messages from her peers or family or both may serve to confirm her relational goals encouraging her to ignore signs that she may be in danger physically and emotionally (see Chapter 1). In summary, examining the onset and perpetuation of violence in a dating relationship from a communication perspective can also enhance our understanding of repetitive patterns of interaction that may develop and how these patterns may entrap the woman in her relationship.

The linkage between romantic fusion and violence in premarital relationships raises a number of interesting questions for future research. In this study, fused relationships that began blissfully became violent in part because partners who were so close could not tolerate their differences and manage conflict. Marks (1986) points out that fused marital relationships are unstable primarily because of gender differences in needs to maintain closeness that surface over time. According to Marks, disturbances in these relationships can lead to affairs, conflict, or the breakup of a relationship. Clearly, all fused relationships do not lead to the expression of violence. What is different about fused relationships that lead to the expression of violence and those that do not? Bartle and Rosen (1994) hypothesized that adults who develop fused relationships may have difficulties in developing differentiated selves. These scholars also suggest that levels of differentiation of self are part of the intergenerational transmission of violence process. The link between the tendency to develop fused intimate relationships, the emergence of violence, and the degree of differentiation from family of origin, however, has not been investigated empirically.

One limitation of this study is that it deals solely with the experiences of women. Understanding how men experience and make sense of their violence would be helpful in the quest to prevent intimate relationship violence or intervene once it begins. Getting both partners' perspective is a useful way to obtain a complete understanding of relationship dynamics (Follingstad, 1990). Such study would also help answer an important question that is seldom addressed directly—why do men stay? Of course, a partial answer is that their relationships fulfill relationship, instrumental, or identity goals or all three (see Chapter 1). There is also evidence, however, that perpetrating violence against their female partners is counterproductive to fulfilling these goals (Denzin, 1984).

The stories of these women have much to contribute to the development of prevention and intervention approaches and strategies (e.g., Rosen & Bezold, 1994; Rosen & Stith, 1993). For example, a clinician who is aware of the "illusion of control" will be careful to consider this illusion when helping an abused woman develop a safety plan because the development of a plan may inadvertently give further credence to this illusion. In prevention or intervention work, the specialist can help women become aware of romantic fantasies and entrapment processes that function to bind them to their relationships. Above all, these women's stories can help the clinician who is pondering the question "Why does she stay?" shift the focus to "How can I empower her to leave or to demand that the violence stop?"

9

Physical Aggression, Distress, and Everyday Marital Interaction

SALLY A. LLOYD

The purpose of this study was to examine the association between everyday marital interaction, physical aggression, and marital distress. Sixty-seven married couples completed two waves of a longitudinal study that included face-to-face interviews, questionnaires, and Huston's telephone interviews for gathering data on marital interaction. At Time 1, differences in positive and negative daily marital interaction between four groups of couples were examined: nondistressed-nonaggressive, nondistressed-aggressive, distressed-nonaggressive, and distressed-aggressive. At Time 2, marital interaction was examined as a function of the stability of aggression in the marriage. Distressed-aggressive couples reported the highest levels of negative interaction, yet they also reported high levels of positive interaction. Distressed-nonaggressive couples, on the other hand, reported low levels of both positive and negative interaction. Couples who reported aggression in the marriage at both Time 1 and Time 2 also reported the highest levels of negative interaction in the marriage.

Physical aggression in marriage is a social problem of far-reaching proportions; nearly 1 in 6 married couples report some type of physical aggression in their marriages and nearly 1 in 15 report the presence of violent behaviors likely to result in an injury (Straus & Gelles, 1990). Indeed, Johnson (1995) argues that enough couples suffer from occasional episodes of physical aggression that the term *common couple violence* is warranted. Although much is known about the personalities, backgrounds, and demographic characteristics of victims and perpetrators of physical aggression, we know relatively little about the nature of

177

the marriage that contains physical aggression (Margolin, John, & Gleberman, 1988). This is unfortunate because evidence suggests that interpersonal factors are better at differentiating between aggressive and nonaggressive relationships (Lloyd & Emery, 1994; Stets, 1992).

The purpose of this research is to examine the everyday marital interaction of spouses in aggressive versus nonaggressive marriages.[1] Previous research clearly indicates that spouses in marriages in which physical aggression has occurred display different patterns of interaction than their nonaggressive counterparts as measured both through detailed observational coding of marital interaction (see Cordova, Jacobson, Gottman, Rushe, & Cox, 1993; Margolin et al., 1988) and survey assessment of communication patterns (see Babcock, Waltz, Jacobson, & Gottman, 1993; Sabourin, Infante, & Rudd, 1993). The present research extends previous work on interaction in the aggressive marriage to the study of everyday marital interaction—that is, the positive and negative socioemotional behaviors exchanged by husbands and wives. As so eloquently stated by Kantor and Lehr (1985), "we shall understand families when we understand how they manage the commonplace, that is, how they conduct themselves and interact in the familiar everyday surroundings of their own households" (p. ix). A second purpose of the study is to look at how aggression and everyday marital interaction change over time.

Physical Aggression and Marital Interaction

Margolin and colleagues have been seminal in the study of marital interaction among physically aggressive couples. Margolin et al. (1988) and Burman, John, and Margolin (1992) discuss the results of their laboratory observation of couples during a marital discussion. This work involves the comparison of four types of couples: nondistressed, physically aggressive, verbally aggressive, and withdrawing (note that the latter three couple types are also distressed). Physically aggressive husbands enacted higher levels of threat, blame, and other negative offensive behaviors. Both husbands and wives in the physically aggressive marriages enacted fewer positive behaviors than did spouses in nonaggressive marriages; they also exhibited patterns that increased the likelihood of further anger responses. In addition, both physically aggressive and verbally aggressive couples had the potential to engage in cycles of attack and defense.

Home observations and diary descriptions of marital conflict yield additional information about physically aggressive marriages. These couples were observed to be high in overt hostility and defensiveness, low in problem-solving skills, and characterized by a pattern of increasing withdrawal and despair over the course of a marital discussion (Margolin, Burman, & John, 1989). Physically aggressive husbands and wives displayed rigid, highly contingent behavior patterns; in particular, hostile, angry behavior from one spouse was likely to trigger hostile, angry behavior by the other spouse. In addition, physically aggressive couples were characterized by anger reactivity; after the expression of anger, spouses were less likely to express positive, neutral, or nonhostile negative behavior (Burman et al., 1993; Margolin, John, & O'Brien, 1989).

The findings of Margolin and colleagues have been corroborated by observational work by Cordova et al. (1993) and Jacobson et al. (1994). Cordova et al. observed higher levels of aversiveness (e.g., criticism, disagreement, and put downs) and lower levels of facilitation (e.g., approval, accepting responsibility, smiling, and paraphrasing) in the physically aggressive marriages than in the nonaggressive marriages. Furthermore, spouses in the aggressive marriages were more likely to reciprocate negative behavior. In comparing aggressive and nonaggressive husbands, Jacobson et al. found higher rates of belligerence, contempt, and anger among the aggressive husbands.

Sabourin et al. (1993) emphasize the role of communication skill deficiencies. Spouses in marriages that contain physical aggression are characterized by low levels of problem-solving and communication skills; they are less willing to argue, they feel less skilled at it, and these deficits may lead to increased verbal aggression (Infante, Sabourin, Rudd, & Shannon, 1990). They also tend to display high levels of inferred reciprocity of verbal aggressiveness (Sabourin et al., 1993). Furthermore, when both husband and wife are low in communication ability, and when the husband is in a less powerful position, there is an increased risk of physical aggression (Babcock et al., 1993). Overt verbal hostility and passive aggression are also precursors to physical aggression (Murphy & O'Leary, 1989; O'Leary, Malone, & Tyree, 1994).

The present study will serve as a complement to previous studies of marital interaction and physical aggression. This study examines the role of "everyday marital interaction"—the positive and negative socioemotional behaviors that make up the daily fabric of marriage. Using the innovative methodology developed by Ted Huston (see Huston, McHale, & Crouter, 1986; Huston, Robins, Atkinson, & McHale, 1987; Huston & Vangelisti, 1991), repeated assessments of the occurrence of both positive and negative socioemotional behaviors were gathered over a 2-week period of time in both aggressive and nonaggressive marriages.

Physical Aggression and Marital Distress

Most studies of the aggressive marriage assume that distress is a necessary condition for aggression. O'Leary (1988) attributes this assumption to clinical work that almost exclusively examined the distressed-aggressive marriage. It is quite apparent that many of the characteristics associated with physical aggression in marriage (e.g., higher rates of negative behavior and hostile actions) are also associated with distress in marriage (cf. Gottman, 1993; Noller, Feeney, Bonnell, & Callan, 1994; Weiss & Dehle, 1994).

The relationship between distress and aggression, however, is not really as simple as "distress is a precursor of aggression." For one reason, the hypothesized link between aggression and distress is not always seen in nonclinical samples. Studies of aggression in premarital relationships have long noted the ability of courting couples to forgive or overlook aggression and in some cases to attribute aggression to feelings of love (Henton, Cate, Koval, Lloyd, & Christopher, 1983). Studies of the early years of marriage evidence a similar trend; a significant proportion of the young couples in O'Leary et al.'s (1989) longitudinal study are aggressive yet nondistressed. Even 2½ years after marriage, there was still no significant relationship between distress and physical aggression for husbands (O'Leary et al., 1994). Thus, temporarily at least (and perhaps particularly for husbands), the occurrence of physical aggression in a close relationship may not affect spouses' evaluations of one another or the relationship.

Understanding the interplay of marital interaction, distress, and aggression is further complicated by the design of previous work. Typically, distressed and nondistressed couples are compared to aggressive couples (the latter are also exclusively maritally distressed). Results from such studies often demonstrate that aggressive and distressed couples have many similarities. For example, Telch and Lindquist (1984) found that aggressive and nondistressed couples differed in terms of sex role stereotypes, jealousy, self-concept, communication skills, assertion, marital anger, alcohol use, and the cycle of family aggression. Aggressive and distressed couples, however, did not differ on the first six of these factors; they differed only in alcohol use and the cycle of aggression. This study highlights a critical problem. Some findings that are viewed as important differences between aggressive and nonaggressive couples may be confounded by the comparison of nondistressed-nonaggressive couples with distressed-aggressive couples (Lloyd, 1990b) or by study designs that use aggressive couple groupings that are significantly lower in marital adjustment than the distressed-nonaggressive group (Cordova et al., 1993) or both.

Ultimately, studies that examine aggressive versus nonaggressive couples have omitted an important comparison group. A full understanding of the role of aggression in marriage requires comparison of four groups of couples: nondistressed-nonaggressive, nondistressed-aggressive, distressed-nonaggressive, and distressed-aggressive. The present study entails such a comparison and examines both the direct and the interaction effects of aggression and distress on everyday marital interaction.

Changes in Aggression Over Time

In addition to assuming that aggression is always accompanied by distress, research on marital aggression also tends to assume that aggression heralds the demise of the marriage. Even marriages that are characterized by severe battering, however, are somewhat stable; estimates from shelter programs indicate that a significant proportion of battered wives return to their husbands (Lloyd, 1990a). Granted, in the long run, marriages that contain physical aggression may dissolve; in the short run, however, they may be relatively stable.

Several recent studies have examined the trajectory of physical aggression in marriage. Feld and Straus (1990) recontacted a subsample of the 1985 *National Family Violence Survey* to assess changes in aggression over the previous 12 months. According to their analyses, minor assaults between spouses tended to encourage subsequent severe aggression; there was great variability in the trajectory of aggression, however, with a sizable proportion of couples ceasing aggression over time.

O'Leary et al. (1989) examined the stability of aggression from 1 month of premarriage to 30 months of marriage. Although they report low yet significant stability of violence in marriage across the 3 years of the study, conditional probabilities reflect considerable movement in and out of aggressive and nonaggressive categorizations. O'Leary et al. (1994) examined the predictors of future use of aggression; the level of husband's physical aggression at 30 months of marriage was predicted by the 18-month assessment of psychological aggression (overt verbal hostility and passive aggressiveness), and the level of wife's physical aggression was predicted by both marital discord and psychological aggression.

The present study will examine aggression, distress, and everyday marital interaction both in the cross section and over time. Of particular interest is the interplay of the stability of aggression with other characteristics of the marriage. How do stable-aggressive marriages differ from stable-nonaggressive marriages? Do the marriages that become nonaggressive over time differ in important ways from stable-aggressive marriages?

Hypotheses

Constructing hypotheses about the relationship between marital adjustment and marital interaction is a relatively simple matter as previous work has established a link between high levels of negative daily interaction and low levels of positive daily interaction and marital distress (Huston et al., 1986; Huston & Vangelisti, 1991). Thus, I hypothesize that there will be significant marital-adjustment main effects, with satisfied couples reporting more positive interaction and less negative interaction than dissatisfied couples. Cordova et al. (1993);

Margolin, John, and O'Brien (1989); and Langhinrichsen-Rohling, Smultzler, and Vivian (1994) found higher levels of negative interaction and lower levels of positive interaction in aggressive marriages; based on these findings, I hypothesize that there will be significant aggression main effects, with aggressive couples reporting less positive interaction and more negative interaction than nonaggressive couples.

Delineating the interaction between aggression and adjustment is more difficult because the literature is limited to the study of the distressed-aggressive marriage. I do predict, however, a significant interaction between aggression and adjustment; I hypothesize that distress and aggression combine to produce a highly negative climate in the marriage. Thus, spouses in distressed-aggressive marriages are expected to report the lowest level of positive interaction and the highest level of negative interaction relative to the other couple groupings. The marital climate among nondistressed-aggressive couples is hypothesized to be less negative (lower levels of negative and higher levels of positive interaction) than the climate for their distressed-aggressive counterparts. This hypothesis rests on the assumption that low levels of negative interaction and high levels of positive interaction somehow "compensate for" or allow the aversive consequences of physical aggression to be downplayed such that the occurrence of aggression is not accompanied by a depression in marital happiness.

Finally, I offer a prediction about the interplay of aggression and marital interaction over time. It is hypothesized that marriages that report aggression at both the first wave of data collection and the second wave of data collection 18 months later (the "stable aggressives") will report higher levels of negative interaction and lower levels of positive interaction at both waves of data collection compared to marriages that report no aggression or that report a move from aggression at Time 1 to nonaggression at Time 2.

Method

Studying Everyday Marital Interaction

In the past two decades, several methodologies have been developed for assessing ongoing behavioral interaction in a natural setting. Beginning with works by Christensen and Arkowitz (1974), Wheeler and Nezlek (1977), and Peterson (1979), social interaction records have been used in a variety of studies of relationships. Essentially, this method entails having participants record and describe significant interactions with specific target persons (e.g., a romantic partner or all friends) over a set period of time (usually 1 or 2 weeks). Interaction records yield rich descriptions of ongoing social behavior; the method, however, is limited to the degree that participants keep accurate daily records.

Both Christiansen and King (1982) and Huston et al. (1987) have adapted daily interaction methodologies specifically to the study of marital interaction. Rather than relying on spouses to record their interaction in diary form, these researchers used telephone calls for data collection. In these telephone interviews, participants were asked to indicate whether specific behaviors had occurred over the past 24 hours. This method retains the descriptive richness of the social interaction method while addressing its limitations (i.e., each participant describes the incidence of the same behaviors, the researcher controls the data collection, and behaviors that are likely to occur only once or twice during a typical 24-hour period can be assessed). The present study used Huston et al.'s telephone interview method to gather data on daily positive and negative interaction in marriage.

Participants

Seventy-eight married couples participated in the first wave of this study.[2] Volunteer couples were solicited through newspaper advertisements that asked for participants for a study of "the stresses and satisfactions of marriage." Interested participants called for more information; during this initial call, participants were screened for eligibility. Criteria for eligibility included being married more than 1 year, being under age 40, and a total family income of $40,000 or less. These sample restrictions were used to ensure demographic comparability across groups of aggressive versus nonaggressive couples because aggression has been found to occur more often among younger spouses and in marriages in which financial stress is characteristic (Straus, Gelles, & Steinmetz, 1980). Each couple was paid $40 for participation.

Mean ages of husbands and wives were 31 and 29 years, respectively. These couples had been married on average 6 years (range 1.5-19 years) and had a median number of two children (range 0-6). Median income for the group was in the $20,000 to $25,000 category; modal education level for both husbands and wives was "some college." All participants were residents of a major city in the intermountain west.

Eighteen months after the first wave of data collection, the 78 couples were recontacted to solicit their participation in a second phase. At this time, 4 couples had separated-divorced, 1 couple declined participation, and 2 couples could not be located. Seventy-one couples completed the Time 2 questionnaires, and 67 couples completed all six Time 2 telephone interviews. Participants were paid an additional $50 on completion of the second wave of data collection.

Procedures

Data were collected for the first wave of the study using two methodologies—a face-to-face interview and a series of behavioral self-report telephone interviews. Participants first came to the university campus for the structured face-to-face interview. Husbands and wives were interviewed separately concerning their use of physical aggression in the marriage and level of marital distress.

After completing the face-to-face interview, arrangements were made for the telephone interviews. The telephone interviews assessed positive and negative interaction in the marriage; the interview protocol was developed by Huston et al. (1987). In the 2 or 3 weeks following the face-to-face interview, participants were called and interviewed by telephone on six different days. Respondents were called three times on weekdays and three times on weekends. Each one of the six telephone interviews asked the same questions on the frequency of occurrence of nine negative and nine positive behaviors during the past 24 hours.

The telephone interviewers were given an instruction sheet for each couple that outlined the days the calls were to be made, that clarified which spouse was to be interviewed first, and that identified which of two forms of interview were randomly assigned. Spouses were asked at the beginning of the interview to go to a quiet spot that was out of hearing of other family members. Spouses' responses were limited to yes, no, and the number of times each behavior occurred. To be absolutely sure that spouses did not influence each other's responses to the questions, two forms of the interview were used. Both forms contained the same questions in different orders. For any given interview, the husband completed one form and the wife completed the other form of the telephone interview. Thus, if one spouse inadvertently was able to overhear the other's answers, it was not possible to ascertain what particular question the other was responding to. Spouses were told that they were receiving the questions in different orders.

The second wave of data collection, which took place 18 months later, involved a mailed questionnaire that assessed level of marital adjustment and occurrence of physical aggression. The telephone interviews were repeated using the same protocol as wave one of data collection.

Measures

Aggressive Versus Nonaggressive Marriages. The Conflict Tactics Scale (CTS; Straus, 1979) was used at both waves of data collection to assess whether physical aggression had taken place between spouses. Eight CTS items, ranging from pushing and shoving to use of a weapon on the spouse, were used in assessing physical aggression. Respondents were asked to indicate how often each behavior had occurred during the past 12 months. Couples who had a combined score of one or higher on the physical aggression scale were classified as aggressive. Internal consistency (Cronbach's alpha) of the CTS physical aggression scale for couple scores is .88 (Straus, 1979). Additional information on the construct, content, and concurrent validity of the CTS is available in Straus (1990).

Distressed Versus Nondistressed Marriages. The distressed versus nondistressed category was determined on the basis of perceived marital quality. Marital satisfaction was assessed with the Dyadic Adjustment Scale (DAS; Spanier, 1976). This scale consists of 32 items that tap the four relationship dimensions of consensus, satisfaction, cohesion, and affection expression. Internal consistency for the scale (Cronbach's alpha) is .96; additional information on construct and criterion validity can be found in Spanier (1976). A score below 100 is considered indicative of marital distress. Couples were assigned to the distressed group if either spouse scored below 100 on the DAS. The nondistressed group consisted of only those couples wherein both partners scored above 100.

Positive and Negative Daily Interaction. Levels of positive and negative daily interaction were assessed during the six telephone interviews. Participants were asked to report on the frequency of occurrence over the past 24 hours of 18 spouse behaviors (Table 9.1). Twelve of these behaviors were identical to the ones used by Huston et al. (1987), and six additional behaviors were drawn from the Spouse Observation Checklist (Weiss & Margolin, 1977). Scores on negative items were averaged across interviews for each spouse to yield a composite daily negative marital interaction score. The composite daily positive marital interaction score was constructed in the same manner with positive interaction frequencies across interviews.

The consistency of the measure of positive and negative interaction was assessed with Cronbach's alpha. The alpha levels of .80 and .79 reveal high internal consistency across the items for positive and negative behaviors, respectively. The positive and negative items were also checked for order effects. This analysis helps determine whether spouses reported differing amounts of positive or negative behaviors as a function of the order of the interview (i.e., first, second, third, etc.). Because spouses spend more time together on weekends (Christiansen & King, 1982), the test for order effects was conducted with a control for day of week. This analysis demonstrated that the composite indices of positive and negative behaviors did not differ significantly across the order of interview for either husband or wife. A final check assessed correspondence between spouses. The correlation between husband's and wife's reports of positive interaction was high, $r = .71, p < .001$; the husband-wife correlation for negative interaction was moderate, $r = .44, p < .001$. (Note that it is not a reliability check because spouses were not reporting on the same behaviors; rather, spouses reported on each other's positive and negative behavior.)

Additional information on the validity of telephone behavioral self-report measures of marital interaction is available in both Christiansen and King (1982) and Huston et al. (1987). In terms of construct validity, Huston et. al. (1986) demonstrated predictable relationships between positive and negative behaviors and marital satisfaction, ambivalence, love, and satisfaction with interaction. In addition, the mea-

TABLE 9.1 Positive and Negative Behaviors Reported on in the Telephone Interviews

Positive behaviors
   Your husband-wife complimented you
   Your husband-wife did or said something to make you laugh
   Your husband-wife comforted you when you were upset
   Your husband-wife said I love you
   Your husband-wife apologized to you
   Your husband-wife did something nice that you didn't expect
   You talked together about good things that happened to each of you during the day
   You expressed physical affection with your husband-wife, such as kissing, hugging, cuddling
   You shared your emotions, feelings, or problems with each other

Negative behaviors
   Your husband-wife seemed bored or uninterested while you were talking
   Your husband-wife got angry and wouldn't tell you why
   Your husband-wife dominated a conversation with you
   Your husband-wife refused to listen to your feelings
   Your husband-wife showed anger or impatience by yelling or snapping at you
   Your husband-wife criticized or complained about something you did or didn't do
   Your husband-wife failed to do something you asked him or her to do, or that you expected to be
      done (such as running errands, coming home late, doing the dishes, etc.)
   Your husband-wife ignored you when you asked for some attention
   Your husband-wife did something, knowing that it annoyed you (habits such as leaving on lights, not
      picking up clothes, etc.)

SOURCE: From Huston, Robins, Atkinson, and McHale (1987) and Weis and Margolin (1977).

sures were predictive of changes in marital satisfaction across time (Huston & Vangelisti, 1991). Further information on the development of this behavioral measure of marital interaction and its relation to other qualities of marriage is available in Huston et al. (1987).

Results

Aggression, Distress, and Everyday Marital Interaction

Crossing aggressive-nonaggressive with distressed-nondistressed groupings yielded four groups. Group sizes were as follows: nondistressed-nonaggressive (ND-NA, $n = 25$), nondistressed-aggressive (ND-A, $n = 19$), distressed-nonaggressive (D-NA, $n = 14$), and distressed-aggressive (D-A, $n = 20$).[3] These groups differed significantly in both dyadic adjustment and frequency of aggression. The two nondistressed groups, however, did not differ (mean DAS for husbands: ND-NA = 115, ND-A = 110; mean DAS for wives: ND-NA = 117, ND-A = 114), and the two distressed groups did not differ (mean DAS for husbands: D-NA = 98, D-A = 93; mean DAS for wives: D-NA = 92, D-A = 92).

There were also significant differences between groups on the CTS. Husbands and wives in the two nonaggressive groups reported zero frequency of aggression. Husbands and wives in the nondistressed-aggressive group reported mean CTS scores of 2.47 and 3.05, respectively; in the distressed-aggressive group, husband and wife scores were 4.45 and 5.80.[4] Nondistressed versus distressed husbands were not significantly different in mean CTS scores, $t = -1.95$; nondistressed versus distressed wives did differ, $t = -2.21, p < .05$.

Repeated measures analysis of variance was used to test the hypothesized differences between groups. This analysis treats the couple as the unit of analysis with spouse as a "within-couple" measure (Kenny, 1988). Because each dependent variable was measured twice (one each for husband and wife), spouse served as the repeated measure. The independent variables were marital adjustment (nondistressed vs. distressed) and physical aggression (nonaggressive vs. aggressive).

Results of the repeated measures analysis of variance are shown in Table 9.2. Analyzing positive interaction, there was a significant spouse main effect and a significant adjustment by aggression interaction. Analyzing negative interaction, there were significant main effects for adjustment, aggression, and spouse, and significant adjustment by aggression and adjustment by spouse interaction effects.

Thus, the hypothesized aggression and adjustment main effects for positive interaction were not supported. The hypothesized aggression and adjustment main effects for negative interaction were supported; distressed couples displayed significantly more negative interaction than did nondistressed couples, and aggressive couples displayed significantly more negative interaction than did nonaggressive couples.

In the aggression by adjustment interaction hypothesis, it was predicted that distressed-aggressive couples would report the highest

TABLE 9.2 Repeated Measures Analysis of Variance on Positive and Negative Behaviors, by Adjustment and Aggression (Time 1)

	Nonaggressive	Aggressive	F Values	
Positive interaction				
Nondistressed				
Husbands	23.04	17.37	F(Agg.)	= 0.32
Wives	16.76	15.37	F(Adj.)	= 1.22
			F(Spouse)	= 18.79***
Distressed			F(Agg. × Adj.)	= 4.14*
Husbands	14.21	21.65	F(Agg. × S)	= 0.21
Wives	10.50	15.55	F(Adj. × S)	= 0.14
			F(A × A × S)	= 2.55
Negative interaction				
Nondistressed				
Husbands	2.28	2.00	F(Agg.)	= 5.22*
Wives	1.92	2.37	F(Adj.)	= 8.29**
			F(Spouse)	= 6.45*
Distressed			F(Agg. × Adj.)	= 4.80*
Husbands	3.71	9.25	F(Agg. × S)	= 0.72
Wives	1.71	4.15	F(Adj. × S)	= 6.48*
			F(A × A × S)	= 1.88

*$p < .05$; **$p < .01$; ***$p < .001$.

levels of negative interaction and the lowest levels of positive interaction. It is clear that only the first part of this hypothesis was supported. Distressed-aggressive couples reported the highest levels of negative interaction; nondistressed-aggressive, nondistressed-nonaggressive, and distressed-nonaggressive couples did not differ in their reports of negative daily interaction. Distressed-aggressive marriages, however, were not characterized by low levels of positive interaction as had been hypothesized. Rather, quite surprisingly, distressed-aggressive couples were characterized by levels of positive interaction that were as high as those of their nondistressed-nonaggressive counterparts. It was the distressed-nonaggressive marriages that were characterized by low levels of positive interaction.

Predicting Changes Over Time

Measurements of physical aggression in the marriage taken during each phase of data collection were used to break the couples into three groups—stable-nonaggressive (husband and wife reported no physical aggression in the marriage at either data collection phase, $n = 30$), *aggressive-to-nonaggressive (physical aggression was reported by husband or wife or both at the first phase of data collection but not at the second phase, $n = 10$),* and stable-aggressive (husband or wife reported some physical aggression in the marriage at both data collection phases, $n = 20$).[5] (Note that a fourth group of couples did occur—nonaggressive-to-aggressive—but was too small for inclusion in the analysis, $n = 7$.)

The husbands and wives in stable-aggressive and aggressive-to-nonaggressive marriages reported significantly different levels of aggression at the first time of data collection, $t = 2.58, p < .05$ and $t = 2.84, p < .01$, respectively. Mean levels of husband aggression in stable-aggressive and aggressive-to-nonaggressive marriages were 4.08 and 1.33, respectively. Mean levels of wife aggression in stable-aggressive and aggressive-to-nonaggressive marriages were 4.78 and 1.73, respectively.

Repeated measures analysis of variance was used to compare husbands and wives in stable-nonaggressive, aggressive-to-nonaggressive, and stable-aggressive marriages. Once again, the couple was the unit of analysis, with spouse as a "within-couple" measure. Results are shown in Table 9.3. There were significant main effects for the change in aggression grouping for negative interaction at both Time 1 and Time 2.

In the hypotheses about changes in aggression over time, it was predicted that higher levels of negative interaction and lower levels of positive interaction at Time 1 would characterize marriages that remained aggressive over time. The results support the first part of this hypothesis; spouses in stable-aggressive marriages were characterized by higher levels of negative interaction at Time 1 of data collection than were their stable-nonaggressive or aggressive-to-nonaggressive counterparts. They did not, however, evidence the predicted lower levels of positive interaction.

TABLE 9.3 Repeated Measures Analysis of Variance on Positive and Negative Behaviors, by Change in Aggression from Time 1 to Time 2

	Stable Nonaggressive	Aggressive to Nonaggressive	Stable Aggressive	F Values
Positive interaction				
Time 1				
Husbands	17.48	16.70	19.39	F(Change) = 0.67
Wives	12.23	12.40	15.43	F(Spouse) = 12.12***
				F(C × S) = 0.14
Negative interaction				
Time 1				
Husbands	2.97	2.40	7.39	F(Change) = 4.82**
Wives	1.18	1.70	4.30	F(Spouse) = 3.00
				F(C × S) = 0.68
Positive interaction				
Time 2				
Husbands	14.03	13.70	14.95	F(Change) = 0.08
Wives	14.17	15.50	14.75	F(Spouse) = 0.17
				F(C × S) = 0.20
Negative interaction				
Time 2				
Husbands	2.77	4.20	7.20	F(Change) = 11.27***
Wives	3.33	3.30	8.35	F(Spouse) = 0.44
				F(C × S) = 1.70

**$p < .01$; ***$p < .001$.

A second hypothesis was that the stable-aggressive marriages would be characterized by the highest levels of negative interaction and the lowest levels of positive interaction at Time 2. This hypothesis was also partially supported; at Time 2, spouses in stable-aggressive marriages reported the highest levels of negative interaction but did not differ from the other groups in levels of positive interaction.

Discussion

The results of this study are in keeping with those of previous work by a variety of scholars. Like Margolin et al. (1988) and Cordova et al. (1993), I found high levels of negative behavior in distressed-aggressive marriages. Previous work is extended, however, by noting that nondistressed-aggressive couples do not show high levels of negative daily interaction. Also, in keeping with Cordova et al.'s (1993) work, nondistressed-nonaggressive and distressed-nonaggressive couples did not differ in levels of negative interaction.

There is one difference between these results and those of previous work. Margolin et al. (1988) found more positive interaction in nondistressed-nonaggressive versus distressed-aggressive couples, whereas I found no differences between these two groups on positive interaction. Langhinrichsen-Rohling et al. (1994) found less positive interaction in distressed-aggressive than distressed-nonaggressive marriages. I attribute these different findings largely to the different methods used to study interaction. In daily marital interaction, distressed-aggressive couples appear to be able to exchange positive behaviors. In a problem-solving situation or conflict discussion, however, such positive interchange may be more difficult for distressed-aggressive couples.

The high levels of negative interaction seen in the distressed-aggressive marriages are not surprising; what was indeed surprising was that such high negativity was accompanied by high levels of positive interaction. Perhaps in aggressive marriages, spouses attempt to compensate for aggression with more positive interaction that offsets the harm done by the abuse, or the high levels of positive interaction may indicate the presence of intense marital attachments. Given potentially intense bonds between husband and wife, the fear of abandonment among aggressive husbands demonstrated by Dutton and Browning (1988) is in character. The results of the present study also hint at the enmeshment of the aggressive-distressed marriage noted by Dutton and Painter (1993). Certainly, the themes of attachment and enmeshment among distressed-aggressive couples bear further scrutiny.

Ultimately, the marital climate of the distressed-aggressive marriage may be characterized as unpredictable. Although these marriages contained as much positive interaction as was seen in the nondistressed marriages, it was accompanied by very high levels of negative interaction. In such a context, it may be difficult to anticipate the valence of the spouse's next behavior, making for a rather volatile relationship.

Also of interest in the present study is the difference between the two distressed groupings. Distressed-nonaggressive marriages, although quite low in negative interaction, were also low in positive interaction; these marriages appeared disengaged rather than volatile. Husbands and wives in the nonaggressive-distressed marriages appeared to have withdrawn their emotional investment in the marriage. Jacobson et al. (1994) found a similar pattern of lower levels of negative interaction patterns among distressed-nonaggressive husbands.

One of the unique features of this study is the examination of nondistressed-aggressive marriages. Nondistressed-aggressive marriages were characterized by high levels of positive interaction and low levels of negative interaction and by a less frequent occurrence of physical aggression. Indeed, their similarity in daily marital interaction to nondistressed-nonaggressive marriages was unanticipated.[6] What produces this group of "happily married, yet aggressive" couples? Perhaps the aggression first occurred in the context of a marriage that overall was very satisfying in most ways; this would allow couples to downplay any negative consequences of the aggression, especially if aggression occurred only occasionally. Studies of premarital couples indicate that "romance and aggression" can easily coexist, and that couples strive to overlook, forgive, or ignore the occurrence of aggression (Henton et al., 1983). Perhaps positive interaction serves to "buffer" the impact of negative events; couples characterized by relatively satisfying interaction patterns may have built up a bank account of positive interaction that mitigates against physical aggression having a longer-term negative impact on the marriage (Huston & Chorost, 1991; Gottman, 1993).

On the other hand, it could be that rather than representing a different dynamic, the nondistressed-aggressive marriage represents an earlier stage of development in which positive feelings about the marriage have not yet eroded. The use of the words "not yet" in the previous sentence is deliberate, for if the physically aggressive behavior continued, it was expected that the quality of marital interaction would deteriorate. There is mounting evidence that although negative behavior in marriage can be overlooked initially, over time it does serve to erode the quality of the relationship (Gottman, 1994; Gottman & Krokoff, 1989; Huston et al., 1986; Noller et al., 1994). Fortunately, such a question was examined in Phase 2 of the study.

Phase 2 of the study demonstrated that couples who remained aggressive over time were characterized by higher levels of negative interaction at both Time 1 and Time 2. On the other hand, couples who moved from being aggressive to nonaggressive over time were characterized by relatively low levels of negative daily marital interaction at Times 1 and 2. This is an important finding because it points to low levels of negative daily interaction as a potential precursor to the cessation of aggression in marriage. Again, the notion of daily marital interaction serving as a buffer seems appropriate here; couples who are characterized by a reserve of positive behavior, relatively minor forms of aggression, and low levels of negative behavior may have the best chance of putting an end to physically aggressive interaction in their marriages. Perhaps these characteristics mitigate against the escalation of marital conflict into aggressive episodes. Couples who are characterized by higher levels of aggression and by high levels of daily negative marital interaction may simply have a very tough time keeping the intensity of conflict and other marital interactions from escalating and erupting into violence.

The longitudinal results of the present study complement the findings of O'Leary et al. (1994) who also demonstrated that negative marital interaction patterns (i.e., overt hostility and passive aggressiveness) were predictive of later physical aggression in the marriage. As Huston and Vangelisti (1991) note, negativity in marriage, particularly that expressed by the husband, may be a primary force in determining later relational climate.

Two other areas of past research are worth mentioning. The gender effects seen in the present study, which picked up on the fact that wives reported significantly greater levels of positive and negative interaction by their husbands than vice versa, are in line with previous work that demonstrates that wives may be more in tune with, and pay more attention to, the positive and negative behaviors displayed by their husbands (Huston & Ashmore, 1986). The significant adjustment main effect corroborates the work of Gottman (1994), Huston et al. (1986, 1987), Noller (1985), and other behavioral researchers who consistently demonstrate that distressed couples, compared to nondistressed couples, display greater negative behavior during problem-solving discussions and in daily interaction. The present study demonstrates, however, that research on marital interaction may do well to incorporate aggression as a variable of interest. Given the differences between distressed-aggressive and distressed-nonaggressive couples seen here, it is clear that grouping couples as simply distressed versus nondistressed may be both limiting and misleading. Indeed, Cordova at al. (1993) note the possibility that previous findings on the significant differences in negativity between nondistressed and distressed marriages may have resulted from the inclusion of aggressive couples in the distressed groupings.

The results of this research must be interpreted cautiously given the limitations of the study design. First, it is important to acknowledge that the differences between the two aggressive groups (distressed and nondistressed) are complicated by the fact that these two groups differed in level of wife's minor aggression in the marriage. Not too surprisingly, it was not possible to construct distressed and nondistressed groupings with equal levels of aggression; conceptually, one would not expect to be able to do so. Despite this limitation, the inclusion of the nondistressed-aggressive marriage is a step ahead of previous work that has not yet acknowledged the possibility of such a marital type. Given the significant adjustment by aggression interaction effect, the importance of including the nondistressed-aggressive marriage in future work is clear.

The pitfalls of having spouses report on one another's behavior and the possible inherent linkages of these reports to marital satisfaction must also be acknowledged (Huston & Vangelisti, 1991). Another limitation of this study is the use of a nonrandom sample, which limits the generalizability of the findings. In particular, recall that these participants were all volunteers, relatively young, and middle to low income. This restriction of the sample in terms of age and income as well as the small sample size must be kept in mind when interpreting the results.

Summary and Conclusions

This study examined daily marital interaction as a function of marital adjustment and physical aggression. It was found that distressed-aggressive marriages were characterized by high levels of both positive and negative interaction, distressed-nonaggressive marriages were characterized by low levels of both positive and negative interaction, and nondistressed-nonaggressive and nondistressed-aggressive marriages were characterized by high levels of positive and low levels of negative interaction. Spouses in stable-aggressive marriages (i.e., reporting physical aggression both at Time 1 and at Time 2) were characterized by higher levels of negative interaction at both Time 1 and Time 2 (compared to their stable-nonaggressive and aggressive-to-nonaggressive counterparts).

The importance of early intervention is clear; working to break patterns of aggression may indeed be most effective when the aggressive behavior has not yet become a stable feature of the marriage, when the members of the couple are characterized by a reserve of positive daily interaction and a relatively low level of negative daily interaction, and when the aggression has not yet served to erode the quality of the marriage.

This study examined four combinations of aggression and distress, including the nondistressed-aggressive marriage, examined everyday marital interaction, and used a longitudinal design. Inclusion of these study designs into future research that examines distressed, nondistressed, and aggressive couples will advance our understanding of the ways in which physical aggression and marital adjustment interact over time to produce particular marital dynamics.

The study of interpersonal factors is critical to our future understanding of the dynamics of the aggressive marriage. I hope the results of the present study will provide an impetus for future work in the area of interpersonal factors and marital aggression. In particular, the use of behavioral self-report data on daily marital interaction seems to be a fruitful area for further research on the aggressive marriage. Understanding the day-to-day interaction of husbands and wives may be the key to understanding why physical aggression occurs in so many marriages.

Notes

1. Throughout the chapter, the perspective is taken that although physical aggression is often reciprocal between husband and wife, wives are typically in the position of responding to husbands' aggression in self-defense. In addition, because wives are at far greater risk of injury from their husband's use of aggression than vice versa, it makes sense to view wives as the more likely victims and husbands the more likely perpetrators (Lloyd & Emery, 1994). The use of the terminology *aggressive marriage* is in no way meant to excuse the perpetrator from responsibility for his actions or the need for stopping his use of aggression on his wife.

2. This research was funded by the Harry Frank Guggenheim Foundation, grants titled "Violence in Marriage: An Interaction Perspective" and "Predicting Changes in Marital Aggression: The Role of Socioemotional Climate." The author gratefully acknowledges the support of the foundation.

3. There were no differences between groups on husband's age, wife's age, family income, length of marriage, number of children, and husband's education. Wives in the nonaggressive-nondistressed group did report significantly greater education than wives in the aggressive-distressed group.

4. For purposes of this analysis, the CTS was scored as suggested by Barling, O'Leary, Jouriles, Vivian, and MacEwan (1987). The husband's score on each CTS item consists of the average of his self-reported use of aggression and his wife's report of his use of aggression; similarly, the wife's score on each CTS item is the average of her self-reported use of aggression and her husband's report of her use of aggression.

5. There were no differences between groups on husband's education, wife's education, number of children, husband's age, wife's age, or length of marriage. The groups did differ significantly in income, with the stable-aggresssive group reporting significantly lower income than the stable-nonaggressive or aggressive-to-nonaggressive couples.

6. Note that although in the present study nondistressed-nonaggressive and nondistressed-aggressive couples were very similar in levels of both positive and negative marital interaction, later analysis of a subset of these couples reveals important transactional differences in relational communication control patterns; see Chapter 11 for details.

10

The Role of Communication in Verbal Abuse Between Spouses

TERESA CHANDLER SABOURIN

This chapter presents a discussion of theory and research on the role of verbal aggression in abusive marriages. Verbal aggression has been studied both as a communication trait and as a relational characteristic. In addition to reviewing both of these approaches, the chapter will examine the various definitions of verbal aggression and some research findings on the relationship between verbal and physical aggression. The chapter concludes with a reflection on the implications of this work for intervening with abusive couples.

Verbal aggression—unlike physical aggression, which is immediately more threatening, more easily identified, and legally prohibited—remains to be fully recognized as a dangerous type of abuse. Furthermore, there is little research on the verbal component of the abuse process due to a belief that its consequences are not severe (Stets, 1990). It will be shown in this chapter, however, that verbal aggression can lead to serious physical, psychological, and relational problems.

Straus and Sweet (1992) have found that verbal aggression is a critical part of the pattern of domestic abuse with antecedents similar to those of physical aggression. Also, through interviews with abusive partners, Sabourin and Stamp (1995) found that abusive couples said so many things in the heat of anger that they felt their relationships were beyond repair. Hence, verbal aggression can permeate and damage the overall quality of a couple's relationship.

Verbal aggression incurs negative consequences for both individuals and their relationships. For example, verbal aggression has been associated with depression, poor physical health, and suicidal thoughts in female victims (Straus, Sweet, & Vissing, 1989). Similarly, Hudson and McIntosh (1981) discovered that female victims of psychological abuse, which results from verbal aggression, have self-esteem problems.

In terms of relational difficulties, verbal aggression can block rational problem solving. Straus (1974) found that verbal aggression inhibited and interfered with the ability to resolve other conflicts. Instead, it produces retaliatory aggression. This retaliatory aggression, which will be discussed later as negative reciprocity, is believed to play a key role in the escalation of verbal aggression into physical aggression as well as being damaging in its own right (Sabourin, 1995). Hence, spouses who use verbal aggression do so with "costly relational side effects such as decreased relational satisfaction" (DeTurck, 1987, p. 107).

Stamp and Sabourin (1995) claim that family communication scholars are especially qualified to examine the relational nuances that may subtly reinforce and contribute to the maintenance of violence between spouses. Thus, this chapter on verbal aggression between abusive spouses is written as a resource for students and scholars as well as practitioners who wish to identify and understand patterns of verbal aggression in their clients. The communication perspective offers a unique vantage point from which to consider the dialectic between verbal aggression as an individual behavior and verbal aggression as a relationally produced and maintained pattern. This means that cognitive, perceptual, and skill explanations for verbal aggression will be presented along with views from systems theory on relational dynamics. The contextualized presentation on verbal aggression will offer insight and direction for future research and theory development.

The chapter will first review the various conceptual and operational definitions of verbal aggression. It will then examine research findings that have explored the relationship between verbal aggression and physical aggression. The theoretical approaches for explaining verbal aggression, including both an individual, skills-based orientation and a relational dynamics one, will be highlighted. The concept of negative reciprocity is discussed as a key concept to explain how verbal aggression can become both dangerous to the individual and damaging to the relationship. Finally, implications for future work will be provided.

Definitions of Verbal Aggression

Although there are many definitions of verbal aggression, most provide a way to identify frequencies of certain acts rather than descriptions of actual behaviors and episodes. Both seem crucial for illustrating the process of verbal aggression. This section of the chapter will discuss conceptual and operational definitions of verbal aggression as well as some of its underlying dimensions.

Conceptual Definitions

Two conceptual definitions of verbal aggression are widely used in the study of verbal aggression between spouses (Infante & Wigley, 1986; Straus, 1979). Straus, who is a family sociologist, and colleagues (1989) define verbal or symbolic aggression as "a communication, either verbal or nonverbal, intended to cause psychological pain to another person or perceived as having that intent" (p. 3). They include the term *symbolic* because they believe that nonverbal communication is also an important component of the abuse process.

In defining verbal aggression, the focus can be placed on either the act being carried out or the injury suffered (Sabourin, 1991; Straus et al., 1989). It is important to consider the focus because if the aggressive act is the defining criterion, it means that acts intended to cause psychological injury would also be counted as verbal aggression even if they were not perceived as aggressive. If the injury suffered is the defining criterion, then mechanisms for measuring the severity and intensity of the resulting abuse become necessary. Hudson and McIntosh (1981) developed such an instrument for measuring both physical and psychological abuse. They determined severity by applying a weighting procedure to subjects' perceptions of various acts of aggression. On the basis of the results, they created a hierarchy of psychologically abusive acts.

Infante and Wigley's (1986), conceptual definition of verbal aggression has also been widely used in communication studies of abuse. They conceptualize verbal aggression as a personality trait that predisposes an individual to attack the character of another individual when discussing conflictual issues rather than attacking the person's ideas or position. Infante, Chandler, and Rudd (1989) further explain that a verbally aggressive message attempts to inflict psychological pain and results in the receiver's feeling less favorable about self.

Operational Definitions

There are more operational definitions for verbal aggression than there are conceptual definitions. Of nine such definitions reviewed for this chapter, variations in terms of whether the measure focused on self, other, or couple behavior were found. Specifically, four of the definitions focus on self-only reports (Buss & Perry, 1992; Gladue, 1991; Maiuro, Vitaliano, & Cahn, 1987; Yudofsky, Silver, Jackson, Endicott, & Williams, 1986), two of the measures focus on self and other (Infante & Wigley, 1986; Straus, 1979), one focuses only on the other's behavior (Hudson & McIntosh, 1981), and two use independent coders to describe couple's verbal behavior (Cordova, Jacobson, Gottman, Rushe, & Cox, 1993: Sabourin, 1991).

In addition to being varied in their focus of description, the measures of verbal aggression also contain both common and distinctive categories of behavior. In a content analysis of these measures, it was found that insults were most commonly included as a type of verbally aggressive behavior (eight of nine measures), followed by threats (five of nine measures), swearing (three of nine measures), disagreement (three of nine measures), and saying something spiteful (three of nine measures).

It is important to be aware of the differences in the operational definitions because results based on these measures may vary according to the definition and not necessarily reflect the actual behavior of the subjects. For example, Infante, Sabourin, Rudd, and Shannon (1990) found that insults were the most frequently used act of verbal aggression. If these results were compared to a study whose operational definition did not even contain a category for insults, the comparison would be invalid. The way in which verbal aggression is measured, therefore, has significant consequences for achieving an accurate understanding of verbal aggression.

The Conflict Tactics Scale. Straus (1979) developed the Conflict Tactics Scale, which contains measures for physical aggression, verbal aggression, and reasoning behavior. Although this scale is widely used, the verbal aggression component contains few items and does not measure corresponding beliefs and attitudes (Schumm & Bagarozzi, 1989). The CTS measures verbal aggression as a self-report variable, asking respondents to identify the number of times in the past year that they or their partner engaged in the following acts: insulting, swearing, saying something spiteful, threatening, leaving the room, and refusing to talk. From a number of studies that have used this measure, it has been found that both males and females are frequent users and recipients of verbally aggressive messages (75%). Also, it has been found that physical aggression occurs less than 1% of the time unaccompanied by verbal aggression (Straus & Sweet, 1992).

A Taxonomy of Verbal Aggression Messages. Infante, Sabourin, et al. (1990) used a taxonomy approach to measure acts of verbal aggression. Their taxonomy includes character attacks, competence attacks, physical appearance attacks, background attacks, accusations, profanity, ridicule, threats, and nonverbal emblems. Subjects respond to this checklist by identifying their use and their partner's use of these behaviors in their last argument.

Instrumental, Relational, and Identity Goals. The goal of verbal aggression has also been used as a way to classify aggressive acts. If the verbal aggression is inflicted as a means to some other end (e.g., to stop an objectionable behavior), it can be classified as "instrumental" (Mack, 1989; Straus et al., 1989). Verbal aggression can also serve relationship and identity goals (see Chapter 1). Determining the purpose of the verbal aggression in terms of whether it is instrumental, relational, or identity seeking has implications for understanding its impact on the marital relationship.

Another distinction to make in defining verbal aggression is whether the criterion is the act carried out or the injury suffered (Sabourin, 1991; Straus et al., 1989). This is important because if the aggressive act is the defining criterion, rather than the injury suffered, it means that acts intended to cause psychological injury would also be counted as verbal aggression, even if they were not successful. If injury suffered is the defining criterion, then mechanisms for measuring the severity and intensity of abuse must be considered. In their operational definition of psychological abuse, Hudson and McIntosh (1981) developed a method for measuring the severity of various acts of verbal aggression, including humiliation and threats.

A final issue in defining verbal aggression has to do with its instrumentality. If the verbal aggression is inflicted as a means to some other end (e.g., to stop some objectionable behavior), it is identified as instrumental (Mack, 1989; Straus et al., 1989). Verbal aggression, however, can also be used expressively as an end in itself. For example, a spouse may criticize another out of anger. Determining the purpose of the verbal aggression, in terms of whether it is instrumental or expressive, has implications for understanding how verbal aggression impacts the relationship as a whole. It also has implications for treatment.

The conceptual and operational definitions of verbal aggression discussed here have been used in numerous studies of abusive marriages. The next section of this chapter will discuss the research findings from these studies, specifically focusing on how verbal aggression and physical aggression have been found to be related to each other.

Research Findings on Verbal Aggression

Little is known about how spouses who experience abusive relationships communicate with each other in nonabusive situations. Hence, much of our knowledge about the verbal behavior of abusive partners reflects how they are aggressive. From the research on verbal aggression per se, some conclusions can be drawn about its relevance, its relation to physical aggression, including its effects on both the individual and the marital relationship, and some gender differences in perceptions of verbal aggression. This section will discuss these findings in more detail.

Prevalence of Verbal Aggression

Straus and Sweet (1992) used data from a nationally representative sample of 5,232 individuals to measure the incidence, chronicity, and correlates of verbal aggression operationalized as the subjects' responses to the CTS. The Conflict Tactics Scale is a self-report measure that contains items on both verbal and physical aggression. From this study, it was discovered that 75% of both male and female subjects reported that they engaged in 1 or more verbally aggressive attacks per year. The median was 3 or 4, and the mean was 10 for both male-initiated and female-initiated incidents of verbal aggression. Furthermore, they found a strong correlation between male-to-female and female-to-male verbal aggression ($r = .67$), concluding that when one spouse becomes verbally aggressive, the other usually responds in kind. Although males and females are both engaged in verbal aggression, however, women report more acts of verbal aggression both as victim and perpetrator. The authors suggest that males may be as active in verbal aggression but not as self-revealing.

Straus and Sweet (1992) also examined the demographic correlates of verbal aggression. As in Golin and Romanowski's (1977) study, Straus and Sweet found gender to be a nonsignificant variable when accounting for verbal aggression. The variables that were found to be significant covariates included age, with younger subjects reporting more verbal aggression, number of children, with couples who have more children reporting less verbal aggression, and alcohol use, in which there was a positive relationship between this variable and verbal aggression. In summary, they report that verbal aggression and physical aggression are similar in their relationship to specified social psychological variables.

Several studies have found that incidents of verbal aggression and physical aggression are highly correlated (Hudson & McIntosh, 1981; Straus & Sweet, 1992). This implies that verbal and physical aggression may tend to be intertwined, occurring at the same time. Verbal aggression is also reported to be higher for couples who reported high levels of conflict (Straus, 1974). Together, these findings point to the need to examine the relationship between physical and verbal aggression. Indeed, to encourage more research on verbal aggression and an awareness of its damaging potential, it becomes critical to understand how these variables are related. The following discussion will provide a summary of research and theory development in this direction.

The Relationship Between Verbal and Physical Aggression. In his seminal study of the role of verbal aggression in marriage, Straus (1974) tested a venting theory of verbal aggression, which posited that the expression of verbal aggression would reduce the incidence of physical aggression because of a catharsis effect. Using social learning theory as an explanation for a counterprediction, Straus states that "the more frequently an act is performed, the greater the likelihood that it will become a standard part of the behavior repertoire of the individual and of the expectations of others for the behavior of that individual" (p. 14). Hence, Straus tested the venting theory using self-report data from 385 couples who recalled an aggressive experience. He found that instead of the catharsis effect, verbal aggression acted as an escalator toward further aggression. He also found that physical aggression increased at a more rapid pace given increases in levels of verbal aggression. Similar findings were found by Sabourin (1991) in her examination of the relation between the rate of verbal aggression and physical aggression in abusive incidents.

Researchers disagree on whether verbal aggression is an independent form of aggression—hence separate from physical aggression—or whether verbal and physical aggression represent polarities along a continuum of aggression. Stets (1990) maintains that verbal and physical aggression are separate phenomena but operate in a two-step process and have different underlying causes. In the first step of the process, Stets believes that individuals move from nonaggression to verbal aggression. The second step of the process entails movement from verbal aggression to physical aggression. This linear portrayal of the abuse process implies a logical progression from verbal aggression to physical aggression. As such, "verbal aggression carries the seed of physical aggression later in a marriage" (Stets, 1990, p. 513).

The causal nature between verbal and physical aggression is difficult to determine. Although the nature of his data prevented Straus (1974) from specifying a causal nature between verbal and physical aggression, it did suggest the existence of a complex relationship. For example, social circumstances could influence the threshold between verbal and physical aggression such that a high level of insult exchange might activate cues that signal a perceived need for physical aggression. It is possible that in this type of situation, the level of threat from verbal aggression is experienced as a physical force as well as a threat to the self-concept (Stamp & Sabourin, 1995). Hence, although verbal aggression may serve as an immediate release for tension, it is also likely to reinforce the aggression that preceded it (Straus, 1974). Some studies have considered the similarities between verbal aggression and physical aggression. Stamp and Sabourin, who examined accounts from men who abused their wives, found that these males experienced their spouse's verbal aggression as having a physical force. Statements such as "She put me down" or "It was a real blow" reflect how verbal aggression could be experienced in a physical way. Yudofsky et al. (1986) developed an operational measure of verbal aggression that contained a hierarchy of acts from less to more severe. This hierarchy notion reinforces the idea that verbal and physical aggression may reflect differences in degree of aggression rather than kind. This means that the line between self-concept attack and bodily attack may not be as distinctive as some definitions suggest

Straus and Sweet (1992) posit that a verbally aggressive attack may be fundamentally similar to one that is physically aggressive. They are similar in that verbal aggression is intended to cause psychological pain (or is perceived as such) and physical aggression is intended to cause both physical and psychological harm. In other words, both attempt to cause deliberate pain. Hence, although verbal aggression does not replace physical aggression, it acts as part of the maladaptive behavioral process and is very similar to that of physical aggression in the family.

The relationship between verbal and physical aggression can also be explained as an outcome of cultural influences. Montgomery (1992) describes how couples participate, both implicitly and explicitly, in a reproduction of the relational ideology presented by the culture. For example, rules that prohibit the expression of verbal aggression in public may encourage it in private. Similarly, Straus (1974) stated, over 20 years ago, that "although we have clear norms and values restricting violence and emphasizing the values of peace and harmony—especially between family members—simultaneously there also exists a high level of actual violence and also norms fortifying aggression and violence" (p. 25).

Several researchers theorize that the relation between verbal and physical aggression is more of a two-step process (Infante et al., 1989; Stets, 1990). Stets, for example, maintains that as a two-step process, verbal and physical aggression are different phenomena with different underlying causes. She explains that the first step contains a movement from nonaggressive behavior to verbally aggressive behavior. In the second step, due to conditional factors, some individuals who are verbally aggressive become physically aggressive. Hence, verbal aggression may be seen as a necessary but not sufficient cause of physical aggression.

Similarly, Infante et al. (1989) purport that verbally aggressive behavior, when combined with other instigators, can influence the behavioral intention to use physical aggression. As such, physical aggression is a response that can occur after verbal aggression has taken place. Interestingly, they found that an argumentative skill deficiency was one of the contributing factors to verbal aggression. Thus, the move from nonaggressive to verbally aggressive behavior was influenced by a lack of verbal skills to manage conflict. This finding is supported by other research (DeTurck, 1987; Watkins, 1982). Hence, among abusive partners, "communication may be lacking or distorted, due to limited personal skills in communication or due to a fear of the consequences of honest communication" (Watkins, 1982, p. 54).

It appears that verbal aggression creates negative arousal, which is a physiological response, and that couples may become physiologically linked—getting "locked into a destructive pattern" (Infante et al., 1989, p. 167). The lack of communication skills, then, contributes to the incidence of both physical and verbal aggression. Accordingly, with a lack of verbal skills, the victim of verbal aggression may feel that physical force is the only way to defend his or her self-image and to discourage a future attack (Infante, Sabourin, et al., 1990). Furthermore, research has shown that certain acts, especially character attacks, are perceived as more catalytic than other types of verbal aggression, perhaps because they most directly deliver psychological pain (Infante, Sabourin, et al., 1990). There is additional research to support the catalytic nature of verbal aggression on physical aggression (Coleman, 1980; Goldstein & Rosenbaum, 1985; Straus, 1974).

Verbal aggression has been defined as both a psychological trait (Infante & Wigley, 1986) and as a relational pattern (Cordova et al., 1993; Gage, 1988; Sabourin, 1995; Sabourin, Infante, & Rudd, 1993). Because much of the research relies on unilateral, self-report data, the relational pattern of verbal aggression has been relatively underexamined. The relational approach, however, is important to show that verbal aggression is damaging in its own right.

Negative Reciprocity

The concept of negative reciprocity is important to understanding verbal aggression as a relational pattern. Negative reciprocity occurs when couples match aversive behavior with aversive behavior (Cordova et al., 1993). From a communication perspective, the dynamic underlying the negative reciprocity may be relational control. According to Millar and Rogers (1987), relational control is a process by which the couple attempts to establish their individual and joint rights to define and direct the actions of the dyad. When both partners attempt to direct, and neither submits to the other's attempt at control, a pattern of escalation, similar to negative reciprocity, emerges. The relational control model explains how behavior is mutually produced, with one partner's behavior contingent on the other's.

The incidence of negative reciprocity among distressed couples has been widely reported in the marital communication literature (Billings, 1979; Gottman, 1982; Jacobson, Follette, & McDonald, 1982; Raush, Barry, Hertel, & Swain, 1974). Typically, couples who are distressed escalate negative behavior and withhold positive behavior. Billings (1979), for example, found that distressed couples display more negative communication reciprocity and less reciprocity of positive communication. Jacobson et al. (1982) found that distressed couples engage in more negative reciprocity and also perceive more negativity in each other's behavior. Hence, the presence of verbal aggression impacts the quality of marital life in both direct and indirect ways. Directly, it creates harm to the self-concepts of marital partners; indirectly, it creates a withholding of support and a lack of positive communication (Sabourin et al., 1993). The lack of support statements was also found in Sabourin and Stamp's (1995) study of abusive couples' conversations. Unlike the nonabusive couples, the abusive partners countered negativity with negativity. The nonabusive couples offered countercompliments to each other. These findings are consistent with the relational control perspective in which a lack of support, and the presence of reciprocity, leads to a rigid control pattern. As such, couples may respond to any type of argument as an attack.

To view verbal aggression as a catalyst to physical aggression, from the relational control perspective, means considering how the partners' responses to others' aggression function at the dyadic level. Several studies have specifically examined the interactions between abusive partners to describe this relational control pattern. Gage (1988), for example, examined the conversations of 29 abusive couples from her private therapy practice using a relational control analysis. She expected to find a complementary pattern, in which the husband would dominate and the wife would submit to relational control attempts, given that this was the traditional notion of spouse abuse. Instead, she found an extremely high prevalence of escalating symmetry (85% of all exchanges), indicating that both partners attempted to control but neither supported the other's attempt. The escalating symmetry means that couples were engaged in negative reciprocity, exchanging like negative behavior.

Cordova et al. (1993) also examined the interactions of abusive couples for negative reciprocity, defined as "the tendency to continue negative behavior once it begins" (p. 559). Using lag sequential analysis to examine conversational examples of interaction from a sample of 29 couples with a physically abusive husband, Cordova et al. tested to see if aversive verbal behavior by the husband would curtail the wife's aversive behavior. According to their coding system, aversive behavior is defined as criticism, disagreement, and putting the other down. Instead of curtailment, they found that the wife reciprocated her husband's aversive behavior with more aversive behavior. Similar to Straus (1974), this means that verbal aggression did not vent aggression but created more of it. The threshold of arousal, at which the male becomes physically aggressive, may be reached as an attempt to intensify control efforts. As such, the husband's inability to get what he wants through verbal means may shape his reliance on physical aggression until he relies on it exclusively to get control and subservience from his spouse.

In a study of relational control patterns among abusive couples, Sabourin (1995) recruited 10 abusive couples to complete a discussion on a topic that was not biased toward conflict. She examined the conversational data using Rogers and Farace's (1975) relational coding scheme. The study examined the conversations for patterns of negative reciprocity and its impact on the relational satisfaction of partners. Similar to other interactional studies, Sabourin found that both husband and wife were equally likely to initiate and respond with control attempts and were less likely to respond with support than nonabusive couples. The specific types of nonsupport statements that were reciprocated included disagreement, disapproval, and nonacceptance.

The abusive couples also reported significantly less marital satisfaction than did the nonabusive couples. This may be due to the fact that negative reciprocity is associated with a lack of positive communication and a reduction in mutual affection as well as being directly damaging (Zietlow & VanLear, 1991). It may be that negative reciprocity creates an enmeshed system in which the autonomy of the individual is subjugated to the negative bonding between spouses. Boundaries and the capacity for empathy are lost, and the verbal aggression contributes to a mutual state of negative arousal (Sabourin, 1995).

In summary, the research findings on the relationship between verbal and physical aggression support the idea that verbal aggression acts as a catalyst to physical aggression. As a catalyst, it appears that when negative arousal from verbal attack reaches a threshold, it calls forth a physical defense. It may also be used when skills for constructive argument are lacking. There is some evidence to suggest that verbal and physical aggression are linked in a nonlinear relationship. When damage to self-concept becomes experienced as a physically painful situation, the boundary between words as words and words as weapons (e.g., "going for the jugular") may dissolve. Either way, verbal aggression has been proven to be damaging to the individual, in terms of increased depression, lowered self-esteem, and suicidal thoughts, as well as to the relationship. The relationship is damaged through a destruction of affection and the creation of a schismogenetic pattern, meaning that the couple is locked into a dysfunctional way of relating (Zietlow & VanLear, 1991). These results suggest the importance of continuing to study verbal aggression as both an individual and a relational phenomena. Before discussing these approaches further, this section will conclude with a review of findings on gender-related differences in verbal aggression.

Gender Differences in Verbal Aggression. According to Marshall and Vitanza (1994), verbal aggression, unlike physical aggression in which male size and strength means they can cause more harm, is equally likely to cause harm by and to both males and females. Although empirical evidence supports the equivalent prevalence of verbal aggression for both husbands and wives, the literature on attributions for aggression suggests that males and females differ in their perceptions of verbal aggression. For instance, males often attribute their physical aggression to their wives' verbal aggression, hence making external attributions for their behavior. Stamp and Sabourin (1995) found many examples in which the wife's verbal aggression was punctuated by the husband as a cause of his physical aggression. One man said that his wife initiated the verbal aggression, and he "kinda finished it" with physical aggression. He said that he told her to "be still, be quiet, shut up, shut up, and then I charged her, stating that, yelling that, and I sorta busted my lip on her head." Furthermore, he maintained that "this is literally the only way to shut her up" because her verbal aggression became "kinda a personal attack" (p. 297).

Several other studies support the idea that males perceive their spouses as instigating them to physical violence with their verbal behavior (Coleman, 1980). When males blame their spouses, it is more difficult for them to stop because the locus of control is perceived as being outside of themselves. Sugarman and Hotaling (1989b) report that abusive men perceive their spouses' behavior as more insulting than do nonabusive men. Hence, they perceive themselves as not responsible and they perceive a higher degree of aggression in their partner, contributing to their felt need to use physical violence.

Females perceive their husband's violence as either an attempt to control them or as a loss of control (Henderson & Stets, 1991). Frieze (1979) found that abused women attributed their spouses' abuse to both stable and unstable factors. Stable causes include his personality (e.g., she expects that he cannot change) and unstable include temporary, situational conditions (e.g., not having dinner ready on time). As long as the negative behavior is attributed to a stable factor, no attempt is made to hold the abuser accountable for change. Furthermore, when situational factors are ignored, few alternatives are examined to resolve their damaging patterns.

Hence, although both males and females engage in verbal aggression, they tend to perceive its causality and its relation to physical aggression differently. Men are more likely to blame their spouses, whereas females are more likely to excuse their husbands for engaging in violence. These results have implications for intervening into abuse, which will be discussed later. The next section of this chapter will highlight the approaches to viewing verbal aggression as an individual and as a relational phenomena.

Approaches for Studying Verbal Aggression

The two main approaches for studying the role of communication in verbal aggression between abusive partners are the trait-based skills approach, adopted by Infante and colleagues (1989, 1990; Sabourin et al., 1993), and the relational dynamics approach, explored by Sabourin et al. (1995). The approaches will be discussed separately and as part of a dialectical approach, which incorporates both individual trait level and relational dynamics as equally important to understanding verbal aggression.

A Skills-Deficiency Approach to Verbal Aggression

The early work of Bandura (1973) showed that unskilled communicators use more physical force than others. This work provides the basis for Infante et al.'s (1989) study that explored the relationship between an argumentative skill deficiency and abuse between marital partners. Their interactionist model of family violence proposed that this lack of skill was one factor that could contribute to physical aggression, given other social and personal conditions. The trait model, then, sees spouse abuse as culminated by physical aggression but with a basis in verbal aggression. Research substantiates the fact that physical aggression is often preceded by or accompanied by verbal aggression or both (Rancer & Niemasz, 1988; Straus & Sweet, 1992).

Verbal aggression is used as an alternative to constructive argument. In other words, individuals who lack the ability and motivation to argue may resort to verbal aggression (Rancer & Niemasz, 1988, p. 2). Argumentativeness and verbal aggression, respectfully, are defined as generally stable traits that predispose individuals in communication situations to either verbally challenge the positions of or to attack the other's self-concept instead of, or in addition to, their position on an issue. Thus, the locus of attack distinguishes verbal aggression from argumentativeness. Generally, argumentativeness is seen as constructive, whereas verbal aggression is considered to be destructive. This approach measures the trait of verbal aggression using the Verbal Aggression Scale, a self-report instrument (Infante & Wigley, 1986).

From the trait view, the outcome of using verbally aggressive behavior is self-concept damage to the receiver. Verbally aggressive messages can take a variety of forms but generally are experienced as insults and put-downs. Furthermore, the victim of another's trait verbally aggressive behavior is likely to protect and defend his or her self-concept through retaliation. This reciprocity is especially apt to occur when the verbal attack was perceived as intentional or unwarranted. The steady escalation of verbal aggression can become habitual and a preferred mode of interaction. Verbal aggression that is reinforced by escalating reciprocity can become, in this way, a relational pattern. This relational view will be discussed below.

A Relational Approach to Verbal Aggression

As this chapter has indicated, abuse between spouses is complex and multidimensional. Although the trait view focuses on the individual's tendency toward verbal aggression, the relational view considers verbal aggression to be a jointly produced characteristic of interaction that is likely to produce retaliatory aggression. From this view, verbal aggression is seen to cause a reduction in mutual liking and affection between spouses. Therefore, it is not just the danger of verbal aggression contributing to physical aggression that is of concern to students of spouse abuse but its impact on relational quality as well.

In her discussion of defensive communication, Waln (1982) explains that in interpersonal conflict there is a tendency for spouses to model each other's verbal behavior in a spiraling pattern. The spiraling process in verbal aggression means that increasingly stronger defenses are required by the partners to defend themselves against increased threat. DeTurck (1987) reinforces this idea by stating that "when communicators are initially unable to obtain their persuasive goals, their subsequent persuasive messages become more threatening" (p. 106). Hence, the reaction to another's verbal aggression defines the phenomena as much as the type of message initiated.

The repetition of verbally aggressive exchanges is the essence of the relational view of verbal aggression. The couple appears to engage in argument seemingly without an end. In Stamp and Sabourin's (1995) study, one subject said that he and his partner would go back and forth in their verbal aggression. Mack (1989) defines this pattern as an escalating cycle in which the potential victim participates in the exchange—sharing in a positive feedback loop. The symmetrical feedback loop means that each partner does more of the same behavior; when the situation becomes untenable, physical aggression is likely to occur.

Thus, although in functional relationships "the norm of reciprocity implies that relational partners will respond to each other with equity" (Roloff, 1987, p. 13), in abusive relationships the norm of reciprocity means that partners engage in mutual destruction. The escalation of verbal aggression into negative reciprocity, then, can be seen as a function of how the partners respond to each other's communicative acts at a relational control level (Sabourin, 1995).

The views on verbal aggression as a trait and as a relational pattern both provide a basis for intervention with couples who are suffering from abuse. In the final section of this chapter, ideas for intervening at three levels will be presented. First, a cognitive-restructuring method will be discussed. Next, an approach for argumentative skills training will be presented. Finally, intervention into the dyadic pattern will be explored. Together, these ideas help to illustrate how the destructive pattern of verbal aggression can be changed to one that is more constructive for both the individual partners and the relationship between them.

Interventions Into Verbal Aggression

A major concern for intervention into spouse abuse is the safety of the victim. Because of this, marital partners are often treated separately. Once abuse has been stopped and the atmosphere of terror has ceased, however, couples may need to learn together how to relate in a more constructive manner. The following discussion provides some suggestions for treatment at the individual level and the couple level that are grounded in communication principles. Although it may seem naive to suggest that communication can be used to alter abusive patterns, this chapter has shown that communication patterns reinforce abuse. Although the role of communication may vary from couple to couple, its importance for change needs to be recognized.

Cognitive Restructuring

It has been shown how perceptions of self and other can contribute to the creation and maintenance of verbally aggressive behavior. Hence, one way to intervene into the process of verbal aggression is through individual, cognitive restructuring. Such an approach gets to the cognitive sources of conflict and can be used to improve intimacy between partners (Cahn, 1992). Programs designed for treating battering men often begin with cognitive awareness activities to enable the men to see how their attitudes and beliefs contribute to their violence. Furthermore, without intervention at the cognitive level, "intimate partners' training is unlikely to have much impact" (Cahn, 1992, p. 108). Another advantage to the cognitive restructuring approach is that it can be used to help both partners discover what their attitudes and perceptions are regarding conflict. From this point, they can learn how to change their views to enable them to engage in a more constructive problem-solving process.

Argumentative Skills Training

Once an awareness of beliefs and perceptions has been obtained, treatment for abusive individuals could begin to focus on communication skills. Infante and colleagues (1989, 1990; Sabourin et al., 1993) suggest that argumentative skills training could be used to create an alternative for verbal aggression. The argumentative skills training could be used for individuals and couples. This approach would allow individuals to role play and to model argumentative behavior that focuses on the issues of conflict rather than on attacking the individuals' self-concepts. Although some individuals are predisposed toward verbal aggression, the training can alter tendencies. When used with partners, such training could break the pattern of negative reciprocity, enabling them to match constructive behavior with constructive behavior.

Dyadic Treatment

When abuse is expressive as opposed to instrumental, Mack (1989) believes that it is more effective to treat the couple together than it is to separate them. His model of abuse illustrates how coercive exchanges and verbal threats escalate toward physical aggression. As such, tension and anxiety arise "with neither side being able to bring them down to a manageable level" (Mack, 1989, p. 195). According to Mack, if either partner in the abusive relationship could make a complementary move, defined as a tension-reducing behavior, the pattern of abuse could be changed. His method for changing the destructive verbal patterns of aggression includes an emphasis on open communication with explicit negotiations and contracts providing alternatives to verbal aggression.

Summary

This chapter has explored the role of communication in verbal aggression between spouses. There is ample evidence to suggest that verbal aggression is damaging to both individuals' self-concepts and to the quality of their marital relationship. The concept of negative reciprocity, which describes the pattern of escalation that couples evolve into, is a key toward understanding the momentum of destructive communication patterns. When partners begin to perceive all arguments as attacks and believe that they have no control over their behavior, destruction is likely to continue. Through the interventions described in this chapter, the potential of communication to help to rebuild these relationships becomes a real potential.

11

Relational Control and Physical Aggression in Satisfying Marital Relationships

L. EDNA ROGERS
ANNE CASTLETON
SALLY A. LLOYD

This study entails a descriptive analysis of communication patterns that differentiate among aggressive and nonaggressive married couples, all of whom also report high to moderate marital satisfaction. Taped conversations of 25 couples' discussion of four topics, coded according to the Relational Communication Coding System (Rogers, 1972), form the basis of this comparison. Aggressive husbands tended to engage in more one-up and fewer one-down messages than did nonaggressive husbands; dominance ratios characterized the aggressive couples as the most husband dominated. Aggressive couples also displayed higher levels of nonconstructive communication patterns.

Since the late 1970s, researchers have been extensively involved in the investigation of physical aggression in marriage. Starting with landmark studies by Walker (1979), Dobash and Dobash (1979), Straus, Gelles, and Steinmetz (1980), and others, hundreds of research studies have examined the role of personality factors, self-esteem, the intergenerational transmission of violence, stress, and other individual variables in the occurrence of physical aggression. Recently, the role of interpersonal

AUTHORS' NOTE: Dr. Lloyd gratefully acknowledges the support of the Harry Frank Guggenheim Foundation for this longitudinal study of violence in marriage.

factors has been emphasized. This line of research clearly indicates different interpersonal patterns in marriages wherein physical aggression is occurring including greater levels of negative behavior, overt hostility, verbal aggression and conflict, and lower levels of argumentativeness, positive behavior, and problem-solving skill (Babcock, Waltz, Jacobson, & Gottman, 1993; Burman, John, & Margolin, 1992; Sabourin, Infante, & Rudd, 1993). As a result of these and other studies on the interpersonal correlates of physical aggression, researchers are beginning to view physical aggression as a communicative act (Lloyd & Emery, 1994; Planalp, 1993). Indeed, this chapter is predicated on this notion. Infante, Chandler, and Rudd (1989) make this point most eloquently when they state,

> A communication approach to the problem of interspousal violence is illuminating because it reveals that when violence occurs it is not an isolated event in people's lives, but is embedded firmly in the process of interpersonal communication which people use to regulate their daily lives. (p. 174)

Control is a key issue in the study of physical aggression from a communication perspective (Lloyd & Emery, 1994). Control has been identified by various scholars as a central dimension of interpersonal relationships (Danziger, 1976; Kelly et al., 1983) and likewise of marital relationships (Jacob & Tennenbaum, 1988; Markman & Notarius, 1987; Schaap, 1984). The study of control as played out in intimate relations seems particularly appropriate for gaining insight into the dynamics of marital aggression.

Many studies of physical abuse in marriage have focused (and probably appropriately so) on the more violent forms of aggression (Dobash & Dobash, 1979; Johnson, 1995). These studies, however, often emphasize that verbal or more minor forms of aggression or both may lead to more severe acts of violence. The study of less violent forms may provide a key for intervention and alteration of patterns that may escalate toward more serious acts of aggression. The analysis of and potential insight into minor forms of aggression represents the focus of this study. Furthermore, it has been assumed by researcher and layperson alike that acts of physical aggression are present only in more dissatisfied or highly distressed marital couples. Research by Lloyd

(1990b, 1996) and O'Leary et al. (1989) indicates that this is not necessarily the case; well-adjusted engaged and married couples do report incidents of physical aggression.

The present study examines the relationship between patterns of relational control and physical aggression in couples who report different levels of satisfaction but relatively happy marital relationships. This investigation builds on Lloyd's (1990b, 1996) previous work and represents the third phase of a larger, longitudinal study of physical aggression among marital couples. A descriptive comparison of the interaction control patterns of couples, differentiated by level of marital satisfaction and physical aggression, is the aim of this aspect of the research.

Relational Communication Control

Relational communication is an interaction-based approach to the study of interpersonal relationships. Grounded within a systems perspective (Watzlawick, Beavin, & Jackson, 1967), this approach gives primary attention to the patterns of interrelating with one another. The emergent social structurings created in the ongoing communication process between relational members give life and form to their relationships. Through communication, we offer definitions of self in relation to others and simultaneously shape the nature of our relationship. Definitions can be accepted, resisted, or modified; the process of defining relationships is, by its nature, a process of negotiation.

The basic premises of the relational view can be visualized through the use of the metaphor of dance. Different relational dances emerge from the combination of different dance steps. How we move in relation to one another via our communication behavior forms the patterns that underlie and identify our social relationships. Analogous to dance steps, message behaviors combine into sequences of pattern, recurring interactions, that characterize our different relationships. With the relational approach, individual movements (message behaviors) can be analyzed, but the dance (relational pattern) is of central interest.

Relational control refers to the interactive structuring of the regulative function of message exchange. Measures of relational control are designed to index the influencing process of defining and delimiting the interactions of system members. Three types of control maneuvers are identified according to how a message in relation to the previous message defines the nature of the relationship. Messages that attempt to direct or assert definitional rights are designated as one-up control movements; requests and acceptances of another's relational definition are one-down control movements; and nonassertive, nonsubmissive, leveling moves are coded as one-across messages. The interlinking of contiguous control movements produces the transactional patterns depicting relational structure.

The concepts of symmetry and complementarity represent two basic patterns for describing different forms of relational control. Symmetrical and complementary patterns are defined on the basis of message similarity or dissimilarity of sequentially ordered message behaviors. Transitory patterns, based on the combination of one-across messages with one-up or one-down messages, form a midrange of relational structuring between complementarity and symmetry. These three general patterns are further differentiated by subtypes of relational control according to the type and order of the control messages exchanged.

Studies of relational control have been carried out in a variety of contextual settings from large organizations (Fairhurst, Rogers, & Sarr, 1987) to family therapy (Friedlander & Heatherington, 1989), but the bulk of the research has concentrated on marital relationships. In a series of studies relating control to role inequity, dyadic understanding, and marital and communication satisfaction (Courtright, Millar, & Rogers, 1979; Millar, Rogers, & Courtright, 1979; Rogers-Millar & Millar, 1979), an inverse relationship was found between one-up control behaviors and both marital and communication satisfaction. Conversely, patterns of reciprocal complementarity indicating relatively equivalent patterns of dominance were positively related to mutual satisfaction and understanding. With unequal dominance, the more dominant partner had lower levels of understanding than the less dominant member. In addition, couples with higher levels of role inequity had a higher proportion of one-up competitive and one-across symmetry and a lower proportion of one-down transitory patterns. In these studies, one-across/one-down transitory interacts were found to be clearly more characteristic of more satisfied couples. In general, flexible redundancy of control structuring was related to positive indices of marital relationships. A similar set of results, which lends cross-cultural confirmation, was found in studies of clinic and nonclinic Spanish couples of differing levels of marital adjustment (Escudero, Rogers, & Gutierrez, in press; Escudero, Rogers, Gutierrez, & Caceres, in press).

Investigations of different marital types (Fitzpatrick, 1984; Williamson & Fitzpatrick, 1985) found different patterns of control in discussions of high- and low-salient conflict topics. Independent couples, regardless of conflict salience, engaged in more competitive symmetry than other marital types. Separate couples tended to avoid conflict; in both topic situations, they had the least amount of competitive symmetry and the highest proportion of complementarity. In contrast, traditional couples enacted less one-up symmetry and more complementarity with low-salient topics and reversed this pattern in their discussion of high-salient conflict topics. Corollary with these more flexible control patterns, traditional couples also had the highest level of dyadic adjustment.

A study of Spanish couples' discussions of conflict and nonconflict topics found more frequent and longer sequences of competitive symmetry exhibited in conflict-prone interactions and more complementary and one-down/one-across transitory transactions with nonconflict topics (Escudero & Gutierrez, 1987). An investigation of the control dynamics of couples in counseling found that both one-down messages, but in particular one-up control messages, led to sequences of competitive symmetry (Manderscheid, Rae, McCarrick, & Sibergeld, 1982). One-up assertions resulted in stronger competitive escalation, whereas one-down moves resulted in a more gradual escalation. The use of one-across messages, however, decreased the potential for competitive sequences.

Across these studies, several comparative similarities emerge. In general, patterns of complementarity, shared dominance, one-across messages, one-across/one-down transactions, and relatively flexible control patterns are positively related to more satisfying marital relationships. Conversely, high levels of one-up messages, unequal dominance, competitive symmetry, and more redundant patterns of relational control are associated with lower levels of marital satisfaction and adjustments.

To our knowledge, only two studies of relational control in physically aggressive couples have been completed, excluding the present investigation. In an analysis of abusive couples' initial counseling discussions of their latest incident of abuse, Gage (1988) found an overwhelming proportion of competitive symmetry. Although this situation may overly prompt high levels of opposition, the struggle for relational control clearly dominated these interactions, with little evidence of dominance or less competitive transactions as a result of such strong patterns of resistance—that is, nonacceptance of the other's definitional assertions. Sabourin (1995) found high rates of competitive symmetry and nonsupport statements and a tendency toward negative reciprocity among aggressive couples. Her data also suggest that males displayed more one-down moves than females in response to their partners' attempts at relational control.

In contrast to these studies of more extreme situations of abuse, the present study focuses on minor forms of aggression among relatively satisfied, nonclinical couples. The goal of this investigation is to offer a descriptive analysis of communication patterns that differentiates among physically aggressive and nonaggressive couples as a way to gain more understanding of control dynamics that may lead to or hold at bay nonconstructive patterns of conflict interaction. Communication-based studies can help shed light on the interaction processes that may promote physically aggressive episodes between intimate partners.

Method

Participants and Procedures

The sample of 25 couples on which the study is based represents a subset of the 31 couples of the original group of 78 who could still be contacted after a period of 3 years and who agreed to participate in this third phase of Lloyd's (1996) longitudinal study of violence in marriage. The couples reside in a metropolitan area in the intermountain west and, on average, have 1 or 2 years of college education with a family income slightly below $30,000. Married for approximately 11 years, they have an average number of three children. The average ages of wives and husbands are 32 and 34 years old, respectively.

The couples were interviewed in their homes at their convenience. The data-gathering process typically took 2 hours. Each participant completed a set of questionnaires, including the Dyadic Adjustment

Scale (DAS; Spanier, 1976) and the Conflict Tactics Scale (CTS; Straus, 1979), after which each couple's discussion of four marital topics was tape-recorded.

On the basis of their dyadic adjustment and conflict tactics scores, the couples were classified into five different groupings: Group 1, high adjustment-no aggression ($N = 9$); Group 2, moderate adjustment-no aggression ($N = 8$); Group 3, moderate adjustment-physical aggression ($N = 8$); Group 4, low adjustment-no aggression ($N = 3$); and Group 5, low adjustment-physical aggression ($N = 3$). Couples in Group 1 had DAS scores above 118 ($\bar{x} = 123$), Group 2 and 3 couples' DAS scores were between 100 and 117 ($\bar{x} = 113$ and 111, respectively), and the DAS scores for Group 4 and 5 couples were less than 100 ($\bar{x} = 96$ and 75, respectively). Because of the small number of couples in Groups 4 and 5, the description of patterned differences will concentrate on the first three groups. Even so, sample limitations prompt a more descriptive than statistical comparison in our attempt to uncover differences that in combination suggest an integrated set of patterns that differentiate couples in satisfying relationships who are physically aggressive from those who are not.

The four topics that the couples were asked to discuss with one another were how they met and decided to marry, how they related the happenings of their day to one another, how they handled disagreements, and what it takes these days to have a good marriage. Each couple discussed each topic for 10 minutes. The taped conversations were transcribed and coded according to the Relational Communication Control Coding System (Rogers, 1972; Rogers & Farace, 1975).

With this system, the "speaking turn" is used to designate the message code unit. Coding procedures comprise three progressive steps: assigning message code categories, identifying the control direction of the code categories, and indexing the transactional patterns that emerge from the sequentially ordered combinations of message control directions.

In line with the above, each message first receives a three-digit code indicating the speaker (wife or husband), the grammatical form of the message (assertion, question, successful talk over, unsuccessful talk over, incomplete, or other), and the response mode (support, nonsupport, extension, answer, instruction, order, disconfirmation, topic change, self-instruction, or other). Second, based on the combined grammatical and response codes, three control codes are identified: one-up, an attempt to assert definitional rights; one-down, messages that accept or request the other partner's relational definition; and one-across, nonasserting, nonaccepting, control-leveling definitions. Third, the combination of contiguous message control directions forms the basis for indexing patterns of control at the transactional level. Nine transactional patterns result from the three control code combinations: symmetrical transactions of similar paired control codes (competitive ↑↑, submissive ↓↓, and neutralized →→), complementary transactions of opposite paired control codes (one-up complementarity ↑↓ and one-down complementarity ↓↑), and transitory transactions of one-across control in combination with one-up or one-down (↑→, →↑, ↓→, and →↓). Messages may be double coded if they have different regulative functions as a response to the previous message and as a stimulus for the following message.

Two trained coders, working from transcripts, coded the couples' interactions, which totaled approximately 13,000 messages for all 31 couples. Intercoder reliability estimates were based on approximately 10% of the total messages coded. Based on the three-digit message codes, Cohen's kappa estimate of reliability was .86 when checked at the midpoint of the coding procedure and .84 at the completion of the coding.

Results

The findings are based on a comparison of the first three couple groups—Group 1, high adjustment-no aggression (high adj-no agg); Group 2, moderate adjustment-no aggression (mod adj-no agg); and Group 3, moderate adjustment-physical aggression (mod adj-phys agg). All eight Group 3 couples reported incidents of physical aggression within the past 12 months, with a group average of 10.1 incidents in the past year. Over the 3-year period of the research project, five of the eight couples indicated physically aggressive episodes at all three data-gathering phases. Furthermore, the aggression reported by these couples is predominantly mutual; in other words, both husbands and wives report engaging in tactics of conflict that included physically aggressive acts.

The results provide a descriptive analysis of communication behaviors of couple groups across all four topic discussions, with selected group differences by topic. These results include both message-level and transactional-level couple group comparisons. Interaction exemplars that highlight relevant patterns of interaction are also provided.

Message-Level Results

Based on a total of 11,644 messages for the 25 couples in the first three groups, the average number of messages per couple was 465 for Group 1 (high adj-no agg), 502 for Group 2 (mod adj-no agg), and 430 for Group 3 (mod adj-phys agg). The lower Group 3 mean indicates a slightly lower rate of speaker turns due to somewhat longer speaking turns and pauses. In comparison to the low-adjustment couples, however—Groups 4 and 5 with message means of 258 and 175, respectively—all of the couples in Groups 1, 2, and 3 had relatively active and involved conversations.

A comparison of support and nonsupport messages found Group 1 couples (high adj-no agg) to have the highest proportion of support messages (28%) and the lowest enactment of nonsupport messages (8%). Groups 2 (mod adj-no agg) and 3 (mod adj-phys agg) have slightly lower proportions of support (22% and 23%, respectively) and higher rates of nonsupport messages (12% and 13%, respectively). These proportions represent approximately equal rates for husbands and wives, with the exception of Group 2 wives who offer less support to their husbands (18%) than husbands to wives (26%). The contrast between Group 1 and Groups 2 and 3 is particularly evident in the ratio of support to nonsupport messages by couple group. Group 1 has a ratio of 3.5 support messages to 1 nonsupport message, whereas the ratios for Groups 2 and 3 approximate 1.8 to 1.

The distribution of message control in Table 11.1 shows Group 1 couples with the lowest proportion of one-up messages (18%) and the highest proportion of one-down moves (36%), whereas Groups 2 and 3 have higher rates of one-up control (24% and 25%, respectively) and lower proportions of one-down message control (29% and 30%, respectively).

The usage of the three types of message control are equivalent for Group 1 husbands and wives, but a noted difference appears in a

TABLE 11.1 Message Control Average Percentages, by Couple Group, by Wife, Husband, and Dyad

	High Adjustment– No Aggression	Moderate Adjustment– No Aggression	Moderate Adjustment– Physical Aggression
One-up↑			
Wife	18.4	26.0	23.0
Husband	17.6	21.4	27.2
Dyad	18.0	23.6	25.1
One-down ↓			
Wife	35.7	24.0	31.3
Husband	36.1	34.1	28.9
Dyad	35.9	29.1	30.1
One-across →			
Wife	45.9	50.0	45.7
Husband	46.3	44.5	43.8
Dyad	46.1	47.2	44.8
Domineeringness ratio	0.96	0.82	1.19

comparison of Groups 2 and 3 husband and wife behavior. Group 2 wives use more one-up moves (26%) than do husbands (21%) and fewer one-down messages (24%) than do husbands (34%). Although not as pronounced, the reverse is the case with Group 3. Group 3 husbands use more one-up messages (27%) in comparison to wives (23%) and slightly less one-down messages (29%) than do wives (31%).

These message control differences between the couple types are further indicated by an index of the couples' domineeringness ratios. This measure of message behavior refers to a husband-wife ratio based on each person's proportion of one-up messages to their total messages. Thus, dividing the husband's score by the wife's score, a ratio of 1.0 indicates a similar or equivalent usage of one-up control behaviors by the spouses, a score larger than 1.0 signifies the husband is more domineering, and a score less than 1.0 indicates the wife is more domineering. Such a ratio can be obtained for all three types of control, but the domineeringness ratio has proven particularly useful in discriminating between satisfied and less satisfied couples. A consistent finding of previous research has been an inverse relationship between domineeringness and marital satisfaction.

The domineeringness ratio for Group 1 couples is 0.96, indicating a very similar usage of one-up control between the spouses. For Group 2 couples, the ratio is 0.82, indexing a more prevalent wife usage of one-up messages, whereas the ratio for Group 3 is 1.19, indicating the higher domineeringness of husbands.

Transactional-Level Results

As shown in Table 11.2, Group 1 couples engage in relatively few competitive, one-up symmetrical (↑↑) transactions (4.2%), whereas couples in Groups 2 and 3 enact twice the amount as Group 1. The control definition implicated in this type of interaction is one of opposition with one spouse making a one-up assertion and the other resisting this definitional stance with a one-up assertive response of his or her own.

The more "one-up" interactional flavor of Groups 2 and 3 is also indicated by their more frequent enactment of one-up transitory (↑→, →↑) interacts (18.1% and 19%, respectively) than Group 1 (13.7%). What is perhaps more noteworthy, however, is Group 1 couples' higher proportion of one-down transitory (↓→, →↓) patterns (39.1%) than that evidenced in Groups 2 (31.4%) or 3 (31.2%). As previously stated, higher proportions of one-down transitory transactions have consistently been related to indices of higher marital satisfaction. One-down transitory exchanges are representative of communication patterns in which one partner's continuation or extension of an issue or topic is accepted by the other. This pattern allows each spouse to express his or her point of view in a noncompetitive, control-neutralizing manner within a supportive interaction context. Thus, this form of transitory transaction, in combination with a reciprocal pattern of complementarity and relatively predictable, but not overly rigid, patterns of redundancy, result in more harmonious patterns of marital interaction.

These two latter styles of interaction are captured in the transactional indices of dominance and redundancy. Dominance is based on the one-up complementary transaction and indexes the percentage of the time that each spouse responds with a one-down message to the other's one-up message (dominance = given a one-up message, the proportion of contiguous one-down responses). Dividing the husband's score by the

TABLE 11.2 Transaction Type Average Percentages, by Couple Group

	High Adjustment– No Aggression	Moderate Adjustment– No Aggression	Moderate Adjustment– Physical Aggression
Symmetry			
↑↑	4.2	8.4	8.7
↓↓	9.0	6.0	6.3
→→	20.2	23.1	20.0
Complementarity			
↑↓	6.7	6.4	7.4
↓↑	7.1	6.6	7.5
Transitory			
↑→	5.9	7.7	9.0
→↑	7.8	10.4	10.0
↓→	18.3	14.5	14.4
→↓	20.8	16.9	16.8
Dominance ratio	1.10	0.62	1.42
Redundancy	51.0	43.0	35.0

wife's score yields a comparative measure of the couple's dominance pattern expressed as a ratio. Redundancy refers to the level of patterned-ness in the enactment of the different transactional types; operationally, it is an index of the sum of the absolute deviations from random use of the nine possible transactional types.

Both of these measures indicate that the more positive patterns characterize couples in Group 1. The overall dominance ratios for Groups 1, 2, and 3, respectively, are 1.10, 0.62 and 1.42. These ratios show an equivalent or shared pattern of dominance for couples in Group 1 and divergent patterns in Groups 2 and 3, with wives being more dominant in Group 2 and husbands being more dominant in Group 3.

The overall redundancy scores for the couple groups are 51, 43, and 35, respectively, for Groups 1, 2, and 3. Redundancy scores have a potential range from 0, indicating total randomness, to 177, indicating maximum rigidity by the use of only one transactional type; empirically, scores have ranged from 20 to less than 100. Across previous marital interaction studies, the average redundancy score was 54 with a standard deviation of 16. Based on these findings, Group 1 couples' redundancy score suggests a relatively stable, but not overly redundant, pattern of interaction. The score for Group 3 couples is suggestive of an overly flexible, or variant, patterning for a sufficiently stable level of predictability. Group 3 evidences the least redundancy in the two more conflict-prompting topics. For Topic 2, their redundancy score is 34 in comparison to 56 for Group 2 and 45 for Group 1, and for Topic 3, the discussion of disagreements, it drops to 29 in comparison to 32 and 48 for Groups 2 and 1, respectively.

Selected Results by Topic

Support and Nonsupport Messages. The proportion of support message used by the three couple groups described previously remains similar across the four different topic discussions. The proportion of nonsupport message usage, however, alters rather significantly across different topic discussions by couple group. Group 1 couples remain at a relatively low level of nonsupport message use across the four topics. The couples in Groups 2 and 3, however, have a pronounced rise in the percentage of nonsupportive messages in the discussion of disagreements (see Figure 11.1).

Of interest is the rise of nonsupport by Group 3 couples in the discussion of Topic 2, how they tell each other about the events of the day, and they evidence another jump in nonsupport messages—the highest of all three groups—in their discussion of disagreements. Then, all groups seem to "mellow out" in the discussion of the final topic, what it takes to have a good marriage.

One-Up Control Messages and Competitive Symmetry. The percentage of one-up control messages increases notably for Groups 2 and 3 in the discussion of Topic 3, but again Group 1 couples' use of one-up messages remains relatively constant across topics. A similar pattern emerges for competitive symmetry (see Figure 11.2). Although the use of this potentially escalating exchange remains low for Group 1 couples across all topics, Group 2 and 3 couples engage in far greater amounts of this type of transaction with Topic 3 disagreement discussions—again with Group 3 engaging in the highest proportion of competitive

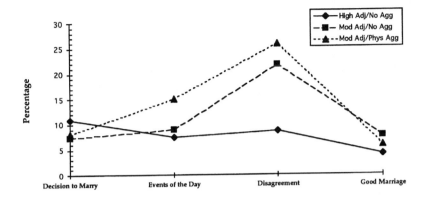

Figure 11.1. Nonsupport Message Percentages, by Topic and by Couple Group

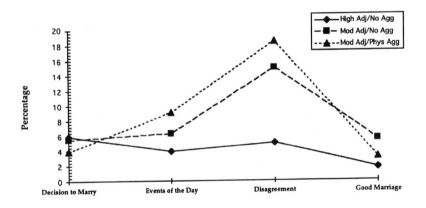

Figure 11.2. Competitive Symmetry Percentages, by Topic and by Couple Group

symmetry. Topic 4 discussions "bring" all couples back to a low level of competitive opposition.

Dominance Ratios. Couple group dominance ratios across the four topics are displayed in Figure 11.3. Topics 1, 2, and 3 show the wide disparity and type of dominance evident in Groups 2 and 3. The dominance ratios are diminished in Topic 3 due to the level of resistance shown by the reciprocal competitiveness of one-up symmetry shown in Figure 11.2. Even so, the dominance differences are still readily apparent. Only in Topic 4 do these differences disappear. Once again, the relatively stable set point of shared dominance patterns is displayed by Group 1 couples across the four different topics.

Discussion

This study describes the relational control patterns of three types of married couples: high adjustment-no aggression, moderate adjustment-no aggression, and moderate adjustment-physical aggression. The study is unique both in its use of relational control coding to study aggressive marriages and in its examination of the communication patterns of physically aggressive marriages that are nondistressed.

Many of the trends noted here corroborate previous research on the communication patterns of high-adjustment couples. In the present study, high adjustment-no aggression couples, compared to both the other couple types, displayed the highest proportion of support messages, one-down moves, and one-down/one-across transitory interacts. They displayed the lowest enactment of nonsupport messages, one-up control, competitive one-up symmetrical transactions, and one-up/one-across transitory interacts. Thus, the work of Rogers and others (see for example Courtright et al., 1979: Escudero & Gutierrez, 1987; Millar et al., 1979) who demonstrate that reciprocal patterns of complementarity and a lack of one-up control behavior are associated with higher marital adjustment is replicated in the present study.

Analysis of dominance and gender patterns yielded some interesting differences between groups. Moderate adjustment-physical aggression husbands tended to use more one-up messages than did either the moderate adjustment-no aggression husbands or the high adjustment-no aggression husbands. This pattern was also evident in the domineeringness ratio and the transactional assessment of dominance; both of these measures demonstrated that moderate adjustment-physical aggression husbands were somewhat more domineering and dominant than their wives. In contrast, high adjustment-no aggression husbands

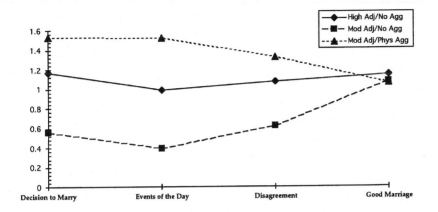

Figure 11.3. Dominance Ratio, by Couple and by Topic

and wives were very similar in their use of one-up control and egalitarian patterns of dominance. In addition, high adjustment-no aggression couples displayed lower levels of both husband and wife use of one-up messages than did the other two couple types.

These findings are quite complementary to the work of Babcock et al. (1993) who studied demand-withdraw patterns among nondistressed, distressed, and distressed-aggressive couples. Distressed-aggressive husbands were more likely to report the husband demand-wife withdraw interaction pattern than were nondistressed or distressed husbands; their wives also reported a high likelihood of wife demand-husband withdraw behaviors. Thus, both spouses in the aggressive marriage report being in the demanding role, and both report withdrawing from the other's demands—a pattern that is likely to lead to a struggle for control. In contrast, the distressed couples tended to report an equally high level of wife demand-husband withdraw behavior and a significantly lower level of husband demand-wife withdraw behavior. The findings of the present study extend Babcock et al.'s results by demonstrating the presence of different dominance patterns in moderately adjusted couples; although clearly tentative, the patterns of husband dominance in physically aggressive couples and wife dominance in nonaggressive couples may have implications regarding the use or nonuse of physical aggression.

Babcock et al. (1993) suggest that physically aggressive husbands lack power in the marital relationship and compensate for that lack through the use of aggression. Alternatively, physically aggressive husbands may use aggression as a tactic of control in situations in which they feel threatened by the demands of their wives. Certainly, the physically aggressive couples in the present study could also be characterized as engaging in a power struggle, given the high level of one-up messages and competitive symmetry they displayed. The use of frequent one-up messages suggests an argumentative stance (Millar & Rogers, 1987), a stance that Sabourin et al. (1993) hypothesize leads aggressive husbands to interpret even neutral messages as a threat to their control of the relationship.

During the discussion of a disagreement, in addition to displaying the tendency toward husband dominance, moderate adjustment-physical aggression couples also displayed the highest levels of nonconstructive communication patterns—nonsupport messages and competitive symmetry. Similar nonconstructive approaches to conflict are seen in other analyses of interaction in the physically aggressive marriage (see Cordova et al., 1993; Lloyd, 1990; Margolin, John, & Gleberman, 1988). Gage (1988) and Sabourin (1995) also note heightened levels of competitive symmetry in physically aggressive marriages.

Perhaps the best way of illustrating the combination of these differences in interactional style between high adjustment-no aggression, moderate adjustment-no aggression, and moderate adjustment-physical aggression couples is to provide examples of the couples' interactions from the transcripts. All three examples are from the couples' discussions of disagreements. The following transcript illustrates the relatively egalitarian, noncompetitive interaction that characterizes the high adjustment-no aggression couples:

Group 1 couple (high adjustment-no aggression)

→ W: I don't think we have major disagreements, just minor ones, like when to sell the car. I think we're pretty considerate of one another's ideas and feelings.

↓ H: Uh huh, I think we're both willing to compromise and listen to each other's ideas and in the majority of cases, willing to meet halfway.

↓ W: Yeah.

→/ H: Like there's times when I'm, I don't know, sort of impulsive and
↓   then it gets tempered with time, but probably at the moment I might
          be difficult to discuss something with. But . . . am I?

→ W: Oh maybe, like with that car, but over time I think that if we needed
          to, you would buy a new car, even if you said you wouldn't.

→ H: Humm.

↓ W: I think you're a pretty reasonable person.

↓/ H: Yeah, I am . . . and I'm really committed to keeping that car another
→   year. (laugh)

↑ W: [You're so full of it. (laughs)]

→ H: I think we do a good job though, of working, trying to find
          solutions. And if there are times when we don't, we just agree that
          we don't agree.

↓ W: That's true.

→ H: You know . . . I really don't want to buy a new car.

↑ W: [You're just waiting for air bags to come out on the passenger's side.]

→ H: Do you know what though, it doesn't make sense to do that.

↓ W: To wait?

↓ H: Yeah, I mean, why wait for a safer car when you're driving one that's
          not? That's paradoxical thinking.

↓ W: It is kind of odd.

→ H: You're driving a death trap until the safer car comes out.

Brackets indicate successful talk over.

The noncompetitive and largely one-across, one-down nature of
this interaction sequence is further illustrated in the cumulative mapping of control movements shown in Figure 11.4.

The interaction of the moderate adjustment-no aggression couple
stands in some contrast to the example provided above. In the following
example and the sequential map in Figure 11.4, the more competitive
nature of the interaction comes through as well as a tendency toward
more attempts at dominance:

Group 2 couple (moderate adjustment-no aggression)

↑ W: Every house we lived in you put your fist through the wall.

↑ H: [Oh come on, give me a break. I did not. I didn't do it in Phoenix.]

↑ W: (Yes you did.)

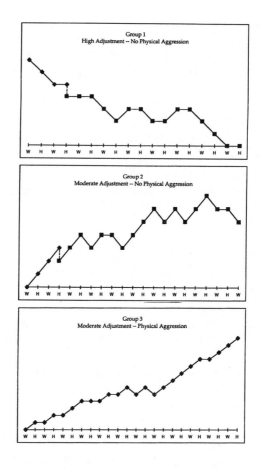

Figure 11.4. Cumulative Control Mapping

↑/↓   H: Did not, when?

↑   W: [Yes you did . . . you did it in Phoenix in the hall.]

↑   H: Did not, did not.

↓   W: Didn't you do it in Phoenix?

↑   H: No.

→   W: You did it in Oregon.

↓   H: Oregon, did I?

↑   W: Uh huh. You did it in our apartment over there at . . .

↑   H: [I did not.]

↑   W: Yes you did.

↓   H: Maybe at the . . . did I?

↑   W: [At the apartment and I was so shocked, cause here was this wonderful man . . .]

↓   H: I have a, I have a bad temper, don't I?

↑   W: [Yeah, I think you've controlled it over the years real well.]

↑   H: [I think it takes a lot for me to get there . . .]

↓   W: I think so too.

→   H: But if I get there, then whew. I try, I try to control it.

↓   W: [Don't you think we deal with our problems a lot better than we used to?]

Brackets indicate successful talk over; parentheses indicate unsuccessful talk over.

The final transcript highlights the more nonconstructive and competitive nature of interaction seen in the moderate adjustment-physical aggression couples. The cumulative map in Figure 11.4 reflects the competitive symmetry of this couple as well. Note also the tendency of this husband to respond to his wife with one-up assertions:

Group 3 couple (moderate adjustment-physical aggression)

→   W: I think our biggest disagreement is that you have different things on this list than I do. You know, on our list.

↑   H: I don't think that's that big a disagreement. I get mad when you let an event take over, instead of family. Like when we went to St. George. You were so uptight about getting out of town on time that you were just short with everybody and upset everybody. We were just going on vacation.

→   W: I don't know, I think I wouldn't have felt like that if we weren't going with someone else.

↑   H: [It's the same . . . like on Thanksgiving.]

→   W: That's the same because someone was waiting for us.

↑   H: Because what's the point?

↑   W: I hate to let people down. I hate to be late.

→   H: Like on Mary Ann's birthday you got all upset.

→   W: Because we were late.

↑   H: [Oh, big deal.]

→ W: I was running around trying to get everybody ready . . .

↑ H: [It's not worth it, making people you care about suffer at the expense of this.]

↓ W: I know that's true, that's a bad point of mine. I try to change but I can't. What do I do?

↑ H: [I don't know. You just lighten up.]

↓ W: Well, I agree, that's a problem I've got to work on, but I also think that your . . . um this invisible list that we have . . .

↑ H: Your invisible list.

↑ W: [My list is different than what your list is.]

↑ H: (I don't have a list. You have a list.)

↑ W: [I have a list and your stereo wasn't on it; we needed a kitchen table and you went and bought a dang stereo.]

↑ H: I'll tell you the other thing that bugs me . . . is when you go charge up all the credit cards.

→ W: But see, I, I don't like to charge, but I have to when it's such a good deal and on sale.

↑ H: [You don't like to charge? How come all my cards are maxed out?]

↑ W: This is what bugs me about you, is when you go and buy the most expensive thing for the car. And it doesn't really matter.

↑ H: It does too matter.

Brackets indicate successful talk over; parentheses indicate unsuccessful talk over.

The cumulative patterns identified in the present study, in tandem with the work of other researchers studying interaction patterns and aggression, help sketch an emerging portrait of the communication patterns of the physically aggressive marriage. Based on the present study, and Sabourin's (1995) work, couples who report physical aggression in a context of either moderate or low marital happiness are characterized by higher levels of nonsupport messages and competitive symmetry—a pattern of both husband and wife attempting to exert control. When physical aggression is accompanied by marital distress, marital interaction is characterized by high levels of aversiveness, reciprocity of negative behavior and anger responses, overt hostility, defensiveness, both husband and wife engaging in patterns of demand-withdraw, and poor problem-solving skills (Babcock et al., 1993; Burman, Margolin, & John, 1993; Cordova et al., 1993; Margolin, Burman, & John, 1989). Certainly, an interesting question for future investigation is whether the patterns of competition and control seen in these moderately adjusted-aggressive couples sow the seeds for a highly aversive marital climate over time.

It is important to keep in mind that the relational control patterns of aggressive couples described in this chapter all occurred in a context of relative marital satisfaction. Indeed, in the analysis of daily marital interaction, adjusted-aggressive couples were highly similar to their adjusted-nonaggressive counterparts, with both groups evidencing high levels of positive daily interaction and low levels of negative interaction (see Lloyd, 1996). Certainly, we think it is safe to speculate that a positive marital climate, one characterized by positive daily interaction and feelings of satisfaction with the relationship, may serve to buffer or mediate the negative impact of competing for relational control and dominance that was evident in the transactional analysis. Thus, these couples remain relatively happy with each other and their relationship despite some nonconstructive and negative interaction patterns (not the least of which is the aggression itself).

Again, the importance of early intervention is clear (see also Lloyd, 1996). Breaking patterns of aggression before they have been linked to highly rigid interaction patterns and marital distress seems paramount. Assessing and addressing issues of dominance and control in the marriage may be an important avenue for changing patterns of aggression, particularly given that aggression serves as a highly potent strategy of exerting control (Lloyd & Emery, 1994). It seems that we can indeed learn a great deal even from such paradoxes as the coexistence of physical aggression and marital happiness.

References

Abel, G., Mittleman, M., & Becker, J. (1984). *Sexual offenders: Results of assessment and recommendations for treatment.* Unpublished manuscript available from New York State Psychiatric Institute, Sexual Behavior Clinic.

Acitelli, L. K., & Antonucci, T. C. (1994). Gender differences in the link between marital support and satisfaction in older adults. *Journal of Personality and Social Psychology, 67,* 688-698.

Ainsworth, M. D. S., Blehar, M. C., Waters, E., & Wall, S. (1978). *Patterns of attachment.* Hillsdale, NJ: Lawrence Erlbaum.

Aizenman, M., & Kelley, G. (1988). The incidence of violence and acquaintance rape in dating relationships among college men and women. *Journal of College Student Development, 29,* 305-311.

Allbritten, W. L., & Bogal-Allbritten, R. B. (1985). The hidden victims: Courtship violence among college students. *Journal of College Student Personnel, 26,* 201-204.

Allen, R., & Oliver, J. (1982). The effects of child maltreatment on language development. *Child Abuse and Neglect, 6,* 299-305.

Ammerman, R. T., & Hersen, M. (Eds.). (1990). *Children at risk: An evaluation of factors contributing to child abuse and neglect.* New York: Plenum.

Andersen, P. A., Lustig, M. W., & Andersen, J. F. (1987). Regional patterns of communication in the United States: A theoretical perspective. *Communication Monographs, 54,* 128-144.

Anson, O., & Sagy, S. (1995). Marital violence: Comparing women in violent and nonviolent unions. *Human Relations, 48,* 285-305.

Apt, C., & Hurlbert, D. F. (1993). The sexuality of women in physically abusive marriages: A comparative study. *Journal of Family Violence, 8*(1), 57-69.

Arias, I., Samios, M., & O'Leary, K. D. (1987). Prevalence and correlates of physical aggression during courtship. *Journal of Interpersonal Violence, 2,* 82-90.

Atkin, C., & Greenberg, B. (1977, August). *Parental mediation of children's social behavior learning from television.* Paper presented at the 60th annual meeting of the Association for Education in Journalism, Madison, WI.

Averill J. R. (1983). Studies on anger and aggression: Implications for theories of emotion. *American Psychologist, 38,* 1145-1160.

Avni, N. (1991). Battered wives: The home as total institution. *Violence and Victims, 6*(2), 137-149.

Awad, G. A., Saunders, E., & Levene, J. (1985). A clinical study of male adolescent sexual offenders. *International Journal of Offender Therapy and Comparative Criminology, 28*(1), 105-115.

Babcock, J. C., Waltz, J., Jacobson, N. S., & Gottman, J. M. (1993). Power and violence: The relation between communication patterns, power discrepancies, and domestic violence. Special section: Couples and couple therapy. *Journal of Consulting and Clinical Psychology, 61*(1), 40-50.

Baily, T., & Baily, W. (1986). *Operational definitions of child emotional maltreatment.* Augusta, ME: Department of Human Services.

Bandura, A. (1969). *Principles of behavior modification.* New York: Holt, Rinehart & Winston.

Bandura, A. (1973). *Aggression: A social learning analysis.* Beverly Hills, CA: Sage.

Barling, J., & O'Leary, K. D., Jouriles, E. N., Vivian, D., & MacEwan, K. E. (1987). Factor similarity of the conflict tactics scales across samples, spouses, and sites: Issues and implications. *Journal of Family Violence, 2,* 37-54.

Barnes, H. L., & Olson, D. H. (1982). *Parent-adolescent communication scale.* St. Paul: University of Minnesota, Family Social Science.

Barnes, H. L., & Olson, D. H. (1985). Parent-adolescent communication and the circumplex model. *Child Development, 56,* 438-447.

Baron, R. (1977). *Human aggression.* New York: Plenum.

Baron, R. A. (1988). Negative effects of destructive criticism: Impact on conflict, self-efficacy, and task performance. *Journal of Applied Psychology, 73,* 199-207.

Bartle, S. E., & Rosen, K. H. (1994). Individuation and relationship violence. *American Journal of Family Therapy, 22,* 222-236.

Bateson, G., Jackson, D. D., Haley, J., & Weakland, J. H. (1981). Toward a theory of schizophrenia. In R. J. Green & J. L. Framo (Eds.), *Family therapy: Major contributions* (pp. 41-104). New York: International Universities Press.

Bauer, W. D., & Twentyman, C. T. (1985). Abusing, neglectful, and comparison mothers' responses to child-related and non-child-related stressors. *Journal of Counseling and Clinical Psychology, 53,* 335-343.

Baum, G. (1994, July 20). The forgotten victims. *Los Angeles Times,* pp. E1, E6.

Baumrind, D. (1975). The contributions of the family to the development of competence in children. *Schizophrenia Bulletin, 14,* 12-37.

Baumrind, D. (1991). Effective parenting during the early adolescent transition. In P. A. Cowan & M. Hetherington (Eds.), *Family transitions* (pp. 111-163). Hillsdale, NJ: Lawrence Erlbaum.

Baumrind, D., & Black, A. E. (1967). Socialization practices associated with dimensions of competence in preschool boys and girls. *Child Development, 38,* 291-327.

Bavelock, S. J. (1984). *Handbook for the adult-adolescent parenting inventory.* Eau Claire, WI: Family Developmental Resources.

Baxter, L. (1988). A dialectical perspective on communication strategies in relationship development. In S. Duck (Ed.), *Handbook of personal relationships* (pp. 257-274). Chichester, UK: Wiley.

Baxter, L. A. (1985). Accomplishing relationship disengagement. In S. Duck & D. Perlman (Eds.), *Understanding personal relationships: An interdisciplinary approach* (pp. 243-65). London: Sage.

Bayer, C. L., & Cegala, D. J. (1992). Trait verbal aggressiveness and argumentativeness: Relations with parenting style. Special issue: Communication in personal relationships. *Western Journal of Communication, 56*(3), 301-310.

Becker, J. V., & Abel, G. G. (1985). Methodological and ethical issues in evaluating and treating adolescent sex offenders. In E. M. Otey & G. D. Ryan (Eds.), *Adolescent sex offenders: Issues in research and treatment* (pp. 109-129). Rockville, MD: U.S. Department of Health and Human Services.

Bell, C. C., & Jenkins, E. J. (1993). Community violence and children on Chicago, southside. In D. Reiss, J. E. Richters, M. Radke-Yarrow, & D. Scharff (Eds.), *Children and violence* (pp. 46-54). New York: Guilford.

Belsky, J. (1993). Etiology of child maltreatment: A developmental-ecological analysis. *Psychology Bulletin, 114*(3), 413-434.

Beneke, T. (1982). *Men who rape.* New York: St. Martin's.

Benoit, W. L., & Benoit, P. J. (1990). Aggravated and mitigated opening utterances. *Argumentation, 4,* 171-183.

Benoit, W. L., & Cahn, D. D. (1994). A communication approach to everyday argument. In D. D. Cahn (Ed.), *Conflict in personal relationships* (pp. 163-182). Hillsdale, NJ: Lawrence Erlbaum.

Bera, W. H. (1985). *A preliminary investigation of a typology of adolescent sex offenders and their family systems.* Unpublished master's thesis, University of Minnesota.

Berger, P., & Luckmann, T. (1967). *The social construction of reality: A treatise in the sociology of knowledge.* Garden City, NY: Doubleday.

Bergman, L. (1992). Dating violence among high school students. *Social Work, 37,* 21-27.

Billingham, R. E. (1987). Courtship violence: The patterns of conflict resolution strategies across seven levels of emotional commitment. *Family Relations, 36,* 283-289.

Billingham, R. E., & Sack, A. R. (1987). Conflict tactics and the level of emotional commitment among unmarrieds. *Human Relations, 40*(1), 59-74.

Billings, A. (1979). Conflict resolution in distressed and non-distressed married couples. *Journal of Consulting and Clinical Psychology, 47,* 368-376.

Bird, G. W., Stith, S. M., & Schladale, J. (1991). Psychological resources, coping strategies, and negotiation styles as discriminators of violence in dating relationships. *Family Relations, 40,* 45-50.

Bischof, G., Stith, S., & Whitney, M. (1995). Family environments of adolescent sex offenders and other juvenile delinquents. *Adolescence, 30,* 157-170.

Bischof, G., Stith, S., & Wilson, S. (1992). A comparison of the family systems of adolescent sexual offenders and nonsexual offending delinquents. *Family Relations, 41,* 318-323.

Block, J. H., Block, J., & Morrison, A. (1981). Parental agreement-disagreement in child-rearing orientations and gender-related personality correlates in children. *Child Development, 49,* 1163-1173.

Bograd, M. (1984). Family systems approaches to wife battering: A feminist critique. *American Journal of Orthopsychiatry, 54,* 558-568.

Bograd, M. (1990). Why we need gender to understand human violence. *Journal of Interpersonal Violence, 5,* 132-135.

Bonanno, G. A., Davis, P. J., Singer, J. L., & Schwartz, G. E. (1991). The repressor personality and avoidant information processing: A dichotic listening study. *Journal of Research in Personality, 25,* 386-401.

Boszormenyi-Nagy, I., & Spark, G. (1973). *Invisible loyalties.* New York: Harper & Row.

Bousha, D. M., & Twentyman, C. T. (1984). Mother-child interactional style in abuse, neglect, and control groups: Naturalistic observations in the home. *Journal of Abnormal Psychology, 93,* 106-114.

Bowlby, J. (1982). *Attachment and loss. Vol. 1: Attachment* (2nd Rev. ed.). New York: Basic Books.

Brassard, M., Hart, S., & Hardy, D. (1993). The psychological maltreatment rating scales. *Child Abuse and Neglect, 17,* 715-729.

Breines, W., & Gordon, L. (1983). The new scholarship on family violence. *Signs: Journal of Women in Culture and Society, 8*(3), 490-531.

Bretherton, I. (1993). Theoretical contributions from developmental psychology. In P. Boss, W. Doherty, R. LaRossa, W. Schumm, & S. Steinmetz (Eds.), *Sourcebook of family theories and methods: A contextual approach* (pp. 275-297). New York: Plenum.

Briere, J. (1987). Predicting self-reported likelihood of battering: Attitudes and childhood experiences. *Journal of Research in Personality, 21,* 61-69.

Briere, J., & Runtz, M. (1988). Multivariate correlates of childhood psychological and physical maltreatment. *Child Abuse and Neglect, 12,* 331-341.

Brown, P., & Elliott, R. (1965). Control of aggression in a nursery school class. *Journal of Experiential Child Psychology, 2,* 103-107.

Brown, S. (1984). Social class, child maltreatment, and delinquent behavior. *Criminology, 22,* 259-278.

Burgdorf, K. (1980). *Recognition and reporting of child maltreatment.* Rockville, MD: Westat.

Burgess, R., & Conger, R. (1977). Family interaction patterns related to child abuse and neglect. *Child Abuse and Neglect, 1,* 269-277.

Burgess, R. L., Anderson, E. A., Schellenbach, C. J., & Conger, R. D. (1981). A social interactional approach to the study of abusive families. In J. P. Vincent (Ed.), *Advances in family interaction: Assessment and theory: Vol. 2* (pp. 1-46). Greenwich, CT: JAI.

Burgoon, M. (1991). Verbal aggression: A critical reply to reported gender differences. *Psychological Reports, 69,* 1202.

Burke, P. J., Stets, J. E., & Pirog-Good, M. A. (1989). Gender identity, self-esteem, and physical and sexual abuse in dating relationships. In M. A. Pirog-Good & J. E. Stets (Eds.), *Violence in dating relationships* (pp. 72-93). New York: Praeger.

Burman, B., John, R. S., & Margolin, G. (1992). Observed patterns of conflict in violent, nonviolent, and nondistressed couples. *Behavioral Assessment, 14*(1), 15-37.

Burman, B., Margolin, G., & John, R. S. (1993). America's angriest home videos: Behavioral contingencies observed in home reenactments of marital conflict. *Journal of Consulting and Clinical Psychology, 61*(1), 28-39.

Buss, A., & Durkee, A. (1957). An inventory for assessing different kinds of hostility. *Journal of Consulting Psychology, 21,* 343-349.

Buss, A. H., & Perry, M. (1992). The aggression questionnaire. *Journal of Personality and Social Psychology, 63,* 452-459.

Buss, D. M., Gomes, M., Higgins, D. S., & Lauterbach, K. (1987). Tactics of manipulation. *Journal of Personality and Social Psychology, 52,* 1219-1229.

Buttny, R. (1990). Blame-account sequences in therapy: The negotiation of relational meanings. *Semiotica, 78,* 219-247.

Cahn, D. D. (1987). *Letting go: A practical theory of relationship disengagement and reengagement.* Albany: State University of New York Press.

Cahn, D. D. (1992). *Conflict in intimate relationships.* New York: Guilford.

Cahn, D. D. (1996). A communication perspective on family violence. In D. Cahn & S. Lloyd (Eds.), *Family violence from a communication perspective* (pp. 1-19). Thousand Oaks, CA: Sage.

Campbell, A., & Muncer, S. (1987). Models of anger and aggression in the social talk of women and men. *Journal for the Theory of Social Behaviour, 17,* 489-511.

Campbell, A., Muncer, S., & Coyle, E. (1992). Social representation of aggression as an explanation of gender differences: A preliminary study. *Aggressive Behavior, 18,* 95-108.

Camras, L., & Rappaport, S. (1993). Conflict behaviors of maltreated and nonmaltreated children. *Child Abuse and Neglect, 17,* 455-464.

Carlson, B. E. (1984). Children's observations of interpersonal violence. In A. R. Roberts (Ed.), *Battered women and their families* (pp. 147-167). New York: Springer.

Carpenter, B. N. (1987). The relationship between psychopathology and self-disclosure: An interference/competence model. In V. J. Derlega & J. H. Berg (Eds.), *Self-disclosure: Theory, research, and therapy* (pp. 203-227). New York: Plenum.

Carter, J. (1994, Spring). The contagiousness of verbal abuse. *Mothering,* 108-110.

Cate, R. M., Henton, J. M., Koval, J., Christopher, F. S., & Lloyd, S. (1982). Premarital abuse: A social psychological perspective. *Journal of Family Issues, 3*(1), 79-90.

Cate, R. M., & Lloyd, S. A. (1992). *Courtship.* Newbury Park, CA: Sage.

Caulfield, M. B., & Riggs, D. S. (1992). The assessment of dating aggression: Empirical evaluation of the Conflict Tactics Scale. *Journal of Interpersonal Violence, 7*(4), 549-558.

Chilamkurti, C., & Milner, J. S. (1993). Perceptions and evaluations of child transgressions and disciplinary techniques in high- and low-risk mothers and their children. *Child Development, 64,* 1801-1814.

Chodorow, N., & Contratto, S. (1982). The fantasy of the perfect mother. In B. Thorne & M. Yalom (Eds.), *Rethinking the family: Some feminist questions* (pp. 54-75). White Plains, NY: Longman.

Christensen, A., & Arkowitz, H. (1974). Preliminary report on practice dating and feedback as treatment for college dating problems. *Journal of Counseling Psychology, 21,* 92-95.

Christensen, A., & King. C. E. (1982). Telephone survey of daily marital behavior. *Behavioral Assessment, 4,* 327-338.

Clark, M. L., Beckett, J., Wells, M., & Dungee-Anderson, D. (1994). Courtship violence among African-American students. *Journal of Black Psychology, 20,* 264-281.

Clark, R. A., & Delia, J. G. (1979). Topoi and rhetorical competence. *Quarterly Journal of Speech, 65,* 187-206.

Claussen, A. H., & Crittenden, P. M. (1991). Physical and psychological maltreatment: Relations among types of maltreatment. *Child Abuse and Neglect, 15,* 5-18.

Clearinghouse of Child Abuse Prevention. (1994). *Fact sheet #2: National and local child abuse statistics '94*. Cincinnati, OH: Planned Parenthood Association of Cincinnati, Inc., 2314 Auburn Ave., 45219.

Cloven, D. H., & Roloff, M. E. (1993). The chilling effect of aggressive potential on the expression of complaints in intimate relationships. *Communication Monographs, 60*, 199-219.

Coleman, D. H., & Straus, M. A. (1986). Marital power, conflict, and violence in a nationally representative sample of American couples. *Violence and Victims, 1,* 141-157.

Coleman, K. H. (1980). Conjugal violence: What 33 men report. *Journal of Marital and Family Therapy, 6*, 207-213.

Coley, S. M., & Beckett, J. O. (1988). Black battered women: A review of empirical literature. *Journal of Counseling and Development, 66*(6), 266-270.

Cooley, C. H. (1922). *Human nature and the social order*. New York: Scribner.

Cordova, J. V., Jacobson, N. S., Gottman, J. M., Rushe, R., & Cox, G. (1993). Negative reciprocity and communication in couples with a violent husband. *Journal of Abnormal Psychology, 102*(4), 559-564.

Coser, L. (1956). *The functions of social conflict*. New York: Free Press.

Courtright, J. A., Millar, F. E., & Rogers, E. (1979). Domineeringness and dominance: Replication and expansion. *Communication Monographs, 46*, 179-192.

Courtright, J. A., Millar, F. E., Rogers, E., & Bagarozzi, D. (1990). Interaction dynamics of relational negotiation: Reconciliation versus termination of distressed relationships. *Western Journal of Communication, 54*, 429-453.

Cox, H. (1994). Excising verbal abuse. *Today's OR Nurse, 16*(1), 38-42.

Crelinsten, R. D. (1987). Terrorism as political communication: The relationship between the controller and the controlled. In P. Wilkinson & A. M. Stewart (Eds.), *Contemporary research on terrorism* (pp. 3-23). Aberdeen, Scotland: Aberdeen University Press.

Crittenden, P. (1992). Children's strategies for coping with adverse home environments: An interpretation using attachment theory. *Child Abuse and Neglect, 16*, 329-343.

Crittenden, P. M. (1993). An information-processing perspective on the behavior of neglectful parents. *Criminal Justice and Behavior, 20*(1), 27-48.

Crosbie-Burnett, M., & Lewis, E. A. (1993). Theoretical contributions from social and cognitive-behavioral psychology. In P. Boss, W. Doherty, R. LaRossa, W. Schumm, & S. Steinmetz (Eds.), *Sourcebook of family theories and methods: A contextual approach* (pp. 531-558). New York: Plenum.

Cummings, E. M., & Davies, P. (1994). *Children and marital conflict: The impact of family dispute and resolution*. New York: Guilford.

Danziger, K. (1976). *Interpersonal communication*. New York: Pergamon.

Daro, D., Abrahams, N., & Robson, K. (1988, May). *Reducing child abuse 20% by 1990: 1985-1986 baseline data*. Chicago: National Center on Child Abuse Prevention Research.

Daro, D., & Wiese, D. (1995). *Current trends in child abuse reporting and fatalities: NCPCA's 1994 annual fifty state survey*. Chicago: National Committee to Prevent Child Abuse, 332 S. Michigan Ave., Suite 1600, 60604.

Davidovich, J. R. (1990). Men who abuse their spouses: Social and psychological supports. *Journal of Offender Counseling, Services and Rehabilitation, 15*(1), 27-44.

Davies, P., & Cummings, E. M. (1994). Marital conflict and child adjustment: An emotional security hypothesis. *Psychological Bulletin, 116,* 387-411.

Davis, G. E., & Leitenberg, H. (1987). Adolescent sex offenders. *Psychological Bulletin, 101,* 417-427.

Dean, D. (1979, July-August). Emotional abuse of children. *Children Today,* 18-22.

Dekovic, M., & Janssens, J. M. A. M. (1992). Parent's child-rearing style and child's sociometric status. *Developmental Psychology, 28(5),* 925-932.

Dell, P. F. (1988). Violence and the systemic view: The problem of power. *Family Process, 28(1),* 1-14.

DeMaris, A. (1987). The efficacy of a spouse abuse model in accounting for courtship violence. *Journal of Family Issues, 8,* 291-305.

Denzin, N. K. (1984). Toward a phenomenology of domestic family violence. *American Journal of Sociology, 90,* 483-513.

DeTurck, M. A. (1987). When communication fails: Physical aggression as a compliance-gaining strategy. *Communication Monographs, 54(1),* 106-112.

Dietrich, D., Berkowitz, L., Kadushin, A., & McGloin, J. (1990). Some factors influencing abusers' justification of child abuse. *Child Abuse and Neglect, 14(3),* 337-345.

Dobash, R., & Dobash, R. (1988). Research as social action: The struggle for battered women. In K. Yllö & M. Bograd (Eds.), *Feminist perspectives on wife abuse* (pp. 51-74). Newbury Park, CA: Sage.

Dobash, R. E., & Dobash, R. P. (1979). *Violence against wives: A case against patriarchy.* New York: Free Press.

Dominick, J., Richman, S., & Wurtzel, A. (1979). Problem solving in TV shows population with children. *Journalism Quarterly, 56(3),* 455-463.

Dornbusch, S. M., Ritter, P. L., Leiderman, P. H., Roberts, D. F., & Fraleigh, M. J. (1987). The relation of parenting style to adolescent school performance. *Child Development, 58,* 1244-1257.

Downs, W., Miller, B., & Gondoli, D. (1987). Childhood experience of parental physical violence for alcoholic women as compared with a randomly selected household sample of women. *Violence and Victims, 2(4),* 225-240.

Dreikurs, R. (1964). *Children the challenge.* New York: Duell, Sloan and Pearce.

Driscoll, R., Davis, K. E., & Lipetz, M. E. (1972). Parental interference and romantic love: The Romeo and Juliet effect. *Journal of Personality and Social Psychology, 24,* 1-10.

Duhon-Haynes, G. M., & Duhon-Sells, R. M. (1991). *Domestic violence: Its past, causes and effects, and implications for society* (Historical materials 060; Reports—Descriptive 141). Louisiana.

Dutton, D., & Painter, S. L. (1981). Traumatic bonding: The development of emotional attachment in battered women and other relationships of intermittent abuse. *Victimology: An International Journal, 6,* 139-155.

Dutton, D. G. (1988). *The domestic assault of women: Psychological and criminal justice perspectives.* Boston: Allyn & Bacon.

Dutton, D. G., & Browning, J. J. (1988). Power struggles and intimacy anxieties as causative factors of violence in intimate relationships. In G. Russell (Ed.), *Violence in intimate relationships* (pp. 163-176). Newbury Park, CA: Sage.

Dutton, D. G., Saunders, K., Starzomski, A., & Bartholomew, K. (1994). Intimacy-anger and insecure attachment as precursors of abuse in intimate relationships. *Journal of Applied Social Psychology, 24,* 1367-1386.

Dutton, D. G., & Starzomski, A. J. (1993). Borderline personality in perpetrators of psychological and physical abuse. *Violence and Victims, 8,* 327-337.

Dutton, D. L., & Painter, S. L. (1993). Emotional attachments in abusive relationships: A test of traumatic bonding theory. *Violence and Victims, 8,* 105-120.

Easterbrooks, M. A., & Emde, R. N. (1988). Marital and parent-child relationships: The role of affect in the family system. In R. A. Hinde & J. Stevenson-Hinde (Eds.), *Relationships within families: Mutual influences* (pp. 83-103). Oxford, UK: Clarendon.

Eddy, D. (1990, March). *Strategic therapy with juvenile sex offenders.* Paper presented at the Thirteenth Annual Family Therapy Network Symposium, Washington, DC.

Edleson, J. L., Eisikovits, Z., & Guttmann, E. (1985). Men who batter women: A critical review of the evidence. *Journal of Family Issues, 6,* 227-249.

Edleson, J. L., Eisikovits, Z. C., Guttmann, E., & Sela-Amit, M. (1991). Cognitive and interpersonal factors in woman abuse. *Journal of Family Violence, 6*(2), 167-182.

Edmunds, G., & Kendrick, D. (1980). *The measurement of human aggressiveness.* New York: John Wiley.

Egeland, B., Sroufe, A., & Erickson, M. (1984). The developmental consequence of different patterns of maltreatment. *New Directions for Child Development, 7*(4), 459-469.

Eisikovits, Z., & Peled, P. (1990). Qualitative research on spouse abuse. In D. J. Besharov (Ed.), *Family violence: Research and public issues* (pp. 1-13). Washington, DC: AEI Press.

Ekman, P., & Friesco, W. (1982). Felt, fault, and miserable smiles. *Journal of Nonverbal Behavior, 6*(4), 238-258.

Else, L., Wonderlich, S. A., Beatty, W. W., & Christie, D. W. (1993). Personality characteristics of men who physically abuse women. *Hospital and Community Psychiatry, 44*(1), 54-58.

Emery, R. E. (1982). Interparental conflict and the children of discord and divorce. *Psychological Bulletin, 92,* 310-330.

Emery, R. E., Fincham, F. D., & Cummings, E. M. (1992). Parenting in context: Systemic thinking about parental conflict and its influence on children. *Journal of Consulting and Clinical Psychology, 60,* 909-912.

Engfer, A. (1988). The interrelatedness of marriage and the mother-child relationship. In R. A. Hinde & J. Stevenson-Hinde (Eds.), *Relationships within families: Mutual influences* (pp. 104-118). Oxford, UK: Clarendon.

Erel, O., & Burman, B. (1995). Interrelatedness of marital relations and parent-child relations: A meta-analytic review. *Psychological Bulletin, 118,* 108-132.

Escudero, V., & Gutierrez, E. (1987). *A sequential perspective on the relational control dimension of communication: Interpersonal control and conflict.* Unpublished manuscript, Universidad de Santiago de Compostela, Departmento de Psicologia y Psicobiologia, Santiago de Compostela, Espana.

Escudero, V., Rogers, L. E., & Gutierrez, E. (in press). Patterns of relational control and nonverbal affect in clinic and nonclinic couples. *Journal of Social and Personal Relationships.*

Escudero, V., Rogers, L. E., Gutierrez, E., & Caceres, J. (in press). Relational control and nonverbal affect in marital conflict: An exploratory study. *Journal of Family Therapy.*

Fairhurst, G. T., Rogers, L. E., & Sarr, R. (1987). Manager-subordinate control patterns and judgments about the relationship. In M. Burgoon (Ed.), *Communication yearbook 10* (pp. 395-415). New Brunswick, NJ: Transaction Books.

Fantuzzo, J. W., & Lindquist, C. V. (1989). The effects of observing conjugal violence on children: A review and analysis of research methodology. *Journal of Family Violence, 4,* 77-93.

Fauber, R. L., Forehand, R., Thomas, A. M., & Wierson, M. (1990). A mediational model of the impact of marital conflict on adolescent adjustment in intact and divorced families: The role of disrupted parenting. *Child Development, 61,* 1112-1123.

Fauber, R. L., & Long, N. (1991). Children in context: The role of the family in child psychotherapy. *Journal of Consulting and Clinical Psychology, 59,* 813-820.

Fein, G. G. (1979). Play with actions and objects. In B. Sutton-Smith (Ed.), *Play and Learning* (pp. 69-82). New York: Gardener Press.

Feld, S. L., & Straus, M. A. (1990). Escalation and desistance from wife assault in marriage. In M. A. Straus & R. J. Gelles (Eds.), *Physical violence in American families* (pp. 489-505). New Brunswick, NJ: Transaction Publishing.

Felson, R. B. (1978). Aggression as impression management. *Social Psychology, 41,* 205-213.

Felson, R. B. (1982). Impression management and the escalation of aggression and violence. *Social Psychology Quarterly, 45,* 245-254.

Felson, R. B. (1984). Patterns of aggressive social interaction. In A. Mummendey (Ed.), *Social psychology of aggression: From individual behavior to social interaction* (pp. 108-126). New York/Berlin: Springer-Verlag.

Ferraro, K. J., & Johnson, J. M. (1983). How women experience battering: The process of victimization. *Social Problem, 30*(3), 325-339.

Festinger, L. (1957). *A theory of cognitive dissonance.* Stanford, CA: Standard University Press.

Fincham, F. D., Grych, J. H., & Osborne, L. N. (1994). Does marital conflict cause child maladjustment? Directions and challenges for longitudinal research. *Journal of Family Psychology, 8,* 123-127.

Fincham, F. D., & Osborne, L. N. (1993). Marital conflict and children: Retrospect and prospect. *Clinical Psychology Review, 13,* 75-88.

Finkelhor, D. (1983). Common features of family abuse. In D. Finkelhor, R. J. Gelles, G. T. Hotaling, & M. A. Straus (Eds.), *The darkside of families: Current family violence research* (pp. 17-28). Beverly Hills, CA: Sage.

Finkelhor, D., Hotaling, G., Lewis, I. A., & Smith, C. (1990). Sexual abuse in a national survey of adult men and women: Prevalence, characteristics, and risk factors. *Child Abuse & Neglect, 14*(1), 19-28.

Finkelhor, D., & Yllö, K. (1985). *License to rape: Sexual abuse of wives.* New York: Free Press.

Firestone, R. (1993). *The universality of emotional child abuse.* East Lansing, MI: National Center for Research on Teacher Learning. (ERIC Document Reproduction Service No. ED 369 003)

Fisch, R., Weakland, J. H., & Segal, L. (1982). *The tactics of change.* San Francisco, CA: Jossey-Bass.

Fisher, G., & Chon, K. (1989). Durkheim and the social construction of emotions. *Social Psychology Quarterly, 52*(1), 1-9.

Fitzpatrick, M. A. (1984). A typological approach to marital interaction: Recent theory and research. In L. Barkowitz (Ed.), *Advances in experimental social psychology* 18 (pp. 1-47). San Diego, CA: Academic Press.

Fitzpatrick, M. A., & Ritchie, L. D. (1993). Communication theory and the family. In P. Boss, W. Doherty, R. LaRossa, W. Schumm, & S. Steinmetz (Eds.), *Sourcebook of family theories and methods: A contextual approach* (pp. 565-585). New York: Plenum.

Folkman, S., Lazarus, R. S., Dunkel-Schetter, C., DeLongis, A., & Gruen, R. J. (1986). Dynamics of a stressful encounter: Cognitive appraisal, coping, and encounter outcomes. *Journal of Personality and Social Psychology, 50,* 992-1003.

Follingstad, D. (1990). Methodological issues and new directions for research on violence in relationships. In D. J. Besharov (Ed.), *Family violence: Research and public policy issues* (pp. 13-25). Washington, DC: AEI Press.

Follingstad, D. R., Rutledge, L. L., Polek, D. S., & McNeill-Hawkins, K. (1988). Factors associated with patterns of dating violence toward college women. *Journal of Family Violence, 3,* 169-182.

Follingstad, D. R., Wright, S., Lloyd, S., & Sebastian, J. A. (1991, January). Sex differences in motivations and effects in dating violence. *Family Relations, 40,* 51-57.

Framo, J. L. (1981). The integration of marital therapy with sessions with family of origin. In A. S. Gurman & D. P. Kniskern (Eds.), *Handbook of family therapy* (pp. 133-158). New York: Brunner/Mazel.

Friedlander, M. L., & Heatherington, L. (1989). Analyzing relational control in family therapy interviews. *Journal of Counseling Psychology, 36,* 139-148.

Friedrich, W., & Boriskin, J. (1976). The role of the child in abuse: A review of the literature. *American Journal of Orthopsychiatry, 46*(4), 580-590.

Frieze, I. H. (1979). Perceptions of battered wives. In I. H. Frieze, D. Bar-tal, & J. S. Carroll (Eds.), *New approaches to social problems* (pp. 79-108). San Francisco: Jossey-Bass.

Frieze, I. H., & McHugh, M. C. (1992). Power and influence strategies in violent and nonviolent marriages. Special issue: Women and power. *Psychology of Women Quarterly, 16*(4) 449-465.

Fry, D. (1993, Summer). The intergenerational transmission of disciplinary practices and approaches to conflict. *Human Organization, 52*(2), 176-185.

Gage, R. B. (1988). An analysis of relational control patterns in abusive couples. *Dissertation Abstracts International, 19,* 1034-1048.

Galvin, K. M., & Brommel, B. J. (1986). *Family communication: Cohesion and change* (2nd ed.). Glenview, IL: Scott, Foresman.

Garbarino, J., Dubrow, N., Kostelny, K., & Pardo, C. (1992). *Children in danger.* San Francisco: Jossey-Bass.

Garbarino, J., & Gilliam, G. (1980). *Understanding abusive families.* Lexington, MA: Lexington Books.

Garmzy, N., & Tellegren, A. (1984). Studies of stress resistant children. In F. Morrison (Ed.), *Advances in applied developmental psychology* (pp. 126-138). New York: Academic Press.

Gelles, R. (1973, July). Child abuse as psychopathology: A sociological critique and reformulation. *American Journal of Orthopsychiatry, 43*(4), 611-621.

Gelles, R. J. (1972). *The violent home: A study of physical aggression between husbands and wives.* Beverly Hills, CA: Sage.

Gelles, R. J. (1989). Child abuse and violence: Parent absence and economic deprivation. *American Journal of Orthopsychiatry, 59,* 492-501.

Gelles, R. J., & Conte, J. R. (1990). Domestic violence and sexual abuse of children: A review of research in the eighties. *Journal of Marriage and the Family, 52,* 1045-1058.

Gelles, R. J., & Cornell, C. P. (1990). *Intimate violence in families, 2nd Ed.* Newbury Park, CA: Sage.

Gelles, R. J., & Straus, M. (1979). Family experience and public support of the death penalty. In D. Gill (Ed.), *Child abuse and violence* (pp. 538-557). New York: AMS.

Gelles, R. J., & Straus, M. A. (1988). *Intimate violence.* New York: Simon & Schuster.

Ghosh, C. M., Margolin, G., & John, R. S. (1995). *Authoritarian versus authoritative parental behaviors and children's active participation during an interactive play task.* Manuscript submitted for publication.

Gilgun, J. (1988). *Factors which block the development of sexually abusive behavior in adults abused as children.* Paper presented at the National Conference on Male Victims and Offenders, Minneapolis, MN.

Gilmartin, B. (1985, July). Some family antecedents of severe shyness. *Family Relations, 34,* 429-438.

Giovannoni, J. M., & Becerra, R. M. (1979). *Defining child abuse.* New York: Free Press.

Gjerde, P. (1986). The interpersonal structure of family interaction settings: Parent-adolescent relations in dyads and triads. *Developmental Psychology, 22(3),* 297-304.

Gladue, B. A. (1991). Qualitative and quantitative sex differences in self-reported aggressive behavioral characteristics. *Psychological Reports, 68,* 675-684.

Glaser, B. G., & Strauss, A. L. (1967). *The discovery of grounded theory: Strategies for qualitative research.* New York: Aldine.

Goddard, C., & Stanley, J. (1994). Viewing the abusive parent and the abused child as captor and hostage. *Journal of Interpersonal Violence, 9(2),* 258-269.

Goffman, E. (1959). *Presentation of self in everyday life.* New York: Doubleday.

Goldstein, D., & Rosenbaum, A. (1985). An evaluation of maritally violent men. *Family Relations, 34,* 425-437.

Golin, S., & Romanowski, M. (1987). Verbal aggression as a function of sex of subject and sex of target. *Journal of Psychology, 97,* 141-149.

Gordis, E. B., Margolin, G., & John, R. S. (in press). Marital aggression, observed parental hostility, and child behavior during triadic family interaction. *Journal of Family Psychology.*

Gordon, T. (1970). *Parent effectiveness training.* New York: Wyden.

Gormly, J. (1974). A comparison of predictions from consistency and affect theories for arousal during interpersonal disagreement. *Journal of Personality and Social Psychology, 30,* 658-663.

Gottman, J. M. (1982). Emotional responsiveness in marital conversations. *Journal of Communication, 32(3),* 108-120.

Gottman, J. M. (1993). A theory of marital dissolution and stability. *Journal of Family Psychology, 7,* 57-75.

Gottman, J. M. (1994). *What predicts divorce?* Hillsdale, NJ: Lawrence Erlbaum.

Gottman, J. M., & Krokoff, L. J. (1989). Marital interaction and satisfaction: A longitudinal view. *Journal of Consulting and Clinical Psychology, 57,* 47-52.

Graham, D. L. R., & Rawlings, E. I. (1991). Bonding with abusive dating partners: Dynamics of Stockholm Syndrome. In B. Levy (Ed.), *Dating violence: Young women in danger* (pp. 119-135). Seattle, WA: Seal Press.

Groth, A. N., & Loredo, C. M. (1981). Juvenile sexual offenders: Guidelines for assessment. *International Journal of Offender Therapy and Comparative Criminology, 25*(1), 31-39.

Haley, J. (1963). Strategic therapy when a child is presented as the problem. *Journal of the American Academy of Child Psychiatry, 12,* 641-659.

Handelsman, C. D., Cabral, R. J., & Weisfeld, G. E. (1987). Sources of sexual information and adolescent sexual knowledge and behavior. *Journal of Adolescent Research, 2,* 455-463.

Hansen, D. J., & MacMillan, V. M. (1990). Behavioral assessment of child-abusive and neglectful families. *Behavior Modification, 14,* 255-278.

Harnett, P. H., & Misch, P. (1993). Developmental issues in the assessment and treatment of adolescent perpetrators of sexual abuse. *Journal of Adolescence, 16,* 397-405.

Harris, M. B. (1993). How provoking! What makes men and women angry? *Aggressive Behavior, 19*(3), 199-211.

Harris, P., & Olthof, T. (1982). The child's concept of emotion. In G. Butterworth & P. Light (Eds.), *Social cognition: Studies of the development of understanding* (pp. 188-209). Chicago: University of Chicago Press.

Hart, S., & Brassard, M. (1987). A major threat to children's mental health: psychological maltreatment. *American Psychologist, 42*(2), 160-165.

Henderson, D. A., & Stets, J. E. (1991). Contextual factors surrounding conflict resolution while dating: Results from a national study. *Family Relations, 40*(1), 29-36.

Henton, J. M., Cate, R. M., Koval, J. E., Lloyd, S. A., & Christopher, F. S. (1983). Romance and violence in dating relationships. *Journal of Family Issues, 4,* 467-482.

Herbert, T. B., Silver, R. C., & Ellard, J. H. (1991). Coping with an abusive relationship: I. How and why do women stay? *Journal of Marriage and the Family, 5,* 311-325.

Hilberman, E., & Munson, K. (1977-1978). Sixty battered women. *Victimology, 2,* 460-470.

Hinde, R. A. (1987). *Individuals, relationships, and culture: Links between ethology and the social sciences.* Cambridge, UK: Cambridge University Press.

Hinde, R. A., & Stevenson-Hinde, J. (1988). *Relationships within families: Mutual influences.* Oxford, UK: Clarendon.

Hirshi, T. (1969). *Causes of delinquency.* Berkeley: University of California Press.

Hobfoll, S. E., Dunahoo, C. L., Ben-Porath, Y., & Monnier, F. (1994). Gender and coping: The dual-axis model of coping. *American Journal of Community Psychology, 22,* 49-82.

Hoffman, M. L. (1980). Moral development in adolescence. In J. Adelson (Ed.), *Handbook of adolescent psychology* (pp. 295-343). New York: John Wiley.

Hoffman, P. (1984). Psychological abuse of women by spouses and live-in lovers. *Women and therapy, 3*(3), 37-47.

Holden, G. W., & Ritchie, K. L. (1991). Linking extreme marital discord, child rearing, and child behavior problems: Evidence from battered women. *Child Development, 62,* 311-327.

Holtzworth-Munroe, A. (1992). Social skill deficits in maritally violent men: Interpreting the data using a social information processing model. *Clinical Psychology Review, 12*(6), 605-617.

Holtzworth-Munroe, A., & Anglin, K. (1991). The competency of responses given by maritally violent versus nonviolent men to problematic marital situations. *Violence and Victims, 6,* 257-269.

Hornung, C., McCullough, C., & Sugimoto, T. (1981). Status relationship in marriage: Risk factors in spouse abuse. *Journal of Marriage and the Family, 43,* 675-692.

Hudson, W. W., & McIntosh, S. R. (1981). The assessment of spouse abuse: Two quantifiable dimensions. *Journal of Marriage and Family, 43,* 873-885.

Hughes, H. M., Vargo, M. C., Ito, E. S., & Skinner, S. K. (1991). Psychological adjustment of children of battered women: Influences of gender. *Family Violence Bulletin, 7*(19), 15-17.

Hurlbert, D. F., & Apt, C. (1991). Sexual narcissism and the abusive male. *Journal of Sex and Marital Therapy, 17*(4), 279-292.

Huston, T. L., & Ashmore, R. D. (1986). Women and men in personal relationships. In R. D. Ashmore & F. K. Del Boca (Eds.), *The social psychology of female-male relationships* (pp. 167-210). New York: Academic Press.

Huston, T. L., & Chorost, A. (1991). *Behavioral buffers on the effects of negativity on marital satisfaction: A longitudinal study.* Paper presented at the National Council on Family Relations, Denver, CO.

Huston, T. L., McHale, S. M., & Crouter, A. C. (1986). When the honeymoon's over: Changes in the marriage relationship over the first year. In S. Duck & R. Gilmour (Eds.), *The emerging field of personal relationships* (pp. 109-132). Hillsdale, NJ: Lawrence Erlbaum.

Huston, T. L., Robins, E., Atkinson, J., & McHale, S. M. (1987). Surveying the landscape of marital behavior: A behavioral self-report approach to studying marriage. In S. Oskamp (Ed.), *Family processes and problems* (Vol. 7, pp. 45-71). Newbury Park, CA: Sage.

Huston, T. L., & Vangelisti, A. L. (1991). Socioemotional behavior and satisfaction in marital relationships: A longitudinal study. *Journal of Personality and Social Psychology, 61,* 721-733.

Infante, D. A., Chandler, T. A., & Rudd, J. E. (1989). Test of an argumentative skill deficiency model of interspousal violence. *Communication Monographs, 56,* 163-177.

Infante, D. A., Myers, S. A., & Buerkel, R. A. (1994, Spring). Argument and verbal aggression in constructive and destructive family and organizational disagreements. *Western Journal of Communication, 58,* 73-84.

Infante, D. A., & Rancer, A. S. (1982). A conceptualization and measure of argumentativeness. *Journal of Personality Assessment, 46,* 72-80.

Infante, D. A., Riddle, B. L., Horvath, C. L., & Tumlin, S. A. (1992). Verbal aggressiveness: Messages and reasons. *Communication Quarterly, 40,* 116-126.

Infante, D. A., Sabourin, T. C., Rudd, J. E., & Shannon, E. A. (1990). Verbal aggression in violent and nonviolent marital disputes. *Communication Quarterly, 38,* 361-371.

Infante, D. A., Wall, C. H., Leap, C. J., & Danielson, K. (1984). Verbal aggression as a function of the receiver's argumentativeness. *Communication Research Reports, 1,* 33-37.

Infante, D. A., & Wigley, C. J. (1986). Verbal aggressiveness: An interpersonal model and measure. *Communication Monographs, 53,* 61-69.

Izard, C. E., Huebner, R., Risser, D., McGinnes, G., & Doughtery, L. (1980). The young infant's ability to produce discrete emotional expressions. *Developmental Psychology, 16,* 132-140.

Jacob, T., & Tennenbaum, D. L. (1988). *Family assessment: Rationale, methods, and future directions.* New York: Plenum.

Jacobson, N. S., Follette, W. C., & McDonald, D. W. (1982). Reactivity to positive and negative behavior in distressed and non-distressed married couples. *Journal of Consulting and Clinical Psychology, 50,* 706-714.

Jacobson, N. S., Gottman, J. M., Waltz, J., Rushe, R., Babcock, J., & Holtzworth-Munroe, A. (1994). Affect, verbal content, and psychophysiology in the arguments of couples with a violent husband. *Journal of Consulting and Clinical Psychology, 62,* 982-988.

Jaffe, P. G., Hurley, D. J., & Wolfe, D. (1990). Children's observations of violence: 1. Critical issue in child development and intervention planning. *Canadian Journal of Psychiatry, 35,* 466-470.

Jaffe, P. G., Wolfe, D. A., & Wilson, S. K. (1990) *Children of battered women.* Newbury Park, CA: Sage.

Johnson, I. M. (1992). Economic, situational, and psychological correlates of the decision-making process of battered women. *Families in Society: The Journal of Contemporary Human Services, 73*(3), 168-176.

Johnson, M. P. (1995). Patriarchal terrorism and common couple violence: Two forms of violence against women. *Journal of Marriage and the Family, 57*(2), 283-294.

Jorgenson, D. (1985). Transmitting methods of conflict resolution from parents to children: Replication and comparison of blacks and whites, males and females. *Social Behavior and Personality, 13*(2), 109-117.

Jouriles, E. N., & LeCompte, S. H. (1991). Husbands' aggression toward wives and mothers' and fathers' aggression toward children: Moderating effects of child gender. *Journal of Consulting and Clinical Psychology, 59,* 190-192.

Jouriles, E. N., & Norwood, W. D. (1995). Physical aggression toward boys and girls in families characterized by the battering of women. *Journal of Family Psychology, 9,* 69-78.

Jouriles, E. N., Pfiffner, L. J., & O'Leary, S. G. (1988). Marital conflict, parenting, and toddler conduct problems. *Journal of Abnormal Child Psychology, 16,* 197-206.

Kantor, D., & Lehr, W. (1975). *Inside the family.* New York: Harper/Colophon.

Kaplan, M. S., Becker, J. V., & Cunningham-Rathner, J. (1988). Characteristics of parents of adolescent incest perpetrators: Preliminary findings. *Journal of Family Violence, 3,* 183-191.

Kaufman, J., & Zigler, E. (1987). Do abused children become abusive parents? *American Journal of Orthopsychiatry, 57*(2), 186-197.

Kavanaugh, C. (1982). Emotional abuse and mental injury. *Journal of the American Academy of Child Psychiatry, 21*(2), 171-177.

Kavanaugh, K. A., Youngblade, L., Reid, J. B., & Fagot, B. I. (1988). Interactions between children and abusive versus control parents. *Journal of Clinical Child Psychology, 17*(2), 137-142.

Kelly, H., Berscheid, E., Christiansen, A., Harvey, J., Huston, T., Levinger, G., McClintock, E., Peplau, L., & Peterson, D. (1983). *Close relationships.* New York: Freeman.

Kelly, M. L., Grace, N., & Elliott, S. N. (1990). Acceptability of positive and punitive discipline methods: Comparisons among abusive, potentially abusive, and non-abusive parents. *Child Abuse and Neglect, 14,* 219-226.

Kempe, C. H., Silverman, F. N., Steele, B. F., Droegemueller, W., & Silver, H. K. (1962, July 7). The battered-child syndrome. *Journal of the American Medical Association, 181,* 17-24.

Kenny, D. A. (1988). The analysis of data from two-person relationships. In S. Duck (Ed.), *Handbook of personal relationships* (pp. 57-78). London: Wiley.

Kinard, E. (1978). *Emotional development in physically abused children: A study of self concept and aggression.* Palo Alto, CA: R and E Research Associates.

Kirkwood, C. (1993). *Leaving abusive partners.* Newbury Park, CA: Sage.

Knapp, M. L., Stafford, L., & Daly, J. A. (1986, Autumn). Regrettable messages: Things people wish they hadn't said. *Journal of Communication, 36,* 40-58.

Knopp, F. H. (1982). *Remedial intervention in adolescent sex offenses: Nine program descriptions.* Orwell, VT: Safer Society Press.

Knopp, F. H. (1985). Recent developments in the treatment of adolescent sex offenders. In E. M. Otey & G. D. Ryan (Eds.), *Adolescent sex offenders: Issues in research and treatment* (pp. 1-27). Rockville, MD: U.S. Department of Health and Human Services.

Kobosa, S. (1982). The hardy personality: Toward a social psychology of stress and health. In G. S. Sanders & J. Suls (Eds.), *Sociology of health and illness* (pp. 124-133). Hillsdale, NJ: Lawrence Erlbaum.

Kuczynski, L., Kochanska, G., Radke-Yarrow, M., & Girnius-Brown, O. (1987). A developmental interpretation of young children's noncompliance. *Developmental Psychology, 23,* 799-806.

Lackey, C., & Williams, C. (1995). Social bonding and the cessation of partner violence across generations. *Journal of Marriage and the Family, 57,* 295-305.

Laing, R. D., & Esterson, A. (1970). Sanity, madness and the family. Baltimore: Penguin.

Lamborn, S. D., Mounts, N. S., Steinberg, L., & Dornbusch, S. M. (1991). Patterns of competence and adjustment among adolescents from authoritative, authoritarian, indulgent, and neglectful families. *Child Development, 62,* 1049-1065.

Lamphear, V. (1985). The impact of maltreatment on children's psychological adjustment: A review of the research. *Child Abuse and Neglect, 9,* 251-263.

Laner, M. R. (1983). Courtship abuse and aggression: Contextual aspects. *Sociological Spectrum, 3,* 69-83.

Langhinrichsen-Rohling, J., Smultzler, N., & Vivian, D. (1994). Positivity in marriage: The role of discord and physical aggression against wives. *Journal of Marriage and the Family, 56,* 69-79.

Launius, M. H., & Jensen, B. L. (1987). Interpersonal problem-solving skills in battered, counseling, and control women. *Journal of Family Violence, 2,* 151-161.

Lawler, E. J., Ford, R. S., & Blegen, M. A. (1988). Coercive capability in conflict: A test of bilateral deterrence versus conflict spiral theory. *Social Psychology Quarterly, 51*(2), 93-107.

Lazarus, R. S., & Folkman, S. (1984). Stress, appraisal, and coping. New York: Springer.

Leach, E. (1964). Anthropological aspects of language: Animal categories and verbal abuse. In E. H. Lenneberg (Ed.), *New directions in the study of language* (pp. 23-63). Cambridge: MIT Press.

Leavitt, R., & Power, M. (1989). Emotional socialization in the postmodern era: Children in day care. *Social Psychology Quarterly, 52*(1), 35-43.

Leffler, A. (1986). *The invisible scars: Verbal abuse and psychological unavailability and relationship to self esteem.* Paper presented at the 96th annual convention of American Psychological Association, Atlanta, GA.

Lemert, E. (1972). *Human deviance, social problems, and social control.* Englewood Cliffs, NJ: Prentice Hall.

Leonard, K. E., & Senchak, M. (1993). Alcohol and premarital aggression among newlywed couples. *Journal of Studies on Alcohol, 11*(Suppl.), 96-108.

Lindahl, K., Clements, M., & Markman, H. (in press). The development of marriage: A nine-year perspective. In T. Bradbury (Ed.), *The developmental course of marital dysfunction.*

Lloyd, S. A. (1990a). Asking the right questions about the future of marital violence research. In D. J. Besharov (Ed.), *Family violence: Research and public policy issues* (pp. 93-107). Washington, DC: American Enterprise Institute.

Lloyd, S. A. (1990b). Conflict types and strategies in violent marriages. *Journal of Family Violence, 5,* 269-284.

Lloyd, S. A. (1991). The darkside of courtship: Violence and sexual exploitation. *Family Relations, 40*(1), 14-20.

Lloyd, S. A. (1996). Physical aggression, distress, and everyday marital interaction. In D. Cahn & S. Lloyd (Eds.), *Family violence from a communication perspective* (pp. 177-198). Thousand Oaks, CA: Sage.

Lloyd, S. A., & Emery, B. C. (1993). Abuse in the family: An ecological, life-cycle perspective. In T. H. Brubaker (Ed.), *Family relations: Challenges for the future* (pp. 129-152). Newbury Park, CA: Sage.

Lloyd, S. A., & Emery, B. C. (1994). Physically aggressive conflict in romantic relationships. In D. D. Cahn (Ed.), *Conflict in personal relationships* (pp. 27-46). Hillsdale, NJ: Lawrence Erlbaum.

Lloyd, S. A., Koval, J. E., & Cate, R. M. (1989). Conflict and violence in dating relationships. In M. A. Pirog-Good & J. Stets (Eds.), *Violence in dating relationships: Emerging social issues* (pp. 126-142). New York: Praeger.

Lloyd, S. A., Koval, J. E., & Pittman, J. F. (1987, November). *Violence in intimate relationships: The role of individual versus relationship factors.* Paper presented at the annual conference of the National Council on Family Relations, Atlanta, GA.

Luepnitz, D. (1988). *The family interpreted: Feminist theory in clinical practice.* New York: Basic Books.

Lytton, H. (1979). Disciplinary encounters between young boys and their mothers and fathers: Is there a contingency system? *Developmental Psychology, 15*(3), 256-268.

Maccoby, E. E. & Mnookin, R. H. (1992). *Dividing the child: Social and legal dilemmas of custody.* Cambridge, MA: Harvard University Press.

Mack, R. N. (1989). Spouse abuse—A dyadic approach. In G. R. Weeks (Ed.), *Treating couples: The interpersonal model of the marriage council of Philadelphia* (pp. 191-213). New York: Brunner/Mazel.

Maiuro, R. D., Vitaliano, R. P., & Cahn, T. S. (1987). A brief measure for the assessment of anger and aggression. *Journal of Interpersonal Violence, 2,* 166-178.

Makepeace, J. M. (1981). Courtship violence among college students. *Family Relations, 30,* 97-102.

Makepeace, J. M. (1986). Gender differences in courtship violence victimization. *Family Relations, 33*, 383-388.

Manderscheid, R. W., Rae, D. S., McCarrick, A. K., & Sibergeld, S. (1982). A stochastic model of relational control in dyadic interaction. *American Sociological Review, 47*, 62-75.

Margolin, G. (1981). The reciprocal relationship between marital and child problems. In J. P. Vincent (Ed.), *Advances in family intervention, assessment, and theory* (pp. 166-222). Greenwich, CT: JAI.

Margolin, G. (1987). The multiple forms of aggressiveness between marital partners: How do we identify them? *Journal of Marital and Family Therapy, 13*, 77-84.

Margolin, G. (in press). Effects of domestic violence on children. In P. K. Trickett & C. Schellenbach (Eds.), *Violence against children in the family and community*. Washington, DC: American Psychological Association.

Margolin, G., Burman, B., & John, R. S. (1989). Home observations of married couples reenacting naturalistic conflicts. *Behavioral Assessment, 11*(1), 101-118.

Margolin, G., Burman, B., John, R. S., & O'Brien, M. (1990). *Domestic conflict inventory*. Unpublished manuscript, University of Southern California, Los Angeles.

Margolin, G., John, R. S., & Foo, L. (1995). *Interactive and unique risk factors for husbands emotional and physical abuse of the wives*. Manuscript submitted for publication.

Margolin, G., John, R. S., Ghosh, C. M., & Gordis, E. B. (1996). Family interaction process: An essential tool for exploring abusive relations. In D. Cahn & S. Lloyd (Eds.), *Family violence from a communication perspective* (pp. 37-58). Thousand Oaks, CA: Sage.

Margolin, G., John, R. S., & Gleberman, L. (1988). Affective responses to conflictual discussions in violent and nonviolent couples. *Journal of Consulting and Clinical Psychology, 56*(1), 24-33.

Margolin, G., John, R. S., & O'Brien, M. (1989). Sequential affective patterns as a function of marital conflict style. *Journal of Social and Clinical Psychology, 8*(1), 45-61.

Margolin, L. (1992). Beyond maternal blame: Physical child abuse as a phenomenon of gender. *Journal of Family Issues, 13*, 410-423.

Markman, H. J., & Notarius, C. I. (1987). Coding marital and family interaction: Current status. In T. Jacob (Ed.), *Family interaction and psychopathology* (pp. 329-389). New York: Plenum.

Marks, S. (1986). *Three corners: Exploring marriage and the self*. Lexington, MA: Lexington Books.

Marshall, C., & Rossman, G. B. (1989). *Designing qualitative research*. Newbury Park, CA: Sage.

Marshall, L. L. (1994). Physical and psychological abuse. In W. R. Cupach & B. H. Spitzberg (Eds.), *The dark side of interpersonal communication* (pp. 281-311). Hillsdale, NJ: Lawrence Erlbaum.

Marshall, L. L., & Vitanza, S. A. (1994). Physical abuse in close relationships: Myths and realities. In A. L. Weber & J. H. Harvey (Eds.), *Perspectives on close relationships* (pp. 263-284). Boston: Allyn & Bacon.

Martin, H. P., & Beezley, P. (1977). Behavioral observations of abused children. *Developmental Medicine and Child Neurology, 19*, 373-387.

Martinez-Roig, A., Domingo-Salvany, F., & Llorens-Terol, J. (1983). Psychologic implications of the maltreated child syndrome. *Child Abuse and Neglect, 7,* 261-263.

Mason, A., & Blankenship, V. (1987). Power and affiliation motivation, stress, and abuse in intimate relationships. Journal of Personality and Social Psychology, 52, 203-210.

Matthews, W. J. (1984). Violence in college couples. *College Student Journal, 18,* 150-158.

McCall, G. J., & Simmons, J. L. (1978). *Identities and interactions: An examination of human associations in everyday life* (Rev. ed.). New York: Free Press.

McClellend, D. (1973). Testing for competence rather than intelligence. *American Psychologist, 28*(6), 1-14.

McCord, J. (1988). Parental behavior in the cycle of aggression. *Psychiatry, 51*(1), 14-23.

McDonald, R., & Jouriles, E. M. (1991). Marital aggression and child behavior problems: Research findings, mechanisms, and intervention strategies. *The Behavior Therapist, 14,* 189-192.

McGaha, J. E., & Fournier, D. G. (1988). Juvenile justice and the family: A systems approach to family assessment. *Marriage and Family Review, 12,* 155-172.

Mead, G. H. (1962). *Mind, self, and society.* Chicago: University of Chicago Press.

Milardo, R. (1984). A measure of positive and negative social support. Unpublished scale, University of Maine at Orono.

Millar, F. E., & Rogers, L. E. (1987). Relational dimensions of interpersonal dynamics. In M. E. Roloff & G. Miller (Eds.), *Interpersonal processes: New directions in communication research* (pp. 117-139). Newbury Park, CA: Sage.

Millar, F. E., Rogers, L. E., & Courtright, J. A. (1979). Relational control and dyadic understanding: An exploratory predictive regression model. In D. Nimo (Ed.), *Communication yearbook 3* (pp. 213-224). New Brunswick, NJ: Transaction Books.

Miller, P., & Sperry, L. (1987). The socialization of anger and aggression. *Merrill Palmer Quarterly, 33*(1), 1-31.

Mills, T. (1985). The assault on the self: Stages in coping with battering husbands. *Qualitative Sociology, 8*(2), 103-123.

Milner, J. S., & Chilamkurti, C. (1991). Physical child abuse perpetrator characteristics: A review of the literature. *Journal of Interpersonal Violence, 6,* 345-366.

Minuchin, S. (1974). *Families and family therapy.* Cambridge, MA: Harvard University Press.

Minuchin, S., Rosman, B. L., & Baker, L. (1978). *Psychosomatic families.* Cambridge, MA: Harvard University Press.

Monastersky, C., & Smith, W. (1985). Juvenile sexual offenders: A family systems paradigm. In E. M. Otey & G. D. Ryan (Eds.), *Adolescent sex offenders: Issues in research and treatment* (pp. 164-175). Rockville, MD: U.S. Department of Health and Human Services.

Montgomery, B. M. (1992). Communication as the interface between couples and culture. In S. Deetz (Ed.), *Communication yearbook 15* (pp. 475-507). Newbury Park, CA: Sage.

Moos, R. H., & Moos, B. S. (1986). *Family environment scale manual* (2nd ed.). Palo Alto, CA: Consulting Psychologists Press.

Mosher, D., Rose, M., & Grebel, M. (1968). Verbal aggressive behavior in delinquent boys. *Journal of Abnormal Psychology, 73,* 454-460.

Mosteller, F., & Tukey, J. W. (1977). *Data analysis and regression: A second course in statistics.* New York: Addison-Wesley.

Mulcahy, F. D. (1979). Studies in Gitano social ecology: Conflict and verbal abuse. *Maledicta, 3*(3), 87-100.

Murphy, C. M., & O'Leary, K. D. (1989). Psychological aggression predicts physical aggression in early marriage. *Journal of Consulting and Clinical Psychology, 57,* 579-582.

Nagaraja, J. (1984). Noncompliance: A behavior disorder. *Child Psychiatry Quarterly, 17*(4), 127-132.

National Center on Child Abuse and Neglect. (1988). *Study findings: Study of national incidence and prevalence of child abuse and neglect.* Washington, DC: U.S. Department of Health and Human Services.

National Committee for the Prevention of Child Abuse. (1987, Summer). *Emotional abuse: Words can hurt.* Chicago: Author.

National Committee to Prevent Child Abuse. (1995, May). *Memorandum, II,* (5). Chicago: Author, 332 S. Michigan Ave., Suite 1600, 60604.

Ney, P. G. (1987, June). Does verbal abuse leave deeper scars: A study of children and parents. *Canadian Journal of Psychiatry, 21,* 371-378.

Nielson, L. (1989). Victims as victimizers: Therapeutic and professional boundary issues. *Journal of Chemical Dependency Treatment, 3,* 203-226.

Noller, P. (1985). Negative communications in marriage. *Journal of Social and Personal Relationships, 2,* 289-301.

Noller, P., Feeney, J. A., Bonnell, D., & Callan, V. J. (1994). A longitudinal study of conflict in early marriage. *Journal of Social and Personal Relationships, 11,* 233-253.

Oates, R. K., Forrest, D., & Peacock, A. (1985). Self esteem of abused children. *Child Abuse and Neglect, 9,* 159-163.

O'Brien, M. (1985). Adolescent sexual offenders: An outpatient program's perspective on research directions. In E. M. Otey & G. D. Ryan (Eds.), *Adolescent sex offenders: Issues in research and treatment* (pp. 147-163). Rockville, MD: U.S. Department of Health and Human Services.

O'Keefe, M. (1994). Linking marital violence, mother-child/father-child aggression, and child behavior problems. *Journal of Family Violence, 9,* 63-78.

O'Keefe, N. O., Brockopp, K., & Chew, E. (1986). Teen dating violence. *Social Work, 31,* 465-468.

Oldershaw, L., Walters, G. C., & Hall, D. K. (1986). Control strategies and noncompliance in abusive mother-child dyads: An observational study. *Child Development, 57,* 722-732.

Oldershaw, L., Walters, G. C., & Hall, D. K. (1989). A behavioral approach to the classification of different types of physically abusive mothers. *Merrill-Palmer Quarterly, 35,* 255-279.

O'Leary, K. D. (1988). Physical aggression between spouses. In V. B. Van Hasselt, R. L. Morrison, A. S. Bellack, & M. Hersen (Eds.), *Handbook of family violence* (pp. 31-55). New York: Plenum.

O'Leary, K. D., Barling, J., Arias, I., Rosenbaum, A., Malone, J., & Tyree, A. (1989). Prevalence and stability of physical aggression between spouses: A longitudinal analysis. *Journal of Consulting and Clinical Psychology, 57,* 263-268.

O'Leary, K. D., Malone, J., & Tyree, A. (1994). Physical aggression in early marriage: Prerelationship and relationship effects. *Journal of Consulting and Clinical Psychology, 62,* 594-602.

Olson, D. A., & Schultz, K. S. (1994). Gender differences in the dimensionality of social support. *Journal of Applied Social Psychology, 24,* 1221-1232.

Olson, D. H. (1976). *Treating relationships.* Lake Mills: Graphic Publishing.

Olson, D. H. (1986). Circumplex model VII: Validation studies and FACES III. *Family Process, 25,* 337-351.

Olson, D. H., McCubbin, H. I., Barnes, H. L., Larsen, A. S., Muxen, M. J., & Wilson, M. A. (1983). *Families: What makes them work.* Beverly Hills, CA: Sage.

Osborne, L. N., & Fincham, F. D. (1994). Conflict between parents and their children. In D. D. Cahn (Ed.), *Conflict in personal relationships* (pp. 117-141). Hillsdale, NJ: Lawrence Erlbaum.

Osmond, M., & Thorne, B. (1993). Feminist theories: The social construction of gender in families and society. In P. Boss, W. Doherty, R. LaRossa, W. Schumm, & S. Steinmetz (Eds.), *Sourcebook of family theories and methods: A contextual approach* (pp. 591-623). New York: Plenum.

Papini, D. R., Farmer, F. F., Clark, S. M., Micka J. C., & Barnett, J. K. (1990). Early adolescent age and gender differences in patterns of emotional self-disclosure to parents and friends. *Adolescence, 25,* 100, 959-976.

Papini, D. R., Farmer, F. L., Clark, S. M., & Snell, W. E. (1988). An evaluation of adolescent patterns of sexual self-disclosure to parents and friends. *Journal of Adolescent Research, 3,* 387-401.

Patterson, G. R. (1976). A performance theory for coercive family interaction. In R. B. Cairns (Ed.), *The analysis of social interactions: Methods, issues, and illustrations* (pp. 119-162). Hillsdale, NJ: Lawrence Erlbaum.

Patterson, G. R. (1982). *A social learning approach: Vol. 3. Coercive family process.* Eugene, OR: Castalia.

Patterson, G. R. (1986). Performance models for antisocial boys. *American Psychologist, 41,* 432-444.

Patterson, G. R., & Bank, L. (1988). Some amplifying mechanisms for pathologic processes in families. In M. Gunnar (Ed.), *Minnesota symposium on child psychology* (pp. 37-57). Hillsdale, NJ: Lawrence Erlbaum.

Paulson, J. (1983). Covert and overt forms of maltreatment in preschools. *Child Abuse and Neglect, 7*(4), 45-54.

Pedersen, P., & Thomas, C. D. (1992). Prevalence and correlates of dating violence in a Canadian University sample. *Canadian Journal of Behavioral Science, 24,* 490-501.

Peled, E., Jaffe, P. G., & Edleson, J. L. (1995). Introduction. In E. Peled, P. G. Jaffe, & J. L. Edleson (Eds.), *Ending the cycle of violence* (pp. 3-9). Thousand Oaks, CA: Sage.

Pence, E., & Taymar, M. (1993). *Education groups for men who batter: The Duluth Model.* New York: Springer.

Peterson, D. R. (1979). Assessing interpersonal relationships by means of interaction records. *Behavioral Assessment, 1,* 221-236.

Pirog-Good, M. A., & Stets, J. E. (1989). *Violence in dating relationships: Emerging social issues.* New York: Praeger.

Planalp, S. (1993). Communication, cognition, and emotion. *Communication Monographs, 60,* 3-9.

Pollak, L., & Thoits, P. (1989). Processes in emotional socialization. *Social Psychology Quarterly, 52*(1), 22-34.

Power, T. G., McGrath, M. P., Hughes, S. O., & Manire, S. H. (1994). Compliance and self-assertion: Young childrens' responses to mothers versus fathers. *Developmental Psychology, 30,* 980-989.

Ptacek, J. T., Smith, R. E., & Dodge, K. L. (1994). Gender differences in coping with stress: When stressor and appraisals do not differ. *Personality and Social Psychology Bulletin, 20,* 421-430.

Radovanovic, H. (1993). Parental conflict and children's coping styles in litigating separated families relationships with children's adjustment. *Journal of Abnormal Child Psychology, 21*(6), 697-713.

Rancer, A. S., & Niemasz, J. (1988, April). *The influence of argumentativeness and verbal aggression in intrafamily violence.* Paper presented at the meeting of Eastern Communication Association, Baltimore, MD.

Raush, H. C., Barry, W. A., Hertel, R. K., & Swain, M. A. (1974). *Communication, conflict, and marriage.* San Francisco: Jossey-Bass.

Reid, J. B. (1986). Social-interactional patterns in families of abused and nonabused children. In C. Zahn-Waxler, M. Cummings, & M. Radke-Yarrow (Eds.), *Social and biological origins of altruism and aggression* (pp. 238-255). New York: Cambridge University Press.

Reid, J. B., Kavanaugh, K., & Baldwin, D. V. (1987). Abusive parents' perceptions of child problem behaviors: An example of parental bias. *Journal of Abnormal Child Psychology, 15,* 457-466.

Riggs, D. S. (1993). Relationship problems and dating aggression: A potential treatment target. *Journal of Interpersonal Violence, 8*(1), 18-35.

Riggs, D. S., O'Leary, K. D., & Breslin, F. C. (1990). Multiple correlates of physical aggression in dating couples. *Journal of Interpersonal Violence, 5,* 61-73.

Roach, K. D. (1992). Teacher demographic characteristics and levels of teacher argumentativeness. *Communication Research Reports, 9,* 65-71.

Rogers, L. E. (1972). *Relational communication control coding manual.* Unpublished manuscript, Michigan State University, East Lansing.

Rogers, L. E., & Farace, R. V. (1975). Analysis of relational communication in dyads: New measurement procedures. *Family Process, 1,* 222-239.

Rogers-Millar, L. E., & Millar, F. E. (1979). Domineeringness and dominance: A transactional view. *Human Communication Research, 5,* 239-246.

Rohner, R. (1975). *They love me, they love me not: A worldwide study of the effects of parental acceptance and rejection.* New Haven, CT: HRAF.

Roloff, M. E. (1987). Communication and reciprocity in interpersonal relationships. In M. E. Roloff & G. Miller (Eds.), *Interpersonal processes* (pp. 11-38). Newbury Park, CA: Sage.

Roloff, M. E., & Cloven, D. H. (1990). The chilling effect in interpersonal relationships: The reluctance to speak one's mind. In D. D. Cahn (Ed.), *Intimates in conflict: A communication perspective* (pp. 49-76). Hillsdale, NJ: Lawrence Erlbaum.

Rosen, K. H. (1992). *The process of coping with dating violence: A qualitative study.* Unpublished doctoral dissertation, Virginia Polytechnic Institute and State University, Blacksburg, VA.

Rosen, K. H., & Bezold, A. M. (1994). *Dating violence prevention: A didactic support group for young women.* Manuscript submitted for publication.

Rosen, K. H., & Stith, S. M. (1993). Intervention strategies for treating women in violent dating relationships. *Family Relations, 42,* 427-433.

Rosen, K. H., & Stith, S. M. (1995). Women terminating abusive dating relationships: A qualitative study. *Journal of Social and Personal Relationships, 12,* 155-160.

Rosenblatt, P. (1994). *Metaphors of family systems theory: Toward new constructions.* New York: Guilford.

Rosenow, D., & Bachorowski, J. (1984). Effects of alcohol and expectations on verbal aggression in men and women. *Journal of Abnormal Psychology, 93*(4), 418-432.

Rosenthal, R., & Jacobson, L. (1968). *Pygmalion in the classroom.* New York: Holt, Rinehart & Winston.

Rutter, M. (1994). Family discord and conduct disorder: Cause, consequence, or correlate? *Journal of Family Violence, 9,* 170-186.

Ryan, G. (1986). Annotated bibliography: Adolescent perpetrators of sexual molestation of children. *Child Abuse and Neglect, 10,* 125-131.

Ryan, G. (1991). Juvenile sex offenders: Defining the population. In G. Ryan & S. Lane (Eds.) *Juvenile sexual offending: Causes, consequences, and correction* (pp. 3-8). Lexington, MA: Lexington Books.

Sabourin, T. C. (1991). Perceptions of verbal aggression in inter-personal violence. In D. D. Knudsen & J. A. Miller (Eds.), *Abused and battered: Social and legal responses to family violence* (pp. 135-142). New York: Aldine.

Sabourin, T. C. (1995). The role of negative reciprocity in spouse abuse: A relational control analysis. *Journal of Applied Communication Research, 23*(4), 271-283.

Sabourin, T. C., Infante, D. C., & Rudd, J. E. (1993). Verbal aggression in marriages: A comparison of violent, distressed but nonviolent, and nondistressed couples. *Human Communication Research, 20,* 245-267.

Sabourin, T. C., & Stamp, G. H. (1995). Communication and the experience of dialectical tensions in family life: An examination of abusive and nonabusive families. *Communication Monographs, 62,* 213-242.

Sadler, O., & Tesser, A. (1973). Some effects of salience and time upon interpersonal hostility and attraction during social isolation. *Sociometry, 36*(1), 99-112.

Sallinen-Kuparinen, A., Thompson, C. A., & Klopf, D. W. (1991). Finnish and American university students compared on a verbal aggression construct. *Psychological Reports, 69,* 681-682.

Salzinger, S., Feldman, R. S., Hammer, M., & Rosario, M. (1993). The effects of physical abuse on children's social relationships. *Child Development, 64*(1), 169-187.

Satir, V. (1972). *Peoplemaking.* Palo Alto, CA: Science & Behavior Books.

Savin-Williams, R. (1994). Verbal and physical abuse as stressors in the lives of lesbian, gay and bisexual youths. *Journal of Consulting and Clinical Psychology, 62*(2), 261-269.

Scanzoni, J. (1978). *Sex roles, women's work, and marital conflict.* Lexington, MA: Lexington Books.

Schaap, C. (1984). Comparison of interaction of distressed and nondistressed married couples in a laboratory situation: Literature survey, methodological issues, and an empirical investigation. In K. Hahlweg & N. S. Jacobson (Eds.), *Marital interaction: Analysis and modification* (pp. 133-158). New York: Guilford.

Scheff, T. (1984). *Being mentally ill: A sociological theory* (2nd ed.). Hawthorne, NY: Aldine.

Schumm, W. R., & Bagarozzi, D. A. (1989). The conflict tactics scale. *American Journal of Family Therapy, 17,* 165-168.

Seidel, J. V., Kjolseth, R., & Seymour, E. (1988). *The ethnograph.* Littleton, CO: Qualis Research Association.

Semin, G., & Rubini, M. (1990). Unfolding the concept of person by verbal abuse. *European Journal of Social Psychology, 20,* 463-373.

Shettel-Neuber, J., Bryson, J. B., & Young, L. E. (1978). Physical attractiveness of the "other person" and jealousy. *Personality and Social Psychology Bulletin, 4,* 612-615.

Shope, G. L., Hedrick, T. E., & Geen, R. G. (1977). Physical/verbal aggression: Sex differences in style. *Journal of Personality, 45,* 23-42.

Shrout, P. E., & Fleiss, J. L. (1979). Intraclass correlations: Uses in assessing rater reliability. *Psychological Bulletin, 86(2),* 420-428.

Silvern, L., Karyl, J., & Landis, T. Y. (1995). Individual psychotherapy for the traumatized children of abused women. In E. Peled, P. G. Jaffe, & J. L. Edleson (Eds.), *Ending the cycle of violence* (pp. 43-76). Thousand Oaks, CA: Sage.

Smith, M. D. (1990). Patriarchal ideology and wife beating: A test of a feminist hypothesis. *Violence and Victims, 5(4),* 257-273.

Smith, S. (1984). The battered woman: A consequence of female development. *Women and Therapy, 3(3),* 3-9.

Spanier, G. B. (1976). Measuring dyadic adjustment: New scales for assessing the quality of marriage and similar dyads. *Journal of Marriage and the Family, 38,* 15-28.

Spinetta, J., & Rigler, D. (1972). The child abusing parent: A psychological review. *Psychological Bulletin, 77(4),* 296-304.

Spitzberg, B. H., Canary, D. J., & Cupach, W. R. (1994). A competence-based approach to the study of interpersonal conflict. In D. D. Cahn (Ed.), *Conflict in personal relationships* (pp. 183-202). Hillsdale, NJ: Lawrence Erlbaum.

Stamp, G. H., & Sabourin, T. C. (1995). Accounting for violence: An analysis of male spousal abuse narratives. *Journal of Applied Communication Research, 23(4),* 284-307.

Steele, B. (1986). Notes on the lasting effects of early child abuse throughout the life cycle. *Child Abuse and Neglect, 10,* 283-291.

Steele, B., & Ryan, G. (1991). Deviancy: Development gone wrong. In G. Ryan & S. Lane (Eds.), *Juvenile sexual offending: Causes, consequences, and correction* (pp. 83-102). Lexington, MA: Lexington Books.

Steele, P. F., & Pollack, C. B. (1974). A psychiatric study of parents who abuse infants and small children. In R. E. Helfer & R. S. Kempe (Eds.), *The battered child* (2nd ed., pp. 92-139). Chicago: University of Chicago Press.

Steinberg, L., Lamborn, S. D., Dornbusch, S. M., & Darling, N. (1992). Impact of parenting practices on adolescent achievement: Authoritative parenting, school involvement, and encouragement to succeed. *Child Development, 63,* 1266-1281.

Steinmetz, S. (1977, January). The use of force for resolving family conflict: The training ground for abuse. *The Family Coordinator,* 19-26.

Stern, D. (1985). *The interpersonal world of the infant.* New York: Basic Books.

Sternberg, K. J., Lamb, M. E., Greenbaum, C., Cicchetti, D., Dawud, S., Cortex, R. M., Krispin, O., & Lorey, F. (1993). Effects of domestic violence on children's behavior problems and depression. *Developmental Psychology, 29,* 44-52.

Stets, J. E. (1980). Verbal and physical aggression in marriage. *Journal of Marriage and the Family, 52(2),* 501-514.

Stets, J. E. (1988). *Domestic violence and control.* New York/Berlin: Springer-Verlag.

Stets, J. E. (1991). Psychological aggression in dating relationships: The role of interpersonal control. *Journal of Family Violence, 6(1),* 97-112.

Stets, J. E. (1992). Interactive processes in dating aggression: A national study. *Journal of Marriage and the Family, 54,* 165-177.

Stets, J. E. (1993). Control in dating relationships. *Journal of Marriage and the Family, 55,* 673-685.

Stets, J. E. (1995). Modeling control in relationships. *Journal of Marriage and the Family, 57,* 489-501.

Stets, J. E., & Henderson, D. A. (1991, January). Contextual factors surrounding conflict resolution while dating: Results from a national study. *Family Relations, 40,* 29-36.

Stets, J. E., & Pirog-Good, M. A. (1987). Violence in dating relationships. *Social Psychology Quarterly, 50,* 237-246.

Stiles, W. B. (1987). "I have to talk to somebody": A fever model of disclosure. In V. J. Derlega & J. H. Berg (Eds.), *Self-disclosure: Theory, research, and therapy* (pp. 257-282). New York: Plenum.

Straus, M. (1990). *Measuring psychological and physical abuse of children with the conflict tactics scales.* Durham: University of New Hampshire, Family Research Laboratory.

Straus, M., & Gelles, R. J. (1990). *Physical violence in American families: Risk factors and adaptations to violence in 8,145 families.* New Brunswick, NJ: Transaction Publishing.

Straus, M. A. (1974). Leveling, civility and violence in the family. *Journal of Marriage and the Family, 36*(1), 13-29.

Straus, M. A. (1979). Measuring intrafamily conflict and violence: The Conflict Tactics (CT) Scale. *Journal of Marriage and the Family, 41,* 75-88.

Straus, M. A. (1990). The conflict tactics scale and its critics: An evaluation and new data on validity and reliability. In M. A. Straus & R. Gelles (Eds.), *Physical violence in American families* (pp. 49-74). New Brunswick, NJ: Transaction Publishing.

Straus, M. A., & Gelles, R. J. (1990). How violent are American families? Estimates from the national family violence resurvey and other studies. In M. A. Straus & R. J. Gelles (Eds.), *Physical violence in American families* (pp. 95-112). New Brunswick, NJ: Transaction Books.

Straus, M. A., Gelles, R. J., & Steinmetz, S. K. (1980). *Behind closed doors: Violence in the American family.* New York: Doubleday.

Straus, M. A., & Kantor, G. K. (1991). *Physical punishment by parents: A risk factor in the epidemiology of depression, suicide, alcohol abuse, child abuse, and wife beating.* National Institute of Mental Health (DHHS), Bethesda, MD; National Institute on Alcohol Abuse and Alcoholism (DHHS), Rockville, MD.

Straus, M. A., & Smith, C. (1990). Family patterns and child abuse. In M. A. Straus & R. Gelles (Eds.), *Physical violence in American families* (pp. 245-262). New Brunswick, NJ: Transaction Books.

Straus, M. A., & Sweet, S. (1992). Verbal/symbolic aggression in couples: Incidence rates and relationship to personal characteristics. *Journal of Marriage and the Family, 54,* 346-357.

Straus, M. A., Sweet, S., & Vissing, Y. M. (1989, November). *Verbal aggression against spouse and children in a nationally representative sample of American families.* Paper presented at the meeting of the Speech Communication Association, San Francisco.

Strauss, A., & Corbin, J. (1990). *Basics of qualitative research.* Newbury Park, CA: Sage.

Strube, M. J., & Barbour, L. S. (1983). The decision to leave an abusive relationship: Economic dependence and psychological commitment. *Journal of Marriage and the Family, 45,* 785-793.

Strube, M. J., & Barbour, L. S. (1984). Factors related to the decision to leave an abusive relationship. *Journal of Marriage and the Family, 46,* 837-843.

Sugarman, D. B., & Hotaling, G. T. (1989a). Dating violence: Prevalence, context and risk markers. In M. A. Pirog-Good & J. E. Stets (Eds.), *Violence in dating relationships: Emerging social issues* (pp. 3-12). New York: Praeger.

Sugarman, D. B., & Hotaling, G. T. (1989b). Violent men and intimate relationships: An analysis of risk markers. *Journal of Applied Social Psychology, 19,* 1034-1048.

Suh, E. K., & Abel, E. M. (1990). The impact of spousal violence on the children of the abused. *Journal of Independent Social Work, 4*(4), 27-34.

Susman, E. J., Trickett, P. K., Iannotti, R. J., Hollenbeck, B. E., & Zahn-Waxler, C. (1985). Child-rearing patterns in depressed, abusive, and normal mothers. *American Journal of Orthopsychiatry, 55,* 237-251.

Tan, A., & Scruggs, K. (1980). Does exposure to comic book violence lead to aggression in children? *Journalism Quarterly, 57*(4), 579-583.

Tedeschi, J. T., & Felson, R. B. (1994). *Violence, aggression, & coercive actions.* Washington, DC: American Psychological Association.

Telch, C. F., & Lindquist, C. U. (1984). Violent versus nonviolent couples: A comparison of patterns. *Psychotherapy, 21,* 242-248.

Thomas, W. I. (1931). The relation of research to the social process. In M. Janowitz (Ed.), *W. I. Thomas on social organization and social personality* (pp. 289-305). Chicago: University of Chicago Press.

Thompson, L. (1992). Feminist methodology for family studies. *Journal of Marriage and the Family, 54,* 3-18.

Thornburg, H. (1986). Adolescent delinquency and families. In G. K. Leigh & G. W. Peterson (Eds.), *Adolescents in families* (pp. 358-380). Cincinnati, OH: South-Western Publishing.

Tolan, P. H., Cromwell, R. E., & Brasswell, M. (1986). Family therapy with delinquents: A critical review of the literature. *Family Process, 25,* 619-650.

Trickett, P. K., & Kuczynski, L. (1986). Children's misbehaviors and parental discipline strategies in abusive and nonabusive families. *Developmental Psychology, 22*(1), 115-123.

Trickett, P. K., & Susman, E. J. (1988). Parental perceptions of child-rearing practices in physically abusive and nonabusive families. *Developmental Psychology, 24,* 270-276.

Trickett, P. K., Susman, E. J., & Lourie, F. (1980). *The impact of the child-rearing environment on the abused child's social and emotional development* (Protocol No. 80-M-1120). Bethesda, MD: National Institute of Mental Health.

Vissing, Y. M., Straus, M. A., Gelles, R. J., & Harrop, J. W. (1991). Verbal aggression by parents and psychosocial problems of children. *Child Abuse and Neglect, 15*(3), 223-238.

Vondra, J. I. (1990). Sociological and ecological factors. In R. T. Ammerman & M. Hersen (Eds.), *Children at risk: An evaluation of factors contributing to child abuse and neglect* (pp. 149-170). New York: Plenum.

Vuchinich, S. (1987). Starting and stopping spontaneous family conflicts. *Journal of Marriage and the Family, 49,* 591-601.

Walker, L. (1989). Psychology and violence against women. *American Psychologist, 44,* 695-702.

Walker, L. E. (1979). *The battered woman.* New York: Harper & Row.

Waln, V. G. (1982). Interpersonal conflict interaction: An examination of verbal defense of self. *Central States Speech Journal, 33,* 557-566.

Walter, W. O., LaGrone, R. G., & Atkinson, A. W. (1989). Psychosocial screening in pediatric practice: Identifying high risk children. *Developmental and Behavioral Pediatrics, 10*(3), 134-138.

Walters, J., & Walters, L. H. (1983). The role of the family in sex education. *Journal of Research and Development in Education, 16*(2), 8-15.

Warren, C., & Neer, M. (1986). Family sex communication orientation. *Journal of Applied Communication Research, 14,* 86-107.

Watkins, C. R. (1982). *Victims, aggressors, and the family secret.* Minneapolis, MN: Minnesota Department of Public Welfare.

Watzlawick, P., Beavin, J., & Jackson, D. (1967). *Pragmatics of human communication.* New York: Norton.

Weinberger, D. A., & Davidson, M. N. (1994). Styles of inhibiting emotional expression: Distinguishing repressive coping from impression management. *Journal of Personality, 62,* 586-613.

Weinberger, D. A., & Schwartz, G. (1990). Distress and restraint as superordinate dimensions of self-reported adjustment: A typological perspective. *Journal of Personality, 58,* 381-417.

Weiss, R. L., & Dehle, C. (1994). Cognitive behavioral perspectives on marital conflict. In D. Cahn (Ed.), *Conflict in personal relationships* (pp. 95-115). Hillsdale, NJ: Lawrence Erlbaum.

Weiss, R. L., & Margolin, G. (1977). Assessment of marital conflict and accord. In A. R. Ciminero, K. D. Calhoun, & H. E. Adams (Eds.). *Handbook of behavioral assessment* (pp. 555-602). New York: John Wiley.

Werner, E. (1984, November). Resilient children. *Young Children,* 68-72.

Werner, E., & Smith. R. (1983). *Vulnerable but invincible: Study of resilient children.* New York: McGraw-Hill.

Westerman, M. A. (1987). "Triangulation," marital discord, and child behavior problems. *Journal of Social and Personal Relationships, 4,* 87-106.

Wheeler, L., & Nezlek, J. (1977). Sex differences in social participation. *Journal of Personality and Social Psychology, 35,* 742-754.

Whipple, E. E., & Webster-Stratton, C. (1991). The role of parental stress in physically abusive families. *Child Abuse and Neglect, 15,* 279-291.

Whitchurch, G. B., & Constantine, L. L. (1993). Systems theory. In P. Boss, W. Doherty, R. LaRossa, W. Schumm, & S. Steinmetz (Eds.), *Sourcebook of family theories and methods: A contextual approach* (pp. 325-352). New York: Plenum.

White, G. L. (1980). Inducing jealousy: A power perspective. *Personality and Social Psychology, 6,* 222-227.

White, J., & Allers, C. (1994). Play therapy with abused children: A review of the literature. *Journal of Counseling and Development, 72,* 390-394.

White, J. W. (1988). Influence tactics as a function of gender, insult, and goal. *Sex Roles, 18,* 433-448.

White, J. W., & Roufail, M. (1989). Gender and influence strategies of first choice and last resort. *Psychology of Women Quarterly, 13,* 175-189.

Williams, L. M., & Finkelhor, D. (1990). The characteristics of incestuous fathers. In M. L. Marshall, D. R. Laros, & H. E. Barbaree (Eds.), *Handbook of sexual assault* (pp. 231-255). New York: Plenum.

Williamson, R. N., & Fitzpatrick, M. A. (1985). Two approaches to marital interaction: Relational control patterns in marital types. *Communication Monographs, 52,* 236-252.

Wilson, S. (1995). *Marital communication as a function of violence in the family of origin and violence in marriage.* Unpublished master's thesis, Miami University, Oxford, OH.

Wilson, S. R., & Putnam, L. L. (1990). Interaction goals in negotiation. In J. A. Anderson (Ed.), *Communication yearbook 13* (pp. 374-406). Newbury Park, CA: Sage.

Wiseman, R. L., & Schenck-Hamlin, W. (1981). A multidimensional scaling validation of an inductively-derived set of compliance-gaining strategies. *Communication Monographs, 48,* 251-270.

Wolfe, D. (1987). *Child abuse: Implications for child development and psychopathology.* Newbury Park, CA: Sage.

Wolfe, D., & Mosk, M. (1983). Behavioral comparisons of children from abusive and distressed families. *Journal of Consulting and Clinical Psychology, 51,* 702-708.

Wolf-Smith, J. H., & LaRossa, R. (1992). After he hits her. *Family Relations, 41*(3), 324-329.

Yates, A. (1982). Legal issues in psychological abuse of children. *Clinical Pediatrics, 21*(10), 567-590.

Yin, R. K. (1989). *Case study research.* Newbury Park, CA: Sage.

Young, D. M., Beier, E. G., Beier, P., & Barton, C. (1975, Winter). Is chivalry dead? *Journal of Communication, 25,* 57-64.

Yudofsky, S. C., Silver, J. M., Jackson, W., Endicott, J., & Williams, D. (1986). The overt aggression scale for the objective rating of verbal and physical aggression. *American Journal of Psychiatry, 143*(1), 35-39.

Zietlow, P. H., & VanLear, C. A. (1991). Marital duration and relational control: A study of developmental patterns. *Journal of Marriage and the Family, 53,* 773-785.

Zillmann, D. (1990). The interplay of cognition and excitation in aggravated conflict among intimates. In D. D. Cahn (Ed.), *Intimates in conflict: A communication perspective* (pp. 187-208). Hillsdale, NJ: Lawrence Erlbaum.

Author Index

Subject Index

About the Contributors

Linda Ade-Ridder received her PhD from Florida State University in Marriage and Family Therapy. Currently, she is Chair of the Department of Family and Consumer Sciences and Professor in the Department of Sociology, Gerontology, and Anthropology at Miami University, Ohio. Her research, teaching, clinical practice, and community service activities emphasize the treatment and prevention of child maltreatment and other women's family issues.

Walter Baily has a doctorate in social work. He and his wife, Thelma, operate a child-focused consulting firm, Peasefield Associates, in Maine.

Gary H. Bischof is currently a doctoral candidate in marriage and family therapy with Purdue University's Department of Child Development and Family Studies. He obtained his master's degree in marriage and family therapy from Virginia Tech, where he conducted research on families of adolescent sexual offenders that resulted in two published articles. He has also published articles and book chapters related to the clinical practice of family therapy and is a family therapist in Indianapolis, Indiana.

Dudley D. Cahn, who is also known as "Lee," is Professor of Communication at the State University of New York at New Paltz. He holds a PhD in communication from Wayne State University (Detroit, Michigan). As a Fulbright Scholar, he has published articles and books on interpersonal communication, relationship disengagement, communication theory, the role of perceived understanding in relationship growth, and, most recently, interpersonal conflict and violence. He edits a scholarly series for the State University of New York Press.

Colleen M. Carey is a first-year graduate student in the Department of Communication Studies at Northwestern University. She received her BA in both speech communication and psychology from Miami University in 1994. Her research focuses on understanding various aspects of dating relationships. Specifically, she has studied courtship violence, conflict in dating relationships, female date initiation, and long-distance dating relationships.

Anne Castleton has recently completed her PhD in communication at the University of Utah.

Chandra M. Ghosh is a doctoral student in clinical psychology at the University of Southern California (USC). She received a Presidential Fellowship from USC and a National Institute of Aging traineeship. Her research interests include parent-child relationships across the life span and in different ethnic and cultural groups.

Elana B. Gordis is a doctoral student in clinical psychology at the University of Southern California. She received a predoctoral fellowship from the National Institute of Mental Health to conduct her dissertation research regarding the relationships among marital conflict, family interaction, and child behavior problems. She is interested in continuing to examine how patterns of marital interaction relate to parenting and to child development.

Richard S. John joined the faculty at the University of Southern California in 1984 and is currently Associate Professor with a joint appointment in systems management and the Department of Psychology. Before receiving a PhD in quantitative psychology from USC in 1984, he earned an MS degree in applied mathematics from USC in 1983.

Allen R. Jones received his master's of arts degree in psychology from Dusquesne University. Currently, he is a full-time counselor at Miami University Student Counseling Service. He is also a master's level candidate in the family and child studies program at Miami University, Oxford, Ohio. His interests include men's issues, including friendship and family violence, as well as philosophical approaches to psychology.

Sally A. Lloyd is Professor of Family Studies and Social Work and Associate Dean of the School of Education and Allied Professions at Miami University in Oxford, Ohio. She earned her PhD in family studies at Oregon State University in 1982. Since that time, she has published articles and books on conflict and violence in both courtship and marriage.

Gayla Margolin is Professor of Psychology at the University of Southern California. She received a PhD in clinical psychology from the University of Oregon. She received a Guggenheim Career Development Award and the 1993 Award for Distinguished Contribution to Family Research from the American Family Therapy Academy. Her research and writings have focused on marital therapy, family interaction, and marital conflict and its effects on children.

Paul A. Mongeau is Associate Professor of Speech Communication at Miami University in Oxford, Ohio. He received his PhD in communication from Michigan State University in 1988. His primary research interests include social influence, small group communication and decision making, and interpersonal communication. His research on relationships includes areas such as accounts and attributions following relational transgressions, first-date initiation and enactment, and deception.

L. Edna Rogers is Professor of Communication at the University of Utah and a Past President of the International Communication Association. She received her PhD from Michigan State University in 1972. The study of interpersonal and family relations from an interactional perspective represents a central focus of her research.

Michael E. Roloff received his doctorate from Michigan State University in 1975 and is Professor of Communication Studies at Northwestern

University. His area of research is interpersonal influence and he has published numerous articles and several books in the areas of interpersonal conflict management, interpersonal compliance gaining, social cognition, bargaining and negotiation, and persuasion. He is currently a Senior Associate Editor of the *International Journal of Conflict Management* and Editor of the *Communication Yearbook*.

Karen H. Rosen is Assistant Professor of Marriage and Family Therapy in the Department of Family and Child Development at the Northern Virginia Graduate Center of Virginia Polytechnic Institute and State University. She is a clinical member and approved supervisor of the American Association for Marriage and Family Therapy and a licensed professional counselor. Her research interests include violent relationship dynamics, woman abuse intervention and prevention strategies, and countertransference issues related to working with battered women.

Teresa Chandler Sabourin is Associate Professor in the Department of Communication at the University of Cincinnati. She earned her PhD from Purdue University, where she began her study of the role of communication in abusive relationships. A pioneer in the study of communication and spouse abuse, her published work has contributed to knowledge about the verbal dimension of abuse.

Sandra M. Stith holds the PhD in marriage and family therapy from Kansas State University and is Associate Professor in Virginia Tech's Department of Family and Child Development. She also directs the marriage and family therapy program in Falls Church, Virginia. Sandra has published numerous articles in the area of domestic violence and has edited two books. Her recent research focuses on violence in intimate partnerships.

Yvonne Vissing, who holds a doctorate in sociology, is Professor of Sociology at Salem State College in Salem, Massachusetts. Her work has focused on child abuse and how to enhance the child's emotional well-being. She also does independent consulting in child advocacy.